Some Things
Are Simply Meant to Be

Some Things Are Simply Meant to Be

Trudy Wells-Meyer

Copy Editor Lynnette Horner

Final copyedit by Judy Gettig-Gage

A Wells-Meyer Book
2021

First Edition

Printed: October 1**8**, 2021

Library of Congress Control Number: 2021910610

ISBN: 979-8-9850285-1-5

Wells-Meyer Publishing (W̧M)

Scottsdale, Arizona 85258

Dedication

In Memory of

Erwin Josef Meyer
&
Gertrud Brunhilde Meyer-Günther

Their lives nurtured the soul who walked the path
that these words describe.
Thank you for
the courage you gave me
and
for teaching me to always say,
Thank You!

Table of Contents

Acknowledgments

THANK YOU!

Rachel Weaver author, keynote speaker at my first Writers' Conference in Steamboat Springs, Colorado, during my paid critique, Rachel gave me confidence and belief — I am a writer.

Lynnette Horner, copyeditor, for her valued help in correcting mistakes in my second language attempt to write this book.

Jerry Ruehle retired creative writing teacher, hair client still, a huge fan, "You will be published!" Words expressed after he read the first poem I wrote, fiercely waving the paper it was written on.

Members at the Writer's group in Steamboat Springs, Colorado, the Scottsdale, Arizona Writer' Group, and author, Laura Orsini, from the Phoenix Arizona Writers' Group Meetup.

Harriett Freiberger, the author of excellent writing that leaves you wanting more, gave me the courage to read my poetry and essays at the weekly writers' group meetings I attended in Steamboat. Her goodbye words linger on: *You need a good copy editor — do not let anyone change your style of writing.*

Sandy Conlon retired English teacher, who provided undeniable encouragement and early help in editing.

Kit Suman, photographer, whose picture of the Statue of Liberty (available on the Internet, no charge) on the book cover reminds me of that single moment in 1965, on a ship from England, when I first faced the symbol of America with starry eyes.

Above all thank you to Lew, my eternal love, husband for life, for fulfilling a long-ago elusive dream in Tann, Switzerland. With my profound appreciation for his spellbinding computer skills, he taught me not to panic when my 'machine' got stuck and left me with moments of agony. His mastermind handed me my first book, a proof copy with my words and pictures in color in time for our trip to Switzerland, to show family and friends. Without his patience, this book would not be what it is today; nor completed.

Preface

Reading this inspirational book, a memoir written in different forms, a collection of short stories, poetry, prose about the school of life, courage, and adventure, trust in fate, joy, heartache, resilience, and — love — may evoke emotions about what love is — can be. Or simply help someone to believe in love and hope that something good can and does happen.
Real-life stories, poems about a belief something extraordinary is possible — Inspiration laced with love.
Coming to America . . . Living the dream. Fate and faith at work. Finding love beyond the stars — Lew, my husband's words: "This book reveals the key to happiness."

True happiness is . . . to want what you have.

A dare-to-be-different (not chronological) memoir with pictures in color to fit the stories throughout.

Writing . . . at the heart of that ambition is desire and determination to show readers the world through the author's eyes — a somewhat arrogant conviction to have found a way to describe something worth committing to paper.

I cherish the gift of writing . . . a revelation of one's reality, like creating a world by the light of the mind and the heat of the heart and — poetry — the impossible task of making the absent present, like photographing the invisible.
I feel in outstanding company with those who write for joy alone and hope my writing remains necessary — vital in my existence, in a life filled with feelings and emotions where my passionate mind believes in the power of words.

Various essays and poems are about unusual happenings in my life such as The Power of Prayers — (my first story) — To Find What I Was Looking for When I Wasn't Looking — A Rose for Mom — A Reason to Wear a Tie — Dollars from Heaven — Night of Broken Bones — Intuition . . . When it Matters — What Possible is. . .
A Friend Who Wanted Me to Live, one story reads about health, how friends, by example, have educated me to eat right, how it changed my life. To lose weight and keep off, the reason I listened, due to many failed diets. To look better **is** to feel

better. The journey is the reward. I learned to believe: Health is a Choice.

Readers will find one chapter about the author's connection to FIFA, (Federation International Football Association) and *Herr* Sepp Blatter, Ex-President of the *Fussball Weltverband* for seventeen years — World Football — called Soccer in America.

Some names, locations, `and identifying characteristics portrayed in this book have been changed to protect the privacy of people in the writer's life. The stories reflect the author's recollection of events, and the dialogue has been re-created based on memory. Every story, every poem has a human face put on display for the reader.
Thank you for accepting my version of the past — a hunch, a memoir is not after all just memory. . .

Some Things Are Simply Meant to Be.

Scottsdale, Arizona, July 1**8,** 2021

Trudy Wells-Meyer

July 1**8**, 2006, a Zermatt photographer solicited for our picture,
up on the Gornergrat.

The Dog That Could Not Walk

He had no feet, no legs,
   bouncing up steep steps as if he did.
      The leash was brown, a string only, I found in
         hardened mud, next to flowers with no name.

I had a dog in picture-perfect Switzerland,
   where I once lived, loved, and had been young.
      Majestic snow-covered Alps, hidden behind dark clouds,
         it smelled like rain, again . . . no sunshine today.

A dog's playful steps on a lonely country road,
   no sounds of barking, my childish joy making me leap, run.
   Blowing in the wind, thoughts of seldom smiling mom.
   Dog hair on her rug and spotless home, unthinkable!

Not hearing the sounds of Switzerland,
   distant cowbells, church bells ringing, only
      the shrill voice of my oh-so-stern, hard-working mom,
      "No dog hair on my hard-earned couch!"

No dog allowed. I dared to dream. I was six, poor, I made do.
   A child's avoid-trouble eyes can see far-reaching is possible
      radiating amazement at "perfect" not looking like
         imagined. I had a dog, chasing after me on a string.

I had a dog that was a ball, no chance to fall.
   My brother's missing soccer ball.
      A joyous secret, Noah was his name,
         our walks a distant memory.

[The first poem I ever wrote, on the balcony in Coronado, CA. in 2008.
First Prize, Dream Quest One, Chicago, Editor, Andre L. West,
International Poetry Prize, $ 250.00, 3/9/2013.
First Prize, Mid-South Poetry Festival Poetry Society of Tennessee,
10/1/2011.
Second Place, Southwest Manuscripters, California, Poetry Contest,
10/18/2010, on my birthday.)

Haupt Strasse, Tann-Rüti, Zürich, Switzerland,
the street where I grew up.

Coming to America

"We all harbor dreams of greatness; the size will be measured by our memories." — Anonymous

At the airport in Kloten, Zürich, boarding a plane to London, from where I would travel to Southampton and embark on a German ship, the Bremen, for America, I hugged my father Adieu. He held me tighter than he ever had. His hug that day remains an unending feeling, and his words would linger in my ears. "*Udi*" — his nickname for me — "you will not come back."

"*Schgruna*" (my nickname for dad), "I am just going for one year," I whispered in his ear. I was crying now. A father knows.

My name is Trudy. I arrived in New York from the German-speaking part of Switzerland on June 18, 1965. I traveled from England on a massive ocean liner, my home for the longest days of my young life. Surrounded by water, on my own — all by myself. Each moment of the voyage took me farther away from the only home I knew. For hours I gazed at the brilliant glittering sea, like dancing diamonds. Endless time to wonder and doubt the dream of C*oming to America*. Fear, a constant companion.

I was 23.

With an explosion of emotions that could not be explained, only felt, I recalled the waiting, all the opportunities of possibly changing my mind. I had told no one in the family about my plans, only Doris, the older sister, understood my dream. Close friends were in awe when I applied for a visa, filling out endless papers. In early 1960, to obtain a green card — an American work visa — required eleven months, an eternity of waiting.

My first glimpse of the Statue of Liberty in the distance, with a sky-stained pink, her extended arm the first thing to appear on the horizon felt like a welcome. What a goose-bump moment on a ship that took five drawn-out days to reach the United States of America. There she was, the symbol of America, of life unknown. I put my hand on my pounding heart as I stared across the glistening water, mesmerized. A young woman transfixed, with mahogany-colored perfectly teased hair,

3

hoping the wind would not destroy. I leaned against the rail of the balcony on this giant traveling city. I rubbed my eyes and stretched out farther until the sea spray-coated my face. The skyscrapers behind the Statue of Liberty rose huge, came closer. The physical beauty and magnificence jolted me into seeing my simple world in a brand-new way, a vision I would most likely remember for the rest of my days. America, the country dreams are made of for a girl growing up relatively poor in a modest Swiss village, in an old house where even dreaming had its limits, never knowing of Switzerland's admired beauty worldwide.

Illusions, ideas, what-ifs . . . the dream of *Coming to America,* my Swiss friend Maria, a hairdresser, lived all that one year before my departure. Maria left for America in 1964, to work in a suburb of Silver Springs, Maryland, filled with skull-spinning excitement and fear of not speaking much English. Regularly Maria wrote letters to me about life surpassing expectations, about the fancy, humongous salon: Vincent and Vincent, a chain with over fifty beauty shops in the Washington, DC area.

Maria and I had worked at Salon Ulmer, near the lake of Zürich. The owner, Mr. Ulmer, was licensed to teach apprentices for 3 years each, girls who wanted to be hairstylists. Cheap help. Maria finished her apprenticeship one year before I did. I learned endlessly from my mentor, a role model with class and influential in everything: hair, manners, how to dress, how to talk to guys. I looked up to Maria completely during our two years together, in a small salon in Rapperswil, two villages away from Tann. I commuted by train every morning and evening. Maria's parents lived in Jona, close to the beauty shop. She arrived every day, on a worn-out bicycle, looking immaculate even when it rained.

In our late teens, we fantasized day after day about going to America, someday. A dream turned into life-altering events.

I had applied and received an offer for a position while Maria worked at the trendy salon in Silver Springs. As planned, Maria returned to her homeland after one year in the US.

A job, a salon across the ocean waited for another Swiss. Me. In June of 1965, I became Maria's replacement.

Dreams do come true. A story to be written. . ..

Early Days in Switzerland

My authoritarian parents chose my profession in an era when kids, especially sons, were expected to continue in the family business. At sixteen years old they pulled me out of the Catholic boarding school in the French part of Switzerland (against my wishes, I cried for days) to start an apprenticeship, for three years, to become a *Coiffeuse,* a hairstylist for ladies.

I disliked hairdressing while working in Tann at my mother and father's successful, old-world beauty shop and a two-station barbershop located on the noisy main street. Years of struggles when they first opened changed to men lining up and waiting their turn, reading the newspaper at the barbershop — no appointments necessary, simply unheard of in those days. *Tädi*, known as the elite barber in town, attracted clients from miles around.

My family lived above the salon in a small rented two-bedroom apartment. On the same floor, another family with two young boys. A single mother, her teenage boy, and an elderly couple lived in the two apartments on the top floor. Four cramped families.

Mom, the stylist for ladies, ran up the stairs to the tiny kitchen to cook lunch during customers' time, some of them under the hairdryer. Naturally, the kids had to help early on, even cooking. Mom not having time appeared endless.

Mother, a seamstress by trade when she met my dashing father in Davos, newly married the happy couple rented and took over a hair salon for men and women in Tann, Zürich Oberland. While pregnant with my older sister, Mom enrolled in hairdressing, a school at the Coiffeur Fachschule in Zürich. She rode one hour each way, by train, three days a week, for six months.

Working with family, competing with Mother was no fun. Not for Erwin, my insecure one-year-older brother, who never wanted to be a hairdresser and barber. His boy-dream to be a professional football/soccer player is still a dream. The first time a client had the nerve to ask the question that left Mom insulted, "Can Trudy do my hair today?" "Why not Erwin?" she'd snarl, her pride hurt. *What about me?* Nonetheless, Mom served and coiffed plenty of customers, every day proved her success to the fullest.

Her domineering ways expected everything of her three — eleven years later — four children. She waged a constant war of words in daily life, yet we knew the consequences of talking back all too well.

No! No continues to fill my ears.

"No, you can't play after school. You help in the salon."

Continuous sweeping hair from the old tile floor, washing clients' hair, taking rollers out, cleaning the stations for the next customer — a day-to-day routine. Not my 3 years older sister Doris, she had asthma, spared conveniently at precise times.

Mom put me on a wobbly stool when I was six years old to shampoo ladies' hair.

"Don't get Mrs. Zollinger wet," Mother hollered. Of course, I did. Trying hard didn't help — I would go and worry for years.

"No, you can't leave the table. You sit here until you finish all your food. Think of the starving children in China." (Every Friday fish — I hate fish to this day.)

Later, as a teenager:" No, you can't stay out after seven," Dad echoed. "No, you don't kiss a boy or any man. That's how girls get pregnant." One *no* I would come to understand much later. Parents mean well — lessons kids often sadly learn too late after they grow up and begin to grasp the depth of their love and discipline.

Nevertheless, the power of possibilities took over my life at an early age — an urge to go boldly in the direction of my dreams, hopeful for a place that would change my life. I believed something extraordinary was possible. I dared to dream about America, with all its glory and reputation as the home of the strong and the brave.

***

Destiny knocked. A mysterious, unforgettable long-distance call, five months before my *Going to America* departure. I hobbled to answer the shrill ringing one frosty winter evening in February at my parents' second-story apartment. Dad's barbershop and Mom's adjoining beauty salon downstairs had closed for the day. I heard a German voice as I picked up the receiver on a wall phone in our dimly lit, cold hallway.

"This is Mr. Hendreks from Houston, Texas."

"Who?" I wondered in shock, *a phone call from America.*

In High-German the voice continued, "My good friend Johann, owner of Salon Johann in St. Louis, gave me Coiffeur Meyer's phone number."

"Are you Trudy?" Mr. Hendreks asked.

Time to drop the phone.

Too startled to find words, an image of a gigantic salon ad, *Looking for hairdressers from Europe,* flashed in front of me — a Cordes & Hendreks monthly ad in the famous German hairdresser magazine my father subscribed to I knew well. An ad not to be missed, its size downright intimidating, I never attempted to answer and apply for a job; although I sure thought of it a range of times.

"I would love to talk to you," the voice continued.

"You want to do what?" I think I yelled. I told him about my ski accident. "I am on crutches."

"Can I come and visit you?"

Confusion and disbelief swirled in my brain.

I did not dare interrupt Mr. Hendreks's commanding voice as he insisted on using a taxi, a nearly one-hour ride from Zürich, the big city — the cost of it! — to visit my parents' humble home to see and talk to *me.*

Mr. Hendreks is in Switzerland, calls, and wants to see *me?*

He arrived one hour later. Tall, debonair, well-dressed like he was going to a party, he shook my hand with a firm grip. I invited him in. I trembled to open the living room door.

Showing concern for my broken leg he professed, "Johann, my good friend in St. Louis, gave me your letter when you applied for a job at his salon a month ago," he continued, "Well, I am here to offer you employment in my salon either in Atlanta, Georgia, or Houston, Texas." His words spilled out as he sipped strong, hot black tea my mother had offered him, sitting on the worn-out couch in the small living room. Wishing everything to be more glamorous, I watched my mom put her hands on her stunned face when Mr. Hendreks explained he traveled periodically to Europe to find hairstylists. My father breathing hard, with a face like stone, remained reading the newspaper on his favorite chair in the corner.

I stared at this charming stranger like a ghost from outer space. Why me? I listened in total awe. I blurted, "Mr. Hendreks, you need to know, I do have a job already, in Silver Springs, Maryland, at Vincent and Vincent."

On the way out to catch the still waiting taxi to return to Zürich, this handsome blond German with impeccable manners waved his business card nonchalantly. I stood at the top of the squeaky wooden stairs, my crutches not allowing me to walk down to open the heavy entry door for our mystery visitor. He spoke words I would never forget as he handed me a Cordes & Hendreks' card.

"If you don't like working in Silver Springs, call me anytime. I hope you heal real soon."

My mom, peeking around the corner of the freezing hallway, waved to Mr. Hendreks. A firm handshake with both his hands and last words lingering still: "See you in America." He was gone.

Staring at the closed door I felt rooted to the floor. It took time to grasp the strangeness of this evening. I turned to my mother in utter astonishment, hands over my mouth. I vowed obsessing, "This . . . has to have something to do with later."

My innermost feelings could not believe I had heard right. Did I indeed listen to a verbal job offer for a Cordes & Hendreks' salon in Houston or Lenox Square, a shopping mall in Atlanta? Overwhelming words hurled around my dizzy brain with this new situation to wonder about.

At the time, unknown to me, Swiss hairdressers were well-liked in the States. How much in demand, I was soon to find out. One of life's unpredictable events at its finest — a simple phone call that would change my life, although I did not yet know how much. The mystery call I limped to answer that fateful February evening, in a cast up to my knee for eight weeks, was linked to an ad I answered in a fashionable Swiss German hairdresser magazine.

A German name, Johann, had caught my eye: *Salon Johann: Wanted: Swiss Hair Stylists.* I applied, not knowing where St. Louis was. Missouri? Where? I wrote mostly out of curiosity, my love for writing, and simply boredom during my recovery from a broken ankle, the result of a beginner ski crash in deep powder snow with borrowed skis. The binding did not release.

Why, oh why, did I write to a Salon Johann in St. Louis? Today, the answer is only too clear:
Some Things Are Simply Meant to Be.

Two months before my planned departure, my flight to Washington, DC, was booked and managed to fill me with unfamiliar nervousness and overwhelming excitement. Then, another phone call rattled my brain — another job offer.

Holland America Cruise Line called. A voice with an accent informed me my application from over one year ago got accepted. They want me. Now?

Weird timing to say the least, or at its best, a call to fulfill another dream of mine, working aboard a cruise ship in the hair salon. Why now? I had forgotten I wrote and applied. I simply believed I did not get the job when for so many months I hadn't received a response from the world-renowned Holland cruise line.

Now what? My thoughts scrambled about how much I always desired to see the world while working on a ship. What if I journeyed on a ship to New York? Could I possibly change my flight reservation? I did.

Influential advice and persistent help from Els, Mom's long-time friend and client, convinced me. Els had lived in the US for eight years, and her stories filled with remarkable experiences I adored listening to. Together we booked my voyage on the *Bremen,* a German ship out of England, to Ellis Island New York. We canceled the flight to New York on TWA, changed, and rebooked the time and day on a flight to Washington, DC. I tried to ignore worries about how I'd find the airport from the ship once docked. I believed I had the best of two worlds.

Nevertheless, my fear of traveling and finding Silver Springs, Maryland, left me with restless, sleepless nights. Someone — I didn't know who — from the salon would meet me at the airport in D.C. Apprehension about how to contact the salon and use of a not ever-seen-before payphone, would hit me later.

***

Late in the afternoon of my first day aboard the mammoth ship with endless, narrow corridors — too many to count — I found the top deck. I spotted a white-haired, distinguished-looking gentleman leaning against the ship's railing. My watch had stopped; my rumbling belly, however, knew soon to be dinner time. Using my courage, I approached this well-dressed older man to ask in my broken English, "Can you please tell me the time?" Embarrassed but smiling, in Swiss German, he informed me, "*Ich verstah kei Englisch.*" He did not understand English.

I held back my urge to hug this man from joy and elation. A Swiss guy traveling to visit his daughter in New York had the power to let me feel *at home.* This Swiss German-only-speaking gentleman invited me to have dinner together. An assigned

9

table for two in the same corner remained ours throughout the whole journey. Passengers believed us to be a father and daughter crossing together, destination United States.

Across the dining room lit by sparkly crystal chandeliers, a striking stranger glanced over at our table, too often, too obviously. Nervously I sensed him catch me looking back at him. I lowered my eyes each time and tried to concentrate on the delicious food. The third night our eyes met; he held my gaze. When dessert was served, out of the corner of my eyes I saw the tall slender stranger get up. Heads turned as he walked over to our table and introduced himself: Wolfgang von Ravenshausen, a name to perk up my ears, guessing: Royalty? His dark eyes were deep-set and unblinking, and his sun-tanned face and shy smile had the ability to change the beating of my heart.

"Entschuldigung, so sorry. I did not mean to intrude." Herr von Ravenshausen assumed he had met my father sitting next to me. Stunned, when he found out differently, he left the table with an obvious heartfelt *excuse-me.* He not only looked embarrassed; he was. Did he believe he had met an older sugar daddy traveling with his mistress?

The next evening Wolfgang found me alone on the top deck

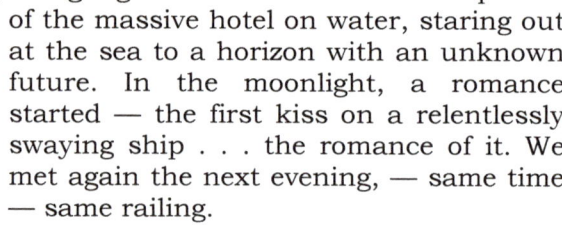

of the massive hotel on water, staring out at the sea to a horizon with an unknown future. In the moonlight, a romance started — the first kiss on a relentlessly swaying ship . . . the romance of it. We met again the next evening, — same time — same railing.

Wolfgang offered to drive me to Washington, DC. "You want to do what?" I answered in awe.

Wolfgang von Ravenshausen journeyed with his new Mercedes on board the *Bremen.* While visiting his family home in Munich, Germany, he purchased a dream car to drive through America to Mexico City via Houston, Texas. Mexico City, his home for ten years while working for Siemens, a huge German company. I found a literal prince, royal by name only, who would take me to my future job and home?

My concern on how to travel to Silver Springs, solved in one instant, one sentence, words of help sounded like music.

More like an alarm going off. If my parents knew. . .

The last evening in our romantic spot, a dark burgundy moon enhanced a passionate kiss, like a so long forever.

Wolfgang confessed, "I am married."

I jolted and pushed him away. Of course. A handsome, tall, sophisticated German; why be surprised?

To this day I love to reminisce about a truly innocent time aboard a rocking ship, the two of us holding hands while countless other passengers were sick and confined to their cabins. The strong ocean wind had me lean on a man who stole my heart for a little while as we listened to the newly released original song by Al Martino with, a haunting melody, "Blue Spanish Eyes."

Fernweh — Wanderlust on our minds and . . . what might have been.

The ship docked in New York at Ellis Island the next morning. Pulled out of the line of travelers moving through customs, an official, with his hand on my arm walked me to a narrow cold room with no furniture and unsmiling immigration personnel sitting at a long table at the end of this daunting room. He pushed me toward a stern woman in her commanding cap. Standing nervously, finally, she acknowledged my presence. Filled with fear, I handed her an envelope. She checked my x-ray which I knew was required to enter the United States of America. I pointed to my doctor's signature on a document provided to me on my last check-up for my broken leg, from the ski accident five months before my voyage.

A voice too scary for my fragile nerves instructed, "Walk to the end of the room and back."

My injury hurt on this particular morning and all the while during the crossing of the Atlantic. Fear of the unknown, nerves playing tricks. I understood one thing: *Walk straight — without limping — do not give them a reason to send me back*. Watched by eagle eyes, I passed the test of America. In 1965, the US did not want any immigrants who would become a burden to their country. How times have changed.

Walking off that ship in New York, understanding and speaking a little English — although not American English — Swiss-chocolate-smitten, extra pounds hiding, I was dressed in my finest: a pink coat left open to reveal a black dress with matching pink flowers. I carried two small suitcases. For the first time I faced endless tall buildings reaching the sky — skyscrapers — the word now made sense, and masses of rushing people — going where? Not ever will I forget the noise — deafening sounds of a bustling city, — New York.

I thought of my stern and oh-so-strict mom, her amazing bragging words I could never believe when I overheard her say to one of her clients, *"My daughter can do anything!"* This was the moment to live up to unmatched words.

"Eventually" had become "Now".

"You gain strength, courage and, confidence by every experience in which you stop looking fear in the face . . . You must do the thing you think you can't do." — Eleanor Roosevelt

While waiting for a brand-new German Mercedes driven off the *Bremen*, Herr von Ravenshausen, Prince Charming, thought about the moment he first set eyes on the girl with fancy hair across the dining room. He had experienced an undeniable spark, as he wondered, *Is she traveling with her father?*

Wolfgang's promise to drive Trudy to Washington, DC, on the way home to Mexico City was still his plan. He had caught up with the starry-eyed girl gazing at her first overpowering American surroundings. He invited her to wait with him at a bar at the harbor, in the middle of the morning, near the dock where ships come and go, in and out, day after day.

Stepping on American soil, Trudy's legs — her whole body —, still felt the rocking, back-forward ship motion. Worries about driving off with a stranger left her mind in disarray; she was excited but scared. In Trudy's heart secretly asked: *What the heck am I about to do?* Dad's face surfaced uninvited, his voice too strict to ignore, and Mom right there with him. *No . . . no.*

"The will of God will never take you where the grace of God cannot protect you." — Anonymous

Trudy clumsily climbed onto a tall barstool, one of many lined up along the gleaming bar with countless bottles, wondering, *why so many?* The young bartender put down a huge glass of ice water in front of her. In shock, she gasped, "I did not order that." A simple girl from Tann believed water is for poor people.

"Please, can I have a soda?" She shoved the glass away, her small English vocabulary not letting her down. The water was never removed. In Switzerland, if you ask for a glass of water, they think you have a headache. The drop-dead handsome American bartender laughed. Prince Charming, his lips wet with beer, joined him, amused by an innocent Swiss girl who was embarrassed Wolfgang drank beer before noon.

Angst and worried to find JFK Airport in the wind, I sat next to Wolfgang, a married gentleman through and through, in his striking car as we drove away from New York toward Baltimore, a turn of events that simply left me impressed beyond words. My whole life stretched out ahead in promise as I gaped at monotonous Interstate highways, cars everywhere, and numerous industrial signs along the road I could not read. His selected route to drive by the White House and the Capitol started pinch-me moments. I was in America! Pictures in an

13

album, impossible to replace, revealing a blue-sky day. I listened to Wolfgang's knowledge of US history all the while I worried sick about how he would find my destination. His pre-organized road map, planned while in Germany, did not include a side trip to a suburb he had never heard of.

We encountered severe hiccups in locating the salon. An effort of finding a payphone, any phone, to let somebody know of my arrival, left me jittery and panicky. Both of us had no American coins. I almost stopped breathing.

Early evening Wolfgang found the salon, *Vincent and Vincent.*

"We don't have to pick you up at the airport!" yelled a voice. "We worried and impatiently waited to hear from you. "

Concerned Phil, the tall, chubby manager, left his client in the chair and rushed toward me with outstretched arms and a most welcome smile. His bear-hug had everyone in the salon staring. He was exactly the kind of boss a frazzled Swiss girl should meet on the first day of her new job in a foreign country, a continent away.

Wolfgang, my driver, my Prince for a little while, stood at the still-open door with my two suitcases. To put where? Shrugging my shoulders, I had no idea.

I turned to him, "*Danke vielmals*, Wolfgang," hoping my simple thank-you adequate. He grabbed me with strong arms and felt my resistance, too tense and uncomfortable about what everybody at the busy salon was thinking. Our eyes locked. With a faint smile, his voice lower than usual he declared, "What will be, will be. I know in my heart I will see you again."

He did.

A year later, out of nowhere in my thrilling American life, while his promise had faded from my mind, Wolfgang, now divorced, flew from Mexico-City to find me, only to discover: a ship romance is what it is . . . a ship romance.

I had moved on.

Silver Springs, Maryland, 1965-1966

Elena, a platinum bleached-blonde Swiss hairdresser at the elegant Vincent and Vincent salon, was expecting the arrival of that new Suisse traveling by ship from Europe. She needed a roommate to split the rent of her one-bedroom/den third-floor apartment on Piney Branch Road, about ten minutes from the beauty shop. My friend Maria's small room was waiting.

The den, with a squeaky accordion door for privacy, became my home for over a year. My bed, a couch — pulled out to cover most of the room, a wall I'd bump into most nights in the dark on my way to the bathroom. The room reminded me of the tiny one I had shared back home with my older sister.

Homesick, one learns the hard way. I never admitted to my parents and family when tears and helpless moments left me sad and downright desperate. To depend on a ride day-after-day — anywhere — no fun. The bus stop was close to the salon yet far from the apartment. I cleaned a lot to make up for the favors.

Lorraine, the receptionist, a stunning, impeccably dressed, middle-aged lady, was my angel of mercy and biggest help in day after day, unknown tasks. My savior, my first American Mom let me borrow her old bike. To have no car in giant America, unheard of. I had to rely on rides and mostly had no guts to ask for.

I still hold dear Lorraine's parting words, accompanied by uncontrollable tears, when I left DC,

"Don't ever forget — if God would give me another daughter, — I would only want you."

The language barrier a constant, "Excuse me, what did you say?" I knew for sure I did not say anything right.

Much later, I would find out people did not understand my scrambled English words because of my soft speaking voice. Answering a phone call especially had me in a tizzy. I had trouble trying to correct myself, to find the right words.

Oh, and all Americans like to spell. Why did I not learn the English ABC sooner? In my country, we did not admit we didn't know how to spell a word. (How I was brought up.) We searched and looked words up. Expected to know, we didn't ask. Is the German language possibly easier to write and know words by sound? I mostly tried to guess. Still do.

My lucky number **8** started in Silver Springs, Maryland, during my homesick, electrifying first year in the US. The day I stepped on American soil was June 1**8**. Up till now memorable things happen when I see **8**. A number can (does) possess magical power.

Urged on by my boss, Phil, the gentle teddy bear-like manager who loved Swiss girls working at his salon, I boldly entered a hair competition in downtown Washington, DC, at the Hilton Hotel. Thirty-four contestants on stage were given ten minutes to finish a hairstyle/comb-out, with hundreds of people watching.

I won.

Excited beyond belief to win the first prize in America, I knew *Everything* that happens in the United States is simply bigger. A gigantic number **8** in front of my model, a red-headed client I colored a rich auburn, reflecting in the mirror remains distinctly in my mind.

Upon a platform, the Master of Ceremony presented a shiny silver and turquoise trophy nearly as tall as me and a certificate in bold, gold letters. I was announced a winner: Potomac Styling Champion 1966.

As I raised the trophy in a triumphant pose, revealing naked emotions, he asked the name of the salon where I worked. Nervously, in my strong accent and still limited English, after nine turbulent months, I said, "Wincent and Wincent."

The MC laughed. In the massive room filled with onlookers and hairdressers, everybody laughed. A burst of loud laughter I had no idea why. Later, much later, I speculated the expressed amusement to be the difference trying the American way to say, Vincent and Vincent, in a strange accent to most people.

Up till now, with a married name of Wells, my pronunciation of Ws and Vs demands a perpetual repeat:

"My name is Vells."

"Oh, you mean Wells."

In the Swiss-German language, W and V are the reverse, one sure *vay,* (way) to detect a German accent.

Due to my win, eligible and invited to enter the competition Monday, the next day, for stylists who had won a trophy in the past, I showed up with a different model. A blonde hairdresser, a friend.

I won second place.

Another tall trophy.

My proud dad back home (I can see his lips trembling) called the Swiss Hairdresser Association and various newspapers. His father, my grandpa, had worked all his life as a typesetter at the local newspaper in Wohlen AG to feed his fourteen children. Dad, the second youngest, number thirteen in the Meyer family, let everyone know about his successful daughter in America. Pictures forever in print, yes, in black and white.

***

Once again, a phone call changed my train of life to a new and different track, a destination written in the stars. One fateful Monday morning, a jolting phone as I entered Vincent and Vincent's salon. I had opened the back door with a borrowed key in search of the jacket I had left behind on Saturday after a busy workday. I rushed to pick up the shrill ringing phone at the front desk.

"This is Mr. Hendreks from Houston." I gasped at the familiar phrase. I recognized that German voice. My dazed feelings intensified, *"Am I dreaming?"* Flabbergasting — since the salon was closed for business on Mondays, and I surely was not supposed to answer or be there at all.

Fate at work. Again.

Mr. Hendreks had called for Trudy. His identifiable *Hoch Deutsch* High German accent once again sounded too cool for words. He showed no surprise I answered the phone. I heard him say, "Let's have dinner. I like to take you to *La Rève* tomorrow, Tuesday evening? I will be in town, a short stop-over in Washington, DC, on the way to Germany."

I hesitated but only for a moment with a babbling answer, "*Ja. Wo — where* — that elegant, posh restaurant?"

The mystery of how he got the number of one of fifty-two Vincent and Vincent salons in Maryland, the one where I worked, seemed as far-fetched as going to the moon. As I sat across from Henry Hendreks, dressed in a stylish suit and tie, I wondered if he was married. No wedding band showing. I anxiously fingered a glass of wine in a classy restaurant in downtown DC. I found out with my mouth open hanging on this sophisticated German's words, "I met Mrs. Silverman."

Natalie Silverman, my divorced, born-in-France client, who once a week had her hair done, (a routine loved by ladies of leisure and money), had plans to fly to Houston to spend a week with her new boyfriend from Texas.

"I need to get my hair done while I am in Houston," she stated worriedly as I finished a striking hairstyle every time putting a smile on Natalie's face.

"Mrs. Silverman, oh, call Salon Cordes & Hendreks, with all European hairdressers," I shouted too loudly.

She wrote down the name as I continued to tell Natalie all about Mr. Hendreks' puzzling phone call as well as his mind-blowing visit by taxi to tiny Tann, in Switzerland, months before I left for America.

My parting words as she left her weekly salon, "If, by chance, you should see Mr. Hendreks, please say hello from Trudy."

It turned out Natalie Silverman met Mr. Cordes, the business partner, as well as Henry Hendreks, who seldom spent time at the Houston salon (mostly at the Dallas or Atlanta location). He happened to be there on the morning of Natalie's hair appointment. The proud German took the time to show Mrs. Silverman around the huge Texas beauty salon and served her coffee in a porcelain cup. Natalie enjoyed the royal European treatment immensely, she reported happily during her regular hair appointment after her return to D.C.

Now sitting across from this attractive German man with intriguing blue eyes, my unbelieving ears listened to Mr. Hendreks's words that changed my life — a job offer.

"How would you like to move to Atlanta and work at the Lenox Square salon?"

I glared at him bedazzled as if he were the angel of mercy. I hardly touched my food but sipped my wine too much.

He continued, "One of my German hairdressers, Monique, is leaving. A station will be available, with an assistant, and far more important — customers waiting for a new European lady hairstylist."

The unreal timing of these unmatched circumstances caused my bewilderment and would continue for days. I clutched my heart with both hands. Words hit my brain . . . I had vowed to my mom obsessively back home in Tann, after Mr. Hendreks slipped into a taxi to return to Zürich after his mysterious visit, *"This has to have something to do with later."* Oh, how it did. . .

What will be . . . will be, one of my life-long favorite lines along with my sincere belief: *Something will happen to show you what to do — with prayers.* These truths — had now transpired and waiting for a sign from God had come to a halt, as monumental as life itself.

A flight to Purdue University in Indiana for the upcoming weekend had been booked for two weeks. Malik, tall, dark, and movie-star-like, my boyfriend since the New Year holidays, anticipated my visit.

Phil, my gentle-bear boss, who was like a father to me and called me *Strudel,* had introduced me to Malik, his nephew, at a glamorous New Year's party at the family's home.

Malik's uncommonly good looks, a gentleman any mother would be proud of, had stolen my heart. He was divorced, with a two-year-old sandy-blond boy, Benjamin, who did not live with Malik's drug-addicted ex-wife.

Facts caused various questions about a future together.

Malik, my Jewish boyfriend, was getting too serious. My parents did not know about a boyfriend. Whereas Malik's mother, who took care of Benjamin, her first and only grandson, agonized about a certain Catholic girl from Switzerland.

On that Saturday late afternoon, with a heavy heart, I flew to visit Malik, to break up and end our relationship, at Purdue, where he finished his studies to become a doctor.

With a deflated face he uttered, "You are leaving for Atlanta?"

I did.

19

Four months before that momentous decision, I had spotted a dreamy white and blacktop convertible automobile, in a showroom at a car dealer in downtown Washington, DC.

"*I want that one,*" I uttered knowing full well I had no cash — payments to a bank for years to come — the American way. My over-bleached Swiss roommate Elena's older boyfriend, a respectable doctor, offered to co-sign his name on a loan agreement. I never really knew this distinguished Swiss man, born in my country, with a flourishing practice in Bethesda Maryland, a ritzy district of Washington, DC. We proudly shared a Swiss trust. The day I returned to the fancy dealership with all the necessary signed papers, — no white car — sold. Oh, no, blue? More like powder blue, spot-on as the white car besides magnificent I had to admit. Driving away, in a state of utter delirium as well as rattled of maneuvering such a gigantic car, I drove on the hectic streets, in rush hour. My 'new, fancy toy' stopped. Yuk, they sold me a bad car, a 'lemon'. Honking everywhere had tears rolling down my face. An eternity later, a young man tapped on the car window. Embarrassed and panicky I searched for how to open it. "Lady, you are out of gas."

In the middle of summer 1966, I drove away in my blue Pontiac Tempest convertible leaving Silver Springs. Aged photos in a drawer show top-down. A lonesome twosome, my imposing car, and me, with marked-in-red AAA maps on my front seat.

"Bravery is being the only person who knows you're afraid." —
Franklin P. Jones

On the long-drawn-out trip toward a new future in the South, Atlanta, Georgia, my mind journeyed back to Switzerland, to a time when I learned to be strong. My Grandma in Davos, whom I admired deeply, boasted, "You are the most courageous one in our family." Her words meant the world.

I recalled a daunting experience, the first time my parents sent me away at age eight, alone, during winter school vacation to visit Grandma. Mom's mother rented out rooms to Germans visiting family at the legendary Lung Sanatoriums in the Grison Alps in Davos. She could use help cleaning. Memories trickled in the back of my mind of Grandma's mirror-like shiny wood floors, surely the shiniest in all the mountain villages.

Unsmiling *Mami*, (Mom) put me on a train to travel all by myself to Davos-Dorf. A trip we had done with the whole family before. Knowing I had to change three times to a different, always-on-time train — Swiss time, gave me train fever.

The second train stop in Ziegelbrücke scared me the most. A two-minute halt only to step on a *Schnellzug*, a fast, nonstop train from Zürich. Next stop Landquart. I endured uncontrollable angst and fear as I sat on the edge of the wooden bench, so as not miss getting out, tense out of my wits. In Landquart, another rush across the train station to connect and catch a waiting, smaller red train, *Rhättische Bahn*, from Chur to Davos.

One never forgets fright on a three-hour *Eisenbahn* train ride. Wondering shakingly if my elegant, persistently wearing a hat when leaving the house Grandma would be waiting at the *Bahnhof* (train station) in Davos-Dorf.

Will the rattling train stop long enough to let me out at that small *Bahnhof,* a two-track train station? A location one day would become famous to prominent world leaders attending the World Economic Forum meetings, held in Davos, every January. Still does. A resort, a vacation destination, known as well to thousands of skiers, from different parts of Switzerland, and the world, to experience the magnificent mountain, named Parsenn, *Weissflu Joch,* with one of the longest ski runs, 12 kilometers. (Skiers still today board the *Zug* in Küblis, back up to Davos, the two-track *Rhätische Bahn.)*

My fear from long ago had developed into courage. Little did I know then, someday I would travel across the ocean, alone . . . and many years later, travel on the very same red train again, to go skiing with my husband, family, and friends at the now fashionable all the rage ski resort Davos, in the Grison Alps.

Haus Rudolf, Davos-Dorf, Grandma Günther's apartment, on the top floor until 1960

If I wondered in those days of my youth growing up how my life would turn out, my boldest guess could not have been near the truth. No knowledge yet of the glamorous world that someday would be mine.

With fascination I learned about everyday life can turn on a small decision — the mystery and myth of fate. A kid from Tann believed early on; something extraordinary is possible and w*hat will be . . . will be.*

Everything in life happens for a reason.

Some Things Are Simply Meant to Be.

"He who submits to fate without complaint is wise." — Euripides

Scottsdale, Arizona — Our Home

To Find What I Was Looking for When I Wasn't Looking

"Years to wonder — one morning to discover — forever to cherish." — Trudy Wells-Meyer

Tombstone, Arizona, a name I knew from reading as a teenager in Switzerland, my passionate, long-held desire to go there, but never finding enough time transformed into a moment that became the center of my memories.

Tombstone, a small Western town compels visitors to think, a place where they are surrounded by boundless history that gives chills. Where it is all about the old way of life: mining, gambling, murder, gunshots, hangings, and certainly bar fights. Now daily shows of gunfights and a long-past lifestyle are repeated over and over, still living this legend. A place where people doubt the phrase, *the good old days* used by countless folks up in years.

Tombstone gives that phrase a whole other meaning.

There, *I found what I was looking for when I wasn't looking.*

Into my husband Lew's first year of retirement in 2005, with a long bucket list of travels, the planned trip had finally arrived, the time was now. I couldn't have been more excited as we drove from Scottsdale through the scenic Arizona desert.

The new, modern Holiday Express, not necessarily the proper place to lodge, gave our Tombstone experience an awareness of today's reality. The downtown streets, where dust followed us everywhere, were filled with people who didn't want to miss one single thing that happened in 1879 —1880. This Western settlement had forty cabins in 1879 and a population of 100. Two years later, the population soared to over 5,000. Then the fires came, twice. Nonetheless, the town was rebuilt immediately.

The direction of my dreams, as a teenager, approached full-circle in this history-filled town on a glorious spring Arizona day, March 14, 2006. My story began fifty-eight years earlier in a small village in Switzerland, where, as far back as I can remember, my underprivileged upbringing affected my dreaming about a different life. No more old newspaper stacked in the bathroom for toilet paper.

Yes, it hurt.

Visiting the old Tombstone Courthouse, a Western Museum today, not my wish of things to do in this desert town; however, my Wisconsin husband's plan, a history lover

fascinated for years with *old stuff* from ages ago. He showed his excitement as we went inside. I followed Lew with a silent sigh, only to experience the leading surprise of my life that shocked me into stunned silence. I had turned to the right on the first floor, into a room filled with tourists, when my eyes caught the sight of a board in the middle of the room. A name in black on white, bold and significant: **KARL MAY!**

With an expression of total disbelief, I stopped and stared long enough for my heart to leap. In front of my unbelieving eyes, I gazed at an exhibit of the famous and legendary German novelist Karl May, a name that had changed my life into my world today.

His name had the ability to bring on an explosion of forceful emotions and memories. I closed my eyes. Karl May, an author who had the talent to write in brilliant ways, such as that Europeans' imaginations were magically inspired and visually knew precisely what the far-away Western places looked like. His books and stories were consistently about the Old West, with cowboys, Indians, and Arizona — the literary details of the Southwest. A renowned novelist, Karl May was known as Europe's window to the West — and mine.

Time stood still. The flush of discovery left me dizzy. *I found what I was looking for when I wasn't looking.* A mere fraction of an instant, I was transported back to my childhood in Switzerland, like crossing over into another dimension, a leap through space and time. A young girl watching mom and astute acting older sister Doris, as they devoured countless books by Karl May. At the turn of the century, he was one of the most celebrated novelists in Germany and Switzerland, and later all over the world.

I recalled the day my mom handed me one of her precious Karl May books. My first. A gift, more like a treasure. *Mami lets me read her cherished book.* With Mother, there was such dignity, an aura of respect, a boundary her four kids did not cross. Mother's somber, often cold, and seldom smiling way stemmed from her enormously strict upbringing high in the mountains in Davos, Switzerland. It included an alcoholic father, German-born in the *Schwarzwald,* Black Forest — and Swiss mother with a temper that created daily fear in eight children, Mom — and seven younger brothers and sisters.

A pregnant daughter — when Grandma found out, she pushed my mom down the steep stairs outside the second-floor apartment. Not married, in 193**8** — the shame of it.

After I finished this magical book, one of many to come, I held it close as if it could break; I gazed at my mom with new admiration. She loved a story about a handsome Apache chief. How a mother can surprise you. Her love for reading and escaping into another world during a hard life after the war started my love affair with a faraway country, a world away, a vision, and inspiration of someday *coming to America.*

As I stood and stared in a room with strangers, I trusted the hand of destiny had brought me here. Memories flooded my heart as I gaped at that name from long ago. Karl May, my hero — a name no American knew. In all the years since my arrival in the USA in 1965, not one person ever answered me with any recognition of his name or any names in those famous stories. Oh, I approached and asked countless people. The answer unfailingly, *'Never heard of him.'* Not even in Arizona.

What about the noble Apache warrior, named Winnetou (Cochise), the atypical Indian hero? What about Old Shatterhand, his virtuous German blood-brother, the white man who loved Indians? Karl May, the author himself was Old Shatterhand, a man who believed in the good of all mankind. He recreated an era when stories of peace, love, and human hearts soared during devastating American cavalry battles — white men against red skins.

How could no one know Old Shatterhand, the heroes and main characters of those books, talked about all over Europe?

Ask any German about these characters — individuals who built an intense relationship with thousands of readers. Uncountable Europeans relived the American-Southwest. Karl May's stories were made into a movie, "*Winnetou*," that would inspire and drive readers to travel to Arizona, a favorite state. Our Swiss friends visited Arizona fourteen times; no other state would do.

Years later, I found out Karl May had *never* visited Arizona himself. His prose was fiction only. *Fiction as wish fulfillment,* an original type of fiction, written in Germany, some while he was in prison.

For a long time, I did not believe it.

Americans enthusiastically claim their own Western author, Zane Grey.

The search for Winnetou the Indian chief, my secret teenage love, had come to a halt. *I found what I was looking for when I wasn't looking.* I stood motionless, incredulous eyes reading and staring at pictures that brought the books vividly to life.

Closeness to my mom, my *Mime*, at this moment had reached beyond intense.

Suddenly, as if struck by a bolt of lightning, my knees went weak. I grabbed a chair and sat down. with a choking feeling in my throat, overpowering tears streamed down my face.

I silently screamed, *"Nein!" Today, March 14th is my mom's birthday."* I shivered with an awareness of earth-shaking magnitude. Mom would have been 91. The day *I found what I almost had given up looking for.*

Happy birthday, *Mime*!

Coincidence or simply God placing me in a Tombstone Courthouse Museum felt overwhelming on this specific day — Mother's spirit reached out on her birthday.

I kept staring at Karl May's exhibit, which had opened in February 2004. A prominent German-writer-world-popular thus the Tombstone State Historic Park had coordinated a partnership with the Karl-May-Foundation in Germany. A large exhibit was built that showed the connection between Germany, Cochise County, and Karl May's legendary books.

Karl May (1842 – 1912) was a prolific author and a favorite

read of several celebrated Germans, including Albert Einstein, Albert Schweitzer, and Herman Hesse. According to the Karl May Press, created by his second wife Klara, his books have sold over 100 million copies across the globe. His sixty novels have been translated into thirty languages, including a recent series in Chinese.

Karl May born in a small town in Germany to an extremely poor family of fourteen children was one of only five to survive infancy. He suffered malnutrition and temporary blindness as a child. He did not travel to the States until 190**8** (never to the west), well after he had written all his famous western novels. The annual two-day Karl May Festival in Bad Segeberg, Germany, is attended by thousands. Clubs in his honor are found around the world. How proud he would have been of such a tribute and exhibit at an old courthouse in Tombstone, Arizona, a result of his passionate fascination with the Old West.

Rooted to the old wood floor, with amazing stillness in my heart, I realized through an unpretentious trip to Tombstone, planned for a long time, my mother had passed down this powerful dream. I have now lived that American dream for years. The clarity of those long-ago, simple days surrounded me with melancholy and nostalgia. I unmistakably now understood the importance of one single moment when Mom handed me that fateful book. Reading and soaring imagination provided a rare escape in our ultimately strict, humble home, where four kids knew demanding work after school. Even hunger was a frequent occurrence when we were small. To dream and read about a land, with no knowledge of where it was and how far away, triggered my love for the magic of words . . . the power of words.

"No, you can't put shoes on. You go barefoot to school." Mom's strict words echoed in my ears, and guilt rose for not obeying her. I was embarrassed, so I hid an old pair behind some bushes halfway to school. Did *Mime* know?

(*Mime,* my lifelong nickname for Mom.)

During days of punishment growing up across the deep ocean, being naughty or misbehaving called for the same consequence each time — locked up in my tiny bedroom. Tiny did not matter, the cold did. Shutters closed the dark had me scared. I hid a flashlight under the covers and one of the Karl May books I had found while sneaking into the attic. I hoped the crack of the old door would not give me away.

How could I have known then, by simply reading about  Winnetou, and dreaming about cowboys and Indians, red rocks, cactus, palm trees, famous sunsets, a place called Arizona would someday become my existence, ultimately my home for over forty years?

Gratitude arose and overwhelmed me for the incredible life I was fortunate to live today.

The day I stepped on foreign soil in New York, my eyes searched for something — anything — that reminded me of Old West movies, of Karl May's books. My visions of America proved to be far from my imagination. However, almost three years later in Atlanta, with destiny and life's astonishing incidents, an unexpected job offer at a new, fancy salon in Scottsdale brought me to Arizona in 1968. A state of breathtaking sunrises and flowers in the desert I had never before seen.

A dream had come true.

The seed planted by my mother soared alive in Tombstone Arizona.

A stranger asked, "Are you all right?"

I trembled. How could I answer about a lifetime flashing in front of my eyes? I smiled at this stranger with a German accent, who will never know what an emotional woman at the age of sixty-four, from a country near his, was feeling. My husband, with a look intense with worry, put his arms around my shoulder in his usual calming way. A touch of most intimate comfort.

My serendipitous rendezvous with destiny at the Tombstone Museum had ended. Lew and I walked out hand in hand, the sky clear, streaked pink toward the west. How I treasure the beauty of this hot country, this jewel of a land I had come to call my own. I found Karl May and Winnetou — eventually — when I wasn't looking. My eyes turned to heaven with a silent prayer.

Thank you, Mime. I could see her rare smile.

At age 80, in 1995, on Saturday, February 28, with a cane for balance, my mom's visit to Arizona finally happened. I had prayed a thousand prayers to my favorite Saint Joseph for that miracle. Oh, the power of prayer. *Tädi* had passed away from Lou Gehrig's disease six years earlier, in 1989.

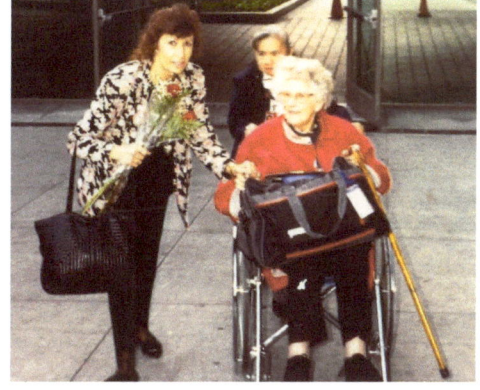

Mom traveled on Swissair, by herself, from Zürich, Switzerland to Los Angeles. Lew had inquired and arranged for a wheelchair. Mom acted like a queen, pushed toward the sounds of an international airport by a smiling Puerto Rican woman. Neither spoke English, but everyone smiles in the same language. Mom knew Lew and I would be waiting, me nervous like never before. On the one-hour flight to Phoenix together, I pinched myself, not believing to have *Mime* so close. At dawn, she'd wake up to a whole new landscape — Arizona — at our home on the lake and golf course in Scottsdale.

Spring in the West, the desert intensely beautiful and the ordinary elevates to turn into the extraordinary. Majestic saguaros on paths stretching as far as the horizon. Witnessing Mother's hidden feelings on the day we drove the Apache-Trail outside Scottsdale — as expected first on *Mime*'s wish list — is a memory I will cherish to the end of time. With the biggest eyes I had ever seen on this regal woman with her sense of stillness and grace, she gazed in amazement at the Sonoran Desert scene from the back seat, her face close to the car window.

Staring at wildflowers in bloom, "*Trunilli*, (one of her nicknames for me) look, flowers on a cactus!" Her voice in a whisper of awe, a scene that boggled her mind. A whole environment known to Mom only from reading Karl May, her favorite, I heard *Mime*'s voice loud and clear, "I can see Winnetou on his horse," I turned around and observed her in dumbfounded silence. What I noticed most were her dreamy eyes. Without a doubt, my mom had a secret-love affair with the Apache hero, as I did, due to an author's world-famous captivation with the Old West.

Driving home I reminded her of "Tom Dooley" by the Kingston Trio. A worldwide popular Western American song that had won a Grammy and Best Song of the Year in 195**8**. A 45 single record Mom played over and over on our treasured turntable in the early sixties. She'd run to turn the volume up. Her eyes each time had a far-away look, like a bird with wings, to escape for a little while. During dinner that evening I put the "Tom Dooley" record on, volume up. I witnessed my mom drop the food on her fork . . . gazing out the bay window in our kitchen, at a glorious sunset in the Arizona west — a special delivery for *Mime* to savor a dream come true. . ..

Mother's dreams of the Wild West never stopped.

***

The morning Lew and I left Tombstone, after a string of discovery-filled Arizona days, we drove away with knowledge and memories bordering on magic. Somehow the beauty of the desert and countless saguaros looked better than ever. Blue skies and desert-earth stretching out to a never-ending nothing filled with burning secrets. As I sat back against the comfortable seat of our fancy Cadillac, I could hear my sullen mom utter: "Why such a big car?" Cars did not fit into her Wild West dream.

I observed my handsome husband Lew in awe, the love of my life, grateful for a spellbinding marriage for thirty-four years to the most intelligent man I know. A power-brained engineer with unconditional caring. He understands and knows a simple act of love, like moving the coffee can one shelf lower in the kitchen cabinet. As to his adored wife would not have to reach too high for coffee, she was not used to making, while he was out of town on a business trip for Motorola. He left a note, *Ich liebe Dich,* I love you written in German.

"Appreciate and enjoy the "little things," for one day you may look back and realize they were the big things." — Anonymous

Although today this drive home from Tombstone belonged to my mom in the big garden in the sky called heaven. Powerful closeness filled my heart and thoughts as I wondered, did *Mime* know her daughter *Nildi*"s vivid fantasy? Did she know my dreams about a faraway land started the day she handed over that first significant book? I never told her. How sad.

My heart hurts, near breaking, knowing Mom and Dad will never know their daughter became a published writer, about her life after hair. They spoke German and Swiss only. I imagine they were spared from not being able to read or understand my work. I write in my second language only — English.

My dreams never included this phenomenal method of communication through the written word, life in poetry, and prose. I stare at my name in print, humbly overwhelming. Every so often I think of Karl May — this influential name — my love for an author, understood now a whole lot more.

When we arrived at our home on the lake in Scottsdale, the sun was low, gliding out of the sky. I stepped out of the car and inhaled a whiff of a familiar scent in the air, orange blossoms. This mesmerizing smell, which left Mom speechless, amazed *Mime* tremendously during her Arizona visit.

I will never forget the day I arrived in Phoenix. It was spring. For weeks, I wondered about a rare fragrance in certain places. In my early letters to family and friends in Switzerland and Europe, my enthusiastic way of bragging about Arizona included words like *It even smells good.*

No orange blossoms in Switzerland. My first Arizona address: *Orange Blossom Lane.*

In early March of 1968, I found Orange Blossom Lane. A moment, a turn, that molded a life, shaped a future, a place where I met Lew — my husband.

My search for a place to live, a studio apartment, remains unforgettable. Driving around in Scottsdale I had checked out a variety of apartments on streets and signs, not knowing how to pronounce most of them, when I turned on Camelback Road heading south on 56th Street in Phoenix. A side street with palm trees caught my eye, Orange Blossom Lane sounded like a song.

My swanky Pontiac Tempest, top-down, turned. . .
Why?

Some Things Are Simply Meant to Be. . .

["To Find What I Was Looking for When I Wasn't Looking": First Place, Chattahoochee Valley Writers, 9/16/2017. First Place, Southwest Manuscripters, California Contest, 10/18/2010, on my birthday.]

Flight Beyond Hearing

Our patio at Heritage Village, October 2008

King of the lake, white shining feathers reflecting in
mirrored water, no ordinary goose or gander.
How does one know — conquers and stays.
Beautiful in a way you seldom see, blue eyes from afar,
claiming a new home at the water's surface,
the lake we live on.
To walk along the grassy hill, the no-trail lake is to face
a shining armor with sounds of protection, scaring others.
A mysterious return, out of nowhere.
Instant adoration given to this out-of-the-blue appearance,
by a man who can see sadness in a white goose's eyes;
no chasing him away.
You should not kick him!
Angry words for a neighbor, a goose-kicking, wild animal hater,
checking for blood, surprised when Goosy attacks, bites his leg.
News of Goosy-on-the-lake travels with the speed of light;
the imperial goose, protector of homes,

a mystery visitor enters our lives — oh, the joy of discovering
a goose's head held high,
as the patio gate opens, for him
only.
Instant walking in, parading and
claiming his territory, he taps on
the window,
his favorite food, grapes out of
a man's aged hand.

One balmy autumn evening, a clear
Arizona desert night, the sun's
nightly
vanishing act and dazzling view
over the lake, Goosy in patio-
heaven,
Lew in his favorite chair,
my fearful-self, I hide behind a
pushed-patio-chair-fence.
Stay out.
Across the lake an open mic-night party at an Arizona Resort
we can see from our kitchen.
Thunderous booms as fireworks strike like lightning,
unfamiliar sounds hissing across the still water scaring Goosy,
near Lew, in the moonlight night.
A cloud of whiteness, a heart-stopping sweep of beauty,
Goose-bird jumps
into the arms of a man that knows the hold of love.
A moment frozen in time.
His flight beyond hearing spells fear. *I am safe now.*
Goosy's reflection in his savior's eyes,
as human hands hold him,
a dazzling lover's posture.
Jaw-dropping, I gasp aloud, only whispers escape my lips,
transfixed I stare,
a silent *wow* witnessing the unthinkable,
the moon is smiling.
Aware of the incredible, uncomprehending eyes gazing,
a sterling-white goose for what seems forever stays motionless,
he does not glide out of a man's gentle hold
until the bangs and thuds stop.

A desperate call at work one blue-sky morning,
our housekeeper yells:
They have come for Goosy, tied him up, taking him away.

Undeniably sad — beyond devastating Lew.
Three days later, a white *ghost* peeking into
our wrought-iron-patio-gate,
I jump, I dance, an explosion of joy.
I search for grapes, stretch out my hand — no fear today —
to welcome blue-eyed Goosy back.
A call in haste, Lew in shock drops everything, speeds home
to witness the incredible home-coming scene: a return
to patio-heaven with rope marks on his legs,
yet, head held high;
luminous eyes catch sight of his savior,
Goosy honks to say hello.
Will Goose-haters come for him, again, to shut him up,
take him where?
They did . . . poor abandoned Goosy,
discarded like an old sock.

Goosey reading the Wall Street Journal on our patio

["Flight Beyond Hearing," *ABSOLOOSE* Volume 1, Loose Moose
Publishing, Prescott, Arizona, October 2016.
Honorable Mention, Poetry Society of Virginia, March 2016.]

Trudy Wells-Meyer

A Reason to Wear a Tie

"May the fountain of youth become the fountain of wisdom." —
Anonymous

In Arizona, blue-sky-perfect on a glorious, sizzling already-summer day in early June 2005, a life-changing day had arrived. My husband Lew retired.

Retire, a word with a sense of "old" creeping in? Most likely for many, or simply "rich"?

Lew's laughter, (weird at times when nobody is laughing), and his smile I know so well beamed huge on this remarkable day; him smiling for days, months, hopefully for years to come.

Retirement means freedom, finding what possible is . . .

To have time, what a gift!

Lew's first retirement party, planned by his coworkers on a Wednesday evening at a trendy, local Mexican restaurant, occurred ten days before his last working day. Most guests came straight from their workplace, General Dynamics. I arrived early, feeling anxious. I had cautiously chosen what to wear, knowing black and white bestows a stunning effect anytime. Numerous men entered this well-known establishment dressed extremely casually — people I had never seen before. *No way,* they can't be here for Lew's party, can they? Dumbfounded, I imagined they must have first gone home and changed.

Lew strolled in looking especially handsome in his customary business attire. I loved my choice of his tie for this specific day, black and white, to coordinate with my outfit — matching — as always in our life together. As the party started, I gaped at his shockingly nonchalant colleagues who dressed like they were attending a ball game. I recalled Lew's words from years past:

"Yes, they do dress too casual at work."

One of Lew's buddies retired for two years, entered. He wore a tie. He shouted with pride as he fingered his tie, "It's for Lew."

My husband at the age of 63, a man who refrains from imitating others, is from the old school of life. Every day for over thirty years he wore a tie to work. I helped pick one out every morning, all the more when "Casual Fridays" started.

"Out of respect for the job," Lew professed. Countless times he was grilled, teased, stared at, and made fun of. In Lew's world, wearing a tie is right there with being on time for work.

Loyalty can't be explained; nonetheless, it explains a lot.

To recount all the praise and admiration — the level of respect shown in a range of speeches before dinner — some filled with humor — is not the reason for my story. Nevertheless, after years of a blissful marriage, I found out on one short evening how much my husband was appreciated, admired, and would be missed. Those are words that will remain a lasting memory, etched in stone. As I drove home, I cried tears of joy. Touching words by numerous coworkers left me all choked up; tears would not stop.

Oh, the power of words. I hoped Lew's 'buddies' knew of his uncanny laughter at some stage of their serious talks. Laughter, Lew explained multiple times during our marriage, is and can be the same emotion as tears.

As this memorable evening neared an end, the party organizer, a lady with stunning blonde hair standing in the corner motioned me over trying hard for Lew not to notice. She whispered, giggling at her secret, "Tomorrow, make sure Lew does not wear a tie you like because we will *cut it off* during his goodbye party at the office. We know he then will have to take it off."

"No, he won't," I insisted with my husky accent. A laugh deep in my throat startled her, though she persisted. "How about we bet money?" I should have.

When Lew came home the next evening, his smile humongous — larger than usual — there was the tie-stub, still around his neck.

June 10th arrived — Lew's last day, Friday — Casual Friday. This emotion-filled morning, as he reached for the tie, I hesitated and suggested,

"How about if you show up with no tie?"

His expression alone, which I know too well, assured, "No!" With a grin, I handed him one of his fine-looking ties to wear one last time.

As Lew arrived at work that final morning, he noticed one of his long-time colleagues wearing a tie. *Him*? Another pal came around the corner, one more — and another one . . . *Why? Someone important coming from Corporate? Nobody told me.*

Lew flashed a smile of surprise. In stunned disbelief he laughed, trying to act cool as he spotted and stared at over one hundred of his coworkers' wearing ties. Yes, Women, some had sewed their own, boasting his name.

After I stopped crying, listening to Lew's astonishing last day at the office, I rushed to my computer. I e-mailed Lew's boss, Kevin, and asked him to please thank EVERYONE for this pinch-me-perfect tribute . . . to an engineer with a compulsive, organized-by-nature attitude. What an exceptional way to  honor Lew. I promised Kevin I would tell the world, everybody, anyone who may listen, and write about that unique spectacle of respect. A movie might be next. . .

In Kevin's prompt e-mail-reply in my inbox, the subject line read:

A reason to wear a tie. . .

["A Reason to Wear a Tie," published in the Swiss *Valley Echo,* Phoenix, Arizona, November 2005.]

Orcas Love — A Gift to Remember

The year was 196**8**, Arizona still new to me and full of wonder with its day after day blue skies and all that sunshine. I stared at one cactus after another as far as I could see, flowers blooming beyond. Flowers in the desert? No sand? Spring in the West even smelled good. Orange blossoms . . . a first for me.

Coming to America, a dream came true when I arrived in Arizona. Its landscape had a front-row seat in my dreams for as long as I could remember where I hoped to see cowboys and Indians. I adored the way the word "Arizona" slid along my tongue, like a song on this humble Swiss girl's lips, an exotic foreign desert state, smelling heavenly.

Watching Mom and Dad as a small kid — doing hair, a given by my parents' talent — I now recognized how much I had learned. Ultimately the reason I ended up in Arizona. My ears perked up when I learned of Carsten's impending move to Scottsdale Arizona, to open his own salon — Coiffure International on 5th Avenue. A small duplicate of the colossal, well-established Cordes & Hendreks in Atlanta, where Carsten and I met and worked together.

The day I reached Atlanta, Georgia, from Silver Springs, Maryland, in 1966, on freeways testing my nerves and mixed with constant anxiety in my needing-a-car-wash Pontiac Tempest convertible, elated I found Lenox Square. A humongous mall, where the salon was located. Mr. Hendreks waited near the fancy door entrance. His welcoming and smiley face helped enormously. He had put on weight since that destiny-filled evening in Tann, Switzerland, when he had arrived on the scene by taxi, a one-hour drive, to deliver news of a job offer that would and did change my life.

Henry Hendreks introduced me to all the staff as we walked through his gigantic salon with twenty-one European hairdressers — mostly German-born males. One girl from Luxemburg and Sandy from England worked in the back of the salon. Sandy's smile promised a future friend. I overheard Carsten tell his German buddies, as he eyed me up and down, too visibly stopping at my not-small breasts, in High German with a loud holler, "A girl will never make it in here."

Carsten did not know I spoke *Hoch Deutsch,* German.

Months later, I would catch him staring at the diverse customers in and out of my chair, all day, each day. At times I had two assistants who helped me. Mr. Hendreks's words had

39

come true big time: Swiss hairstylists are very popular and respected in America.

A dumbfounding day for Carsten when he learned my weekly paycheck was higher than his and all his stylist buddies. Nevertheless, he saw dollars for his future salon in Arizona.

He offered me a job.

"When I am settled, I will pay all your expenses to move and you'll work at my luxurious salon in downtown Scottsdale," he promised. Carsten hugged me with a heartfelt goodbye muttering in my ear "*Auf Wiedersehen* in Arizona "*Glöckleberg.*" (His nickname for me — still is.)

A job offer, a promise, became my life . . . Going West, Arizona, my dream and destination of exciting anticipations, where I would find the life I could never have imagined.

Still, Carsten reminds Lew regularly, "You can thank me."

***

One scorching June morning, when I didn't yet know what "Arizona hot" really meant, solely one can fry an egg on a car hood, a new client, Sonya McKenzie sat in my chair at Coiffure International. A neighbor had told her to call and ask for Carsten; however, he was all booked up. I was her second choice. Sonya and family, new to Arizona, had relocated from Colorado.

How could I have known that day that a bond and long-time relationship had found its beginning? Coincidence? *Some things are simply meant to be.*

For years, whatever salon I moved to — oh, there were a few — Sonya found me and called for my service, even after being gone to California for 14 months.

Lew's job, a contract worker, a job-shopper getting paid more money — not permanent, however — had terminated. Motorola sent him to Chicago. Lew was not laughing.

"Not again," he emphasized frowning. Chicago? I could feel my heart drop, but my disappointment turned into a titanic smile when Lew declined. With no Harvard papers to prove his high IQ, he found employment in Phoenix. The electronic business, in no time, relocated Lew to manage the Los Angeles office.

Everything happens for a reason.

Assailed by panic at leaving my well-paid job, worries at night but ecstatic by day over a developing romance with Lew, I moved to Santa Monica, California, one month later.

Now married, we returned to Scottsdale after fifteen months. Motorola, Lew's previous place of work, had called to offer him a job he would, could not refuse.

Michelle, a classy German lady, owner of Fashion Square's exclusive up-scale dress shop with an adjoining small hair salon called. Martha, one of the fashion sales ladies, my previous ex-customer, knew of our return to Scottsdale. She got me the job. However, I stayed only four months.

The first week in this tiny, hectic salon with noisy chatter and too little space, Sonya was back in my chair, with her mop of hair that could look fabulous well-cut. As usual, she brought new ideas for her hair; some I liked better than others. One request remains vivid: she wanted curls — that meant a perm — her mop of hair enlarged out of control. My new assistant, a licensed hairdresser who could not earn enough money at styling hair, only a week at her job, as she removed the perm rods, she informed Sonya, "Oh, perms are definitely wonderful — it will give you so much more hair and body." Sonya started to worry, all she wanted — be curly — not more hair. Never again!

Sonya, the first one to agree when women talked about how long it used to take to get their hair done, she'd say, "Not because Trudy is slow." The problem: too many requests, too many calls, incompetent receptionists, overbooked! Not having learned how to say *no,* not knowing how, or simply my Swiss upbringing, handed down by my parents, to serve and please everyone, consistently.

Customers were lined up, and my weekly Friday ladies started a book club since getting to my chair, their turn, was rarely an on-time thing. Clients left valued books on my second station to pass on to a certain lady they had met during their standing appointments. The book stack got out of hand, too tall, covering the mirror and in the way of messy hair business at times. I purchased an attractive basket so the books would have a home. Customers walked in and headed right for the basket — Trudy's Library.

The first time Sonya saw the stack and overflow of books in my corner at the new Mahogany salon on Indian School Road, her unbelieving eyes glared at the basket. She shook her head and mumbled, "Not even doctors have books in their office."

One early Saturday morning, Sonya showed up half an hour late. With having-to-wait-for-me-anyway on her mind, she felt safe. Nevertheless, at an early appointment-time first thing in the morning, I needed clients on time. Upset, nervous, hardly talking to her, I worried about the rest of my day. Running behind schedule does not make it easy.

Sonya's next appointment I will remember always. She waltzed in smiling, in a bright red T-shirt printed with bold white letters: **DON'T WORRY — BE HAPPY.**

When I retired, she gave me her shirt that brought a smile every time I styled and cut her hair. A shirt — Sonya's going-to-the-salon-and-getting-her-hair-done-outfit.

***

Early on, Sonya brought her children, Chelsea the oldest, and Stephan. Later, Deena, the baby. Stephan thus far does not like to go to another stylist. He had to when he transferred away, out of town for an exciting new job. He still talks about that unpleasant experience, hating his haircut. When he returned to Scottsdale his hair was long — super long.

Chelsea, at eleven years old, in her shy way, the same innocent girl someday I would do hair for her wedding, asked, "Would you come to my school and teach classmates about hair?"

I did. As I stood in front of twenty-five boys and girls, I trembled, no stopping. I observed all those young faces, their eyes staring at me. Years later I still wondered if they noticed my cracking voice, with a heavy accent, my English vocabulary more limited due to anxiety. Surely one more reason to stare. A grown-up showing nerves, all the while I tried to explain the importance of hair and answer their unique questions.

On the way out, some kids clung to me with more questions. "Can my mom come to see you?" "Yes, of course." Some did.

Deena's long hair, flowing down her back, parted in the middle, didn't change, not even when she moved to Paris, France, for one of her dream jobs. Paris, a city with fashion that women dream about, where fashion trends start. Not Sonya's Deena — Paris did not change her looks. Each trip home, Deena sat in my chair for a necessary trim. Not for looks only but to be kind to hair — split ends — a no-no for long hair.

At her wedding in June, Deena wished and dreamed of curls. Curls to stay in long, straight hair on a sweltering day in Arizona, a nightmare for any hairstylist. However, that day stunning hair emerged — like an advertisement for a new shampoo — and surprisingly curled for a little while.

A dejected day when Chelsea, a teenager now, did not want her mom's hairstylist to cut her hair anymore. Her friends knew better where to go — not Mother's hairdresser. Months later, during mom's hair visit, with lowered eyes, Sonya announced with hesitation, "Chelsea wants to come back. Her idea."

Sonya and her husband Marshall, (still working at 80,) sent Chelsea to a special part-time school called *Plaza Three*, a school that teaches teenagers poise and grace. Some students would go on to become models. A customer of mine, a teacher and mentor at this in-demand place, sent numerous girls to see me for their hair. Students were taught a key lesson: it starts with hair. When your hair looks good, you feel good. The day Chelsea's teacher advised the class to call for an appointment with Trudy at Mahogany's, Chelsea hollered, "That's my mom's hairstylist."

I still today keep a picture in the back of my mind of Sonya's clever smile on her face.

Chelsea turned into one of my major fans. No matter where she lived, on her trips home for holidays, getting her hair done was a must on her to-do list. At some stage of one such salon visit from college in California, a promise started: *Someday I will do your hair for your wedding.*

My promise became reality in August 2005, the reason for this story.

Sonya, the bride's proud mom, began to talk about the wedding of the year while I was cutting her hair.

"Guess where? Orcas Island."

I stopped and asked, "Where? Never heard of Orcas."

On an island near Seattle and Canada — part of the San Juan Islands, the only way to reach Orcas Island is on a ferry.

My husband knew and showed me on a map.

Why there? A romantic reason, no doubt I found out with delight. Chelsea lived near San Francisco, where she met Chris, her husband. Orcas Island was their vacation get-away. When the bride and groom-to-be left the Island, their wedding place had become definite. An outside summer ceremony in August.

The romance of it . . .

I enlightened Sonya, "A promise is a promise. I will be there with hair tools — and Lew?"

"Of course, bring Lew," she gushed as she gave me a hug that spelled gratitude, elation, and meant the world — to both of us.

43

It turned out to be one of the most fun weddings we ever attended. (There were plenty in my career.) Never before, at any wedding did guests have that much in common besides the union of two people in love.

Starting with the ferry, arriving on Orcas Island late Friday afternoon surrounded with dark clouds, concerned about rain on travelers' faces.

At the rehearsal dinner, held at the Orcas Hotel, a variety of guests from the ferry — I recalled their casual outfits, hair flying on the windy water voyage — now were all formally dressed for the celebration. Everyone was invited, ready to eat after a long day of traveling. However, did anyone know vegan food would be on the menu? Eating food many did not recognize? A rehearsal dinner, where cocktail hour started with coconut milk? Coconuts in cardboard boxes had traveled from San Francisco. The vegan chef, a close friend of the groom, brought them in his car.

I loved it all; vegetarians recognize fresh fruits and vegetables anywhere prepared the vegan way.

Most guests and all the kids gathered at the table where pasta was served — pasta never tasted so good — waiting patiently as they ran out multiple times. Stephan, the brother, and a car full of guests slipped away in search of hamburgers.

On Saturday morning, rain puddles dotted the streets and dark clouds were threatening, although getting lighter. Luckily, we had enough time to drive around the picturesque island before I was expected at the Place at Cayou Cove. A rented cottage for the bride and her family, where I would perform the magic of hair on this special day. (Chelsea had come to Scottsdale for a practice run.) Sonya with her striking hair, I managed effortlessly, but for the bridesmaids — a shocking surprise — we had no extra flowers I had planned to put in their hair. Panic. Somebody forgot!

"What about the wildflowers we admired along the roads?" All of the bride's maids and mom embraced Lew's saving words.

My husband, pleased to help, left in search to pick wildflowers. Flowers graced the bridesmaid's hair matching the ones in the field, where the afternoon wedding took place.

Put that on your list all you swanky wedding coordinators.

As we drove to this enchanted setting for a wedding in the middle of nowhere, the sun peeked behind clouds — oh, glorious sunshine. I presumed several guests prayed for the sun to shine when it mattered most. The bluest water in the distance, wildflowers graced the landscape with such beauty an air of unreality submerged. Everybody from the night before, dressed for this grand occasion, walked through a meadow toward chairs set up in the grass. Concerns moist grass might soil everyone's dress shoes gave the impression as not to matter. Nonetheless, not surprisingly, a strong wind from the north, the one thing hairdressers cringe over most. I had secured Chelsea's hair with extra spray, the flowers with additional pins, but no hairspray for Dad. I forgot to offer. He didn't dare ask.

A picture of the elegant bride's smile, on her father's arm, his comb-over hair flying in the wind, a memory that has its own story to tell with a human face on display — Chelsea was floating on grass. Did she worry about her dressy white shoes getting stuck? Chris, the groom, stood proud in his assigned place, with his almost-smile awaiting a life together — everlasting.

Like a movie in color.

The festive reception continued close by, in a white tent ready for a celebration in style. Fortunately, protection from Orcas rain was not needed any longer. Vegan food had changed to all-American food. Nonetheless, a vegan wedding cake, with lots of carrots and ingredients better for everyone's heart, remains a cake to remember doing its name justice.

***

On May 1, 2006, five years later, we traveled back to that magical place. Again, we worried about clouds and smiled when the sun came out. Memories reappeared in our minds. Looking forward to a trip is one thing; we simply were in total amazement of a trip that was a gift. A gift from Sonya, the most exceptional client in my life for thirty-seven years. An America West Airline flight for two and three nights at the cottage where the McKenzie family stayed, "The Place at Cayou Cove".

Plus, Sonya wrote a poem along with my retirement gift . . .

To Trudy..........From '68 to '05

You've trimmed the McKenzie flock.
Chelsea at six; then Stephan, sixteen;
And Deena's first baby lock.

Through years you've shared our special times;
Provided Scout's hair tips,
Supported us through joys and woes,
Last-minute appointment trips.

In early days we read your books
While waiting patiently;
Then donned "Be Happy" red t-shirt
When we arrived "unpromptly"!

So now it's time to show our thanks
For always being there —
Munching melon, with sesame snacks,
With such artistic care.

So fly away with your love Lew
Back to the Orcas spot —
Where you'll relax, dream of hairdos
And pen next writing plot.

With Love & Many Thanks...
Sonya, Chelsea, Stephan, and Deena

Three Nights during February 11 through May 26 or November

How fortunate to know someone like Sonya McKenzie. Gratefulness took on a whole new meaning.

Such is a relationship between a client and a hairstylist.

"Your talent is God's gift to you. What you do with it is your gift back to God." — Leo Buscaglia

Rain in Seattle at the airport let sunshine emerge all the more miraculously driving onto the ferry for Orcas Island. Our second time — radiating sun, surrounded by deep blue sky and water, snow-covered mountains in the distance . . . reminiscent of Switzerland. It was the time of day, illuminated by the setting sun, where the glistening of the water reminds me of dancing diamonds. As we drove off the ferry in our rented car, onto an island where rain is a regular occurrence, we witnessed the splendor of lush green and scenery showing off flowers in a way poets write about. (Lew had inspected the internet, the rainy weather for days before our trip.)

Orcas, the promise of peace. A landscape we seized pleasure in making a part of our souls.

It was spring in the North.

Walking into the cottage, the small house reserved by Sonya, the place where I had arranged everyone's hair for Chelsea's wedding day, the sun filtered through a variety of windows. A lump in my throat, now here I stood mystified. Abundant tears streamed down my face as I watched the leaves on the trees fluttering in the wind — oh, how very green. Later I found a name: *Orcas green.* How did I not remember how magnificent a place . . . on that memorable wedding day in August?

Hair only on my mind.

This enchanting place was *our home* for three glorious

days. Valerie, owner of The Place at Cayou Cove, knocked on our door each morning, at our choice of time, to serve a breakfast we will not ever forget.

Touring the island, the next day, not one cloud in the sky, with the beauty of spring beyond imagination, I intentionally kept an eye on my husband taking in this serene beauty — with eyes like mine — Lew's eyes are my eyes.

A dazzling view becomes your own vision. What you see has everything to do with the stage of your life. Happy people see a view with different eyes . . . thankful eyes.

Another such time to pinch me and smile.

A Gift to Remember . . . always.

"One does not choose the time to write . . . It chooses you." — Trudy Wells-Meyer

By the way . . .

Sonya visits Carsten's Haircutter salon regularly now that I am retired. Carsten still loves doing hair, retirement far from his mind.

Sonya's phone call for a hair appointment at Coiffure International in 196**8**; her first choice: Carsten.

The circle of life.

Retirement Lunch, organized by my customers, at the Chart House, Scottsdale, May 2005

Happy 4ᵗʰ of July 2006

For one month in June 2006, the daily *Scottsdale Tribune* newspaper asked the readers to send in *What is Freedom?* — fifty words or less. The best entries (25) were to be published on the 4ᵗʰ of July Sunday paper.

I sat down and started writing precisely fifty words:

"Freedom is . . . The day 9/11 happened – knowing Life will never be the same . . . But your everyday Life remaining what it was . . . Only the memory makes you wonder . . . The horrors of the world flashing across your television screen . . . Knowing – counting your blessings takes on a whole other meaning.

Freedom is AMERICA." — Trudy Wells, Scottsdale

The office at the *Tribune* called our home three days before Sunday, July 2nd, to congratulate the winner. A profoundly pleasant voice notified me a photographer would come to our home to take pictures, at our convenience, as soon as possible. Lew climbed the ladder on the driveway to take down the American flag that hangs above our garage. During the photoshoot, he stood behind me holding up the flag, in our living room.

"The 4ᵗʰ of July T-shirt with the symbol of America is textbook," shouted the excited young fellow who clicked a bunch of pictures in our home.

"You might be on the front page," he revealed with a wink of his eye on the way out.

When Lew picked up the Sunday paper, in those days heavy and fat, my picture almost covered half of the newspaper's front page — displayed for Arizona to see.

Not my father — not my mom. From heaven?

Lew laughed — his untimely, uncalled quick to laugh — nonetheless, that morning his laughter turned into tears. When his bear hug let me go, I danced in the hallway with arms outstretched to heaven with never before experienced sensations.

I closed my eyes, knowing words do have meaning . . .

SCOTTSDALE
Tribune

ARIZONA'S NEWSPAPER OF THE YEAR

A Freedom Communications
Newspaper © 2006
ScottsdaleTribune.com

An edition of the EAST VALLEY Tribune $1.75

SUNDAY · JULY 2, 2006

Ariz. anti-terrorism funds halved

By MARK FLATTEN
TRIBUNE

Local leaders seek answers from feds, get no response

Arizona's overall allocation will be cut in half, to about $30 million this year. Money allocated to prevent and respond to terrorist attacks in the Valley is being sliced by more than 60 percent, from $50 million last year to $19 million.

Why is Omaha, Neb., a more attractive terrorist target than the Valley?

Or Milwaukee? Or Louisville, Ky.? Or even Columbus, Ohio?

That's what those planning the defense of Arizona and the Valley against terrorist attacks are demanding to know as they scramble to cope with deep cuts in federal anti-terrorism grants from the Department of Homeland Security.

So far they've received no answers.

All of those metropolitan areas will be getting more counter-terrorism funds through the federal grants than the Valley. Yet federal Homeland Security officials refuse to explain how they weighed the risks as they determined how to dole out $1.7 billion meant to help state and local governments prepare for a terrorist attack.

SEE FUNDS · PAGE A2

Activists urge land initiative support

Developers back current state trust use, other measure

By J. CRAIG ANDERSON
TRIBUNE

If voters don't approve a grass-roots initiative to reform the Arizona Land Department, huge swaths of desert could be sold to developers before another conservation measure reaches the ballot.

That's the message of preservationists from Scottsdale to Apache Junction. They say Conserving Arizona's Future, an initiative likely to go before voters in November, is the only way to protect state trust land in the East Valley before developers crank up their bulldozers.

But developers see things differently.

Spencer Kamps, a lobbyist with the Home Builders Association of Central Arizona, said state trust land exists to generate money for public education — and the best way to do that is to sell the land to the highest bidders.

He said setting aside state trust land for conservation is an inappropriate use of the property.

Thousands of acres in the Superstition Mountains, the McDowell Sonoran Preserve and other areas would be protected if voters approve the proposed reform. A competing measure offered by the Legislature would preserve far fewer areas, especially those near urban centers.

What is FREEDOM?

RALPH FREED, TRIBUNE

"Freedom is . . . The day 9/11 happened — knowing life will never be the same . . . But your everyday Life is remaining what it was . . . Only the memory makes you wonder . . . The horrors of the world flashing across your television screen . . . Knowing — counting your blessings takes on a whole other meaning. Freedom is AMERICA."

– Trudy Wells, Scottsdale

AMERICA IN PERSPECTIVE

In their own words: East Valley readers share what freedom means

Perspective

Going Home

Power of Rain . . . Clouds . . . Sunshine

Steady downpour for the entire day, plans change,
moisture curls my hair. A mixture of sadness and desire,
rainfall, again — a blessing — in May?
Where do birds hide when it rains? Robins know.
Fog, clouds take hold of my world, sinking disbelief,
discouraged by the failing light, colorless.
Like a movie in black and white.
Cold and windy, fallen leaves snatched by the wind, muddy,
soggy semi-deserted streets: where does all that water go?
City life bustling, malfunction of wipers on cars,
umbrellas everywhere, people running, a mad dash
for the bus. A time to share the closeness of one umbrella,
for lovers in the morning.

Where is Spring? Flashes of hope for sunshine reach
a state of countless numbers. Nostalgia, the sentimentality
of life without sun, a sense of loss of time,
I pray not to be there long. Memories play tricks in
my muddled, rained-out mind, simply hoping
for pockets of paradise to light up the sky.
Postcard-perfect Switzerland, where? Its unparalleled beauty
disappears for days. Majestic snow-covered Alps, a vision
only in my mind, now behind angry clouds.
Continuous rain, its power clouding my mind and soul,
I hear my father's words: *"You should have come last week."*
A sense of tragedy, enough for angels to weep.
A blanket of gray — time to choose attitude.

Enjoy a day of rain, dance in the rain? Knowing the dark
let vibrant city lights glow, erupt into a skyline
hard to forget. The power of light, time to possibly
understand a blind man for a fleeting moment — gaze
into his blackness, his sun's unseen power,
in his dreams only.

A pouty look, sheer boldness of desire for sunshine,
wishing angry words unsaid. All I can offer myself is
the shell of who I was before the rain. Anxious anticipation
for blue sky, famous beauty, birds singing, an infusion of

glorious change — like a treasured gift from above —
I know will transform my soul.
In the distance, high above the clouds for an instant
a watery gleam of blue, I turn my face —
momentary brilliance — it stopped raining. Rays of light
in never-ending clouds, a howl of surprise; sunshine —
what a magical, spiritual source — after days of rain the sun
decided to shine. Abandoned spirits lift instantly.
My smile has become huge.

Immense joy, total elation as Switzerland turns into
postcard pictures, once again.
The sun, its sparkle of light . . . lets your heart fly,
a state of happy delirium, sun puts you there.
The end of depression, a change of mood — transport
back to serene magnificence,
oh, how we live in our heads more than any place.
The green side of Switzerland's magic, for poets, writers,
a country's glorious sunsets compel me to listen
to nature's most endangered sound, silence. Falling in love
with the circle of life, its many faces, distant cowbells,
church bells ringing — sounds of Switzerland,
my childhood home — Like a movie in color —
aware of sunshine in our hearts, is what truly matters.

*"When it looked like it wouldn't stop raining God put a rainbow
in the clouds."* — Maya Angelou

Matterhorn Zermatt, in 2006, a famously known mountain all over the globe we could see from our hotel room, so close as to almost touch it. A July miracle — 10 days of sunshine and clear sky each day.

"Nailed" at the Bodensee

During one of our yearly trips abroad to Switzerland in May 2007, my older sister Doris and her husband Marc planned a family afternoon starting with lunch at a Swiss restaurant *Seelust am Bodensee*, Lake Constance. We enjoyed Suisse cuisine at its finest on a day where buckets full of rain came down. A steady downpour for the entire day, known to Swiss people only too well and feared by those of us who come to visit.

After a memorable meal at a famous and crowded dining place with a lake view, on a clear day guests can see Germany, not believable when it rains, we stopped at my sister's fantastic new home. From the upstairs room terrace, Doris's winter garden — her pride and joy — you could see the lake. Not today. Plans ruined to sit outside. Doris and Marc apologized for the rain, "You should have come last week," though spoiled us with *Gastfreundschaft* (hospitality) and homemade dessert.

Time for goodbyes, only too soon at 6 p.m., we walked toward my younger sister Beate's car. My brother-in-law saw it first. A rear tire, almost flat. Our faces showed concern and shock. Our one-and-a-half-hour drive home in jeopardy, to Tann/ZH, where Beate and happily divorced brother Erwin live in the old house where we were kids together.

Marc knew who to call — a friend and owner of a BP gas station near their house on the main street in Kesswil. A worried look on Doris' face, she proclaimed, "It's too late . . . closed." *Fyrabig* in Switzerland happens early. Closing time at this garage: 5:30.

The owner answered the phone. Lucky.

What I remember most is this Swiss man's unforeseen smiling face with no evidence of being bothered by an after-hours repair. The minute we drove up, he recognized Marc's car and greeted him with a friendly embrace. Mr. Innauen's confidence and knowledge of what to do was instant as he spotted the tire. His cool, unhurried voice as he pulled out a rusty nail did not suggest the easy way out of patching it in fifteen minutes, to be drivable until we got home to deal with the tire the next morning, no! His idea was to fix it to last forever! His words.

To me, a nail in a tire meant a new tire.

Markus Innauen, the owner of the cleanest garage Lew, the American, had ever seen — "Switzerland-clean" — informed us he needed until about a quarter to eight. "Something" had to dry for a certain time. We left this after-hours, smiling savior, to drive back to Doris's house. Her farewell words, "Come back very soon," had turned into real soon. Smiling all the while she served sandwiches.

My brother-in-law, drove the four of us back to the garage at **8** p.m. Beate, her outstretched hand reaching for the keys to her now perfectly fixed car by that smiling Swiss, "How much?" With her other hand, she pulled out her wallet.

"Forty *Franken*," the man replied.

I could not believe it, and they say Switzerland is expensive?

I had reached for fifty *Stutz*, (Franken) a tip for this overtime-working-owner long before he said, "Forty *Franken*."

Thanking him, everyone got in the car. I handed Mr. Innauen that fifty *Stutz* Swiss bill and his eyes got huge — a grin to remember with his loud *Danke vielmals* echoing in a garage the pinnacle of neatness and cleanliness. We waved to Adieu until we could not see him anymore. At the last turn, with my head out the window, I blew him a kiss.

High above, the clouds parted, a watery gleam of sunshine broke through. I turned my face to this momentary brilliance. The rain had stopped. By the time we got closer to the Zürich Oberland, thanks to daylight saving time in Switzerland, a spectacular sunset displayed itself in front of us. The golden sun appeared as if gliding out of the sky. A sunset streaked with pink and coral, its afterglow indelibly imprinted in my mind — a poetic evening experience.

To experience a flat tire, where customer service is offered with that personal Swiss touch and friendly service, the place — his name: Markus Innauen in Kesswil/TG. His garage is his castle. A deep sigh reflected on my pride to be Swiss.

My Wisconsin-born husband reminded my sister and brother that, at his dad's Shell garage, on the highway between Chicago and Minneapolis, where his after-school hours were filled with work until all kinds of late hours, there was no *Fyrabig* at 5:30. No early closing time in Mauston for a gas station on the main road of a small town.

I caught Lew checking that back tire with watchful eyes for the rest of our days in Switzerland. As for me? I did not worry. I knew when Markus Innauen said *forever,* that meant a long time.

August 19, 1965 Gottlieben, *am Bodensee,* Lake Constance

Sister Doris's, *Oisi* (nickname) wedding, and her 3 siblings. After two months in Silver Springs, MD, I flew home, to be her maid of honor.

["Nailed at the Bodensee," published in the *Swiss Review* (sent to all Swiss abroad), February 2008, and in the Arizona Swiss newsletter *Valley Echo,* January 2008.]

Trudy Wells-Meyer

Rumble of Freedom

Switzerland, a country with a flag of red and white. Swiss colors — a white cross on red. Where national pride emerged when least projected, and the ordinary turned into atypical moments in a little village on a sunny, Swiss picture postcard-perfect morning in May 2007 at **8**:30.

A rumbling thunder caused my jet-lagged eyes to look up in shock. "What's happening to the building, a storm?"

The old house trembled . . . a possible earthquake in Tann? I stared at my sister and Lew, my American husband. His eyes blurred from not enough sleep crossing the Atlantic the night before, jet-lagged Lew aware only too well his body was still on Arizona time. My words echoed in the air as we sat down for breakfast Swiss-style, freshly baked bread and croissants towering in a worn-out basket. My older brother Erwin's run to the local bakery, when it first opens at seven in the morning, an errand he provided daily because of love for early-am, fresh-baked bread. One day old won't do. A routine by foot before Erwin opens his hair salon, located downstairs on the first floor — the family salon, my parent's life, and pride for over fifty years.

As I spread my baby sister's homemade jelly on bread that never tastes better than at the house where we all grew up — each time on our frequent visits I treasure identifying my roots from long ago. I stopped in mid-air, my aged hand wabbly. We all paused in utter disbelief, as vibrations and sounds raised to a crescendo, to levels that compelled one to believe something dreadful was about to happen. Beate, my never-married single sister, jumped up from her chair, her long hair flying. I followed. We dashed to the window, on the third floor, my younger sister's home for years. A promise by our father on his deathbed ensured Beate's right to live in that apartment to the end of her days.

We flung the window open; we leaned out. I felt the smile

fade on my face. I turned profoundly serious as I gawked at Swiss Army tanks approaching up the steep main street of our country village, — a fearful image of the past. I could hardly believe my eyes. In mere seconds, I was transported back to my

56

childhood as memories flooded my heart, sounds of war . . . a young girl again. Tank convoys rattled as we peeked from hidden places, fearful and hoping not to be detected. Kids playing war outside, after school.

Spellbound, left speechless with a silent *wow* on my lips, I became aware of a sight that would remain in my head. I must have looked downright ill. With a soft, pinched voice, I uttered, "What are *they* doing? Where are *they* going?"

I could feel the fear from long ago . . . a memory carried me back to a once child-like, innocent time. A time when a military tank meant a toy for my brother; however, only too clear, the scary knowledge of the real meaning of what tanks represented in 1944, all through World War II.

Recognizing the extreme importance for Lew, the Wisconsin boy, to witness this convoy, I yelled, "Get up, come and look!"

Flustered at the intensity of my emotional state, I watched my husband. I tried to guess his thoughts as he flashed unexplained laughter and smiles of surprise. "Thank God the Swiss have not given up their vigilance. Standing guard, making sure . . . Switzerland, a country ready at all times, means power to the world."

Lew's unexpected words jolted me into stunned silence. I swallowed over the lump in my throat. I simply nodded.

My sister's arm had found my shoulder. With her other arm, she waved. I used both of mine, waving fiercely at a motorcade where the tank commanders, totally focused, unmoving, eyes straight ahead — an act that affirmed this procession of power more dramatic, more serious.

The Rumble of Freedom . . .

As Lew walked away from the window, he shouted, "Don't mess with the Swiss. The Swiss Army can and must provide the security for Switzerland."

His words bestowed a presence of security. Infinite pride swelled my heart. Oh, to be Swiss with its Wilhelm Tell mentality, its unique grandeur, blue lakes, and the famous sounds of Switzerland. Remote cowbells — church bells ringing — the one thing I miss in America on Sundays and holidays. Fear had turned into national pride and honest appreciation for my country's strong defense.

Switzerland — A small country with a huge military.

"Excellence is never an accident. It is always the result of high intention, sincere effort, and intelligent execution; it represents the wise choice of many alternatives — choice, not chance determines your destiny." — Aristotle

Lew had served in the United States Navy during the Vietnam War, on the USS Oriskany CVA34, "Aircraft Carrier Attack," the same ship US Senator John McCain served on when he was shot down in North Vietnam. For my proud American husband, on his mind constantly were questions about the declining US military and the war on the police. What was going on in a once-admired country? The land of the free and the home of the brave . . .

Erwin, my brother explained later, those chilling, Swiss training-only tanks, were on route to an oversized military base. An Army Park near our humble home in Hinwil, only forty-five minutes outside Zürich, a cosmopolitan city and world-famous shopper's-dream.

In Switzerland, all Swiss men are obligated to serve once a year for three weeks, leaving their jobs and undergoing soldiers training that occurs all over this tiny country, famous for its Alps, cows, cheese, and chocolate. At age 34 (officers at 42), they turn in all their military clothing. To keep the rifle at home is a choice. However, a recent political controversy occurred about not keeping the rifle at home any longer. Ongoing Army bashing in the media continues, with the topic of a compelling national tradition at stake. Disarm the descendants of Wilhelm Tell?

Nein. On February 13, 2011, the Swiss voted to keep the weapons at home. A Swiss military tradition, an expression of the Swiss people's trust in its citizens, lives on.

At twenty years old, for four months, most young men attend the recruits' basic training, a mandatory obligation. Unless they are disabled, they perform Civil Service, for the protection of the civilians.

Switzerland preserves freedom for the country and every individual. Switzerland without an Army — Hitler would have loved that.

This impeccable, clear spring morning with its imposing, snow-covered Swiss Alps soaring in the distance, visible from the upstairs windows of my parents' home, left me aware when I was a kid, I did not see this humbling magnificence with the same eyes. Now feelings of pride poured out for the land of my birth. Yet, rumbling sounds of tanks and fear of their power lingered. How much does the universe truly know about *neutral* Switzerland I wondered?

***

San Diego skyline Coronado bay, Memorial Day 201**8**

An American by choice, the first in my huge Swiss/German family, I am an immigrant truly fortunate to own dual citizenship as I live and love the American life I could never have visualized. I stand proud to be an American citizen. Few people in the world can claim citizenship in 2 countries I am Swiss born in one of the most beautiful countries in the world, (even though it rains a lot), and I also value the amazing beliefs, ideals in America, that liberate and protect the entire world. Always.

When you are young, your future is a blaze of dreams and maybes. To become an American never filled my imagination while I dared to dream of *Coming to America.* Imprinted in my mind, nonetheless, remains the day July 19, 1974, when I took the oath and became a citizen of the United States of America — the first naturalized American in my gigantic family. My husband's security clearance, as project leader for a government contractor, required his Swiss wife to be a naturalized citizen. I recall shrugging my shoulder with indifference at the request as if to say, "So — why not," did not seem to matter much at the time. However, in a large, downtown city hall, surrounded by forty-two other want-to-be-

Americans from a mixture of countries, I hesitated on the edge of decision-making. I underwent physical pain. Homesickness? A passionate and bewildering feeling of extreme attachment to my country of origin, as well as astounding closeness to my parents, across the ocean half a world away, overwhelmed me. My strong link to Switzerland would soon be replaced by this vast country called the USA. Especially Arizona, sizzling and breathtaking, a jewel of a state I have come to call my home. No other state would do, due to watching Wild West movies as a teenager; oh, and reading European-known, famous German author Karl May's way of writing, which brought everyone into a world one could visualize.

My key to the future, my mind on the past, instead of joy I experienced sadness. A don't care attitude had turned into tears like the opening of a floodgate. Memories appeared like random photographs: a lifeless privileged early on, my father's unique almost-smile, stars seen from the tiny, cold room I shared with my bossy older sister Doris. My authoritarian parents, who ruled with an iron fist, never really knew the admirable job their "little girl" performed in a faraway country — a daughter filled with knowledge from the school of life and strict parental teachings.

I entered daily life with body and soul to accomplish simply everything. I learned to do something by doing it.

Thank you, Mom and Dad!

Surrounded by the unfamiliar, nervous trembling with traitor-like doubt, I composed myself and welcomed my gift. I signed my name. Welcome to America.

America and Switzerland, now tied together by the future.

On every journey to Switzerland over the years, I still travel with my Swiss passport tucked away in my husband's travel bag. Why? Thoughts of, *Switzerland, what a great country to be from* never leave me, (reminded persistently by Americans that have visited this scenic country). I show my American passport with pride as we enter *Pass Kontrolle* in Zürich. Each time though I surprise myself by hoping the stranger behind the window knows I am Swiss with dual citizenship. I holler, "*Grüezi!*" provoking a smile (every time), yet I know the desire to-come-to-America, leave Switzerland, is simply understood only by immigrants who did.

On certain days, once a year in Switzerland, still true today, you can witness Swiss Military tanks driving on the main village and country roads. Small roads, relative to those in the US. When my brother turned fifty, the age military routine stopped in those days, a routine that spelled duty and honor, left him distraught and feeling old. (The law changed in 2005 to age 34.)

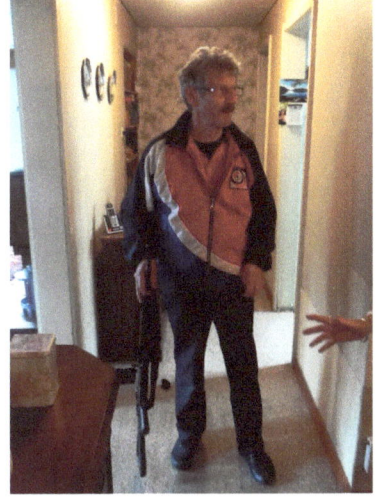

Shooting is a mammoth national Swiss sport. Erwin attends well-organized events regularly, where he wins medals for shooting perfectly. At 75 years old, he leaves the house with his rifle on his arm, as countless Swiss men do — the colossal rifle he keeps in the office/den closet. On our periodic trips over the ocean, my husband, the American, mesmerized he stares and marvels at his brother-in-law, with the rifle, getting in a car to attend a shooting festival. Most times when he returns, a medal is pinned on his coat.

Enthusiastically back in Arizona, Lew shows pictures to his American buddies. They respond with shock and awe hardly believing all year-long festivals are held in a variety of communities all over Switzerland.

Erwin's grand case in his bedroom, filled with medals and prizes, has caught up with the impressive glass cabinet that stores Dad's shooting medals — a lifetime of awards of this gentle, proud Swiss man, my father.

Like father, like son, a tradition lives on. America, wake up!

"Freedom consists not in doing what we like, but in having the right to do what we ought." — Pope John Paul II

Trudy Wells-Meyer

After Days of Rain, The Sun Decides to Shine

For my father — *Tädi*

Master of the tightrope, my father, a barber in a tiny
Swiss village, where even dreaming had its limits.
His smile had no sound but meant everything.
Still does. Always will.
His unspoken words only I can hear.
His pain with its eerie silence.
I pretend to possibly understand the depth of my dad,
carved into my soul.
I remain mesmerized.
The majestic Alps hidden behind angry clouds
soaring — close to heaven.
On the edge of the gray lake, I know can be blue,
a watery gleam of sunshine — a faint outline of snow high up,
my heart skips a beat.
The power of light shining on pure white,
on a mountain, my father's mountain, a giant called Titlis.
His favorite.
The clearing like an opening of the sky,
as I listen to the past,
pockets of paradise ignite the cloudy sky,
Tädi, smiling from Heaven.
The morning sun holding a memory locked in my heart.
A sight, rare because of rain for days, clouds, mysterious fog,
Mein Vater, as big as life.
The irreversible loss of the past illuminates his mountain,
aware of Dad's presence, remembrances from long ago not
necessarily as they were.
I feel his eyes and soul watching me,
until, at last,
I am beyond his range of vision — not Dad's wisdom.
A moment in time in a glamorous hotel on Lake Lucerne,
on a slippery balcony on the fourth floor,
a vision leaves me crying behind my hand.
*The mountain he climbed and conquered as a young man
during the War.*
Sunshine . . . what a magical, spiritual source.

["After Days of Rain, The Sun Decides to Shine", Loose Moose Publishing, Prescott, Arizona. *ABSOLOOSE* Vol. 2, published in April 201**8**; also, 1**8**th place in *Writer's Digest* Popular National Poetry Award, December 2017, with a fifty-dollar gift certificate.]

How I wish my *Tädi* could read my poetry today. He never even knew I wrote poetry (I started in 200**8**).

Dad did not read or speak English.

By the way . . .

In 19**8**9, one Tuesday night on November the 15th in Switzerland, (still the 14th in Arizona), a shrill ringing woke us at 11:30 p.m. With a jolt, I scrambled to pick up the phone and listened to Beate's crying voice. Dad had left for heaven, the garden in the sky, at 6:30 a.m. in Tann, at the new apartment in the *Hochhaus,* a high-rise building that was not very tall.

Mami and *Tädi* had moved to Tann's only towering building, after retiring from hair in 19**8**6. He had agreed, with heavy heart, to Mom's wish to move away from where hair was the number-one language. Our father's emotional words would remain, leaving me melancholy "No more staring out the upstairs window in the old house to check who enters the barbershop and salon."

The complexities of grief, dark and soundless like a ship of nostalgia, spilled over me, tears of loss for days to come. No one truly knows what a person feels to receive a call from so far away, with words like a cold north wind: *"De Tädi isch gstorbe."* Dad died. Distance too colossal and unbearable, my brain was in disarray.

"We must get to Switzerland as soon as possible." I howled in despair. No sleep on such a night.

The following week happened to be the Thanksgiving holiday. Our every year weekend plan, to fly to San Diego, California, on Wednesday evening after work for our first kiss-tradition on Coronado Island, would and did not happen. In exchange, frantic calls to various airlines to fly home for Dad's funeral. The Turkey holiday days off, planned for months, turned out to be helpful.

The morning after that heartbreaking call before midnight, I left for work early, as normal at 5:30, crying — wearing tinted glasses so as not to show smeared eye makeup. My first client at 6 a.m., Doctor Benson, one of my regular every-three-weeks male clients, received a haircut through tears.

Nameless emotions struggled in my heart. Ironic indeed, for this morning to have a male haircut in my chair since my dad never understood how I cut men's hair without the correct Swiss training and appropriate papers to prove I took the necessary test — and passed. I studied only three years as an apprentice and owned a license for ladies. My father's voice in my head unveiled, he could never believe: *How on earth can America allow that?*

In the US, women send their husbands and boyfriends to their stylists. Clients simply trust you if you are from Europe and have a father who was the best barber in town. A father from whom I collected knowledge beyond worth, as a kid while sweeping hair, cleaning two barber stations over and over, and getting waiting male clients ready. I watched and listened.

On this somber Wednesday morning, at my two chairs/stations, a salon-set-up like my dad's two-chair barbershop across the ocean in a faraway land, yet so close, *Schgruna*, my father guided his daughter *Udi* in a unique way only he could. When Dr. Benson walked in three weeks later for his regular early hair appointment on Wednesday, his hello included "That was the best haircut you ever gave me."

***

As I stood at my father's open grave knowing you can't prepare how to feel, a momentary ray of sunshine surged from the gray clouds like a heavenly messenger on a cold, windy November day. My homecoming, with a heart torn in two, had shivers emerge — *If only I had held his hand on that balcony in July a little longer . . . and told him "Ich liebe Dich."*

Throughout our last visit that summer, I witnessed Dad in agony, not from physical pain but, loss of movement. My proud dad thru the last six months of his life sat on the toilet for hours — no control over his bowel movements any longer — ALS, Lou Gehrig's disease at its worst. The last evening, for the first time, *Mami* had to help and manually push Dad into bed. This proud Swiss, who opened car doors for his wife, died the next morning.

Feeling empty in a battle against his illness and gathering pity along the way for what once was, blurred in memory, thoughts keep revisiting my mind of that last hour when I sat next to *Schgruna* on the fourth-floor balcony, together admiring the grand Swiss Alps in the distance. His muted tone of haunting words: "I can't sing anymore. I miss the men's choir." Dad belonged to a local male singing group as far back as a young man when he opened the family business.

As a child, I learned of *Tädi*'s love for Viennese concerts. (He would have loved Andre Rieu's orchestra, the king of waltzes.) The power of music — what a potent bond between people. Music, the world's language — no translation needed. While I had to work and help at the beauty shop, I would sprint down the dark hallway connecting the two salons, whenever one of Dad's favorite songs or tunes played on the old radio. "*Immer nur lächeln* — always smile . . . by Franz Lehar. I ignored all rules, strong words spoken too often by Mom to her kids "Turn down the radio." I could barely reach the buttons located high up in the barbershop. On my toes, I turned up the volume for my dad to hear better while I peeked for his reaction. A slight wink with smiling eyes and an almost nod belonged to his daughter Udi.

Tädi's music remains my music, knowing as beloved sounds washed over his barber-soul during the demands of life, listening to his favorite song . . . he was a happy man. Smiling.

André Rieu's music anywhere, anytime, my profound wish my dad had known of the King of the Waltz. Inside my heart, *Schgruna*, Dad is right there in attendance with me at any of Rieu's live concerts and television performances. Anyplace where his sounds fill the air.

Music is what feelings sound like.

Entrance to the Meyer house, July 1989, last happy picture with *Tädi*

After the funeral, held on a somber November morning the day after we had arrived in Switzerland, — on the flight back to Arizona, through tears I squinted out the window high up on

Delta, close to heaven. I could see my *Schgruna* in the clouds — not gone, yet closer to my heart than ever. Memories flashed with painful intensity. He'd want me to smile and hide emotions. *"Immer nur lächeln"* Always just smile — out of Franz Lehar's operetta, *The Land of Smiles*, one of his favorites had turned into a lifetime teaching, a display of being strong.

Just like Dad.

I tried to relive those last moments at the airport back in July, his last words, his eyes intently on mine, waving with his unmatched smile, his last gesture of love. With his other hand trying to hold on to a railing for support with a bent back, he stood tall. He smiled and waved through the airport glass door. I learned later he had no strength to stand that long. My proud dad, not showing emotions but a smile. My heart still bursting, we both knew it would be the last time. Lew pulled me toward the airline gate — holding my hand, the only comfort.

Memories do sustain us. I stepped through the old door of my childhood and saw *Schgruna*, the way he tipped his hat and lifted it slightly to greet people that crossed his path on the street.

The pride in *Tädi*'s voice when he talked about Switzerland's beauty and majestic Alps and range of snow mountains — some he had climbed.

The hobby he cherished after a long hard day, to repair children's broken dolls — pulled out arms, legs, eyes missing — the *Puppendoktor* — doll doctor of Tann, *Züri Oberland*.

Moms came from everywhere — *"Die chömed eifach inegschneit"* (they simply come without an appointment) words Dad would utter in disbelief, from Uster, Wald, Wetzikon, Tösstal, some by postal mail.

ELLE magazine interviewed our father, published a whole page with his picture, about his unique and only known doll-doctor practice. A variety of arms, legs, parts, and components, ready to fix whatever was broken, filled a storage corner in the dark cellar. Girls of all ages chocking on tears and hopeful eyes held on tightly to their precious, injured dolls and didn't want to let go or leave behind with the adored doctor, who one week later loved to watch the same girl's smile ecstatically embracing their treasure, all healed and fixed.

Technology lets me listen to Dad's interview with a lady journalist of the local newspaper. On a tape I play in my car, his voice already shaken with illness, I hear the pride in his uncommon achievement, the doll doctor that lasted over forty years.

Like a blur, the distance from Tann to Arizona had gotten exceedingly short. Dad in my heart — how close is that. There is something good about everything . . . no more guilt I should visit more often — stay longer. An immigrant across the daunting ocean repeatedly feels the vast remorse of not doing enough. Now a certain comfort lingers to look up to the open freeway to heaven — oh, how I cherish the newfound closeness. streaming

Outside the church in Tann, ZH June **8**, 1972

Even if you could wake up and not feel this pain of immense loss, you respectfully don't want that either. Hurt is a sure reminder of what a loved one truly meant and means for eternity.

One memory, hidden but constant, I wish I could erase, is seeing my father in a tiny cold room, *Aufbewahrungshalle,* a storage hall built with ugly bricks. No flowers, no heaters warmed the burial place, the *Friedhof* (cemetery) that had no resemblance to a fancy funeral home in the US. No sophisticated, expensive caskets. A plain wooden box is the county's last gift to Swiss citizens who pass on. Simply too ordinary for my father, no choice to choose.

Our immediate stop after our flight arrival at eight in the morning was stepping into the *Leichenhaus* (morgue) large enough for one casket only. I screamed uncontrollably . . . my tears fell like rain. The Swiss small size of this dreadfully shabby room had me cringe — the coldest place on earth, literally.

Appalled and yelling, "*No.* Not for my *Schgruna.*" An echo of pain. To compare America's lavishness of funeral homes was so the wrong thing to do, but how could I not?

The feeling of loss changed into merciful knowledge as my faith in God reminded me: *Tädi* is not here. Look up — my *Schgruna* is in heaven.

When we spend time in Switzerland, mostly once a year, and visit our parents' resting place, I am struck with wonder at the location and the view of the Swiss Alps from the fresh-flowered-filled cemetery. On a clear day, I can see one of the mountains that meant everything to Dad: "Vreneli's Gärtli", a snow-covered square nestled between high and pointed mountaintops. I love to reminisce about the days when *Schgruna's* eyes would search for it in the distance, emerging from the clouds. He'd point with exuberance and a dreamy smile. "Look." (Picture below}

Now I am the one searching for Vreneli's garden of snow. Closeness, a bond fills my senses with *Tädi* to last a lifetime.

Thank God for my parent's burial plot with fresh flowers planted every spring and fall by my brother Erwin and sister Beate and attended to regularly with a view of the beloved Swiss mountains — always and forever. Well, not correctly forever. In

Switzerland, after 20 years (25 in Wohlen, AG where Dad is from) they reuse the plot. Tiny Switzerland needs the space, none to spare.

Families are contacted if there is anything like the gravestone candles, vases left on the grave over the years they would like to retrieve. A gold cross decorated Dad's grave for 20 years we added to our Mom's resting place. Comfort in that — Together again — sharing flowers and the beloved Alps in the distance.

Anniversary celebration lunch, 50 years together, at the Panorama Restaurant Chrug, overlooking Lake Zürich.

One of the happiest pictures ever of *Mime* . . . our mom.

Faith

The Power of Prayer

❖ **Monday, November 19, 2001 — Scottsdale, Arizona**

Sainte Léonie Aviat
Mère Françoise de Sales
16 septembre 1844 - 10 janvier 1914

In three days, we will fly to Rome, Italy, where Mother Léonie Frances de Sales Aviat, will be canonized and declared a saint by our Holy Father, Pope John Paul II, on November 25, 2001. The Vatican had cleared the way for the canonization of Léonie Aviat, born on September 16, 1844. A French Sister, Blessed Léonie Françoise de Sales Aviat, is the co-founder, with Blessed Father Louis Brisson, (1817-1908), of the Oblate Sisters of Saint Francis de Sales in Troyes, France. They began a religious order according to the spiritual legacy of St. Francis de Sales to meet the needs of the young girls who found themselves in the city of Troyes during the Industrial Revolution. Léonie Aviat obtained the habit of the new congregation along with her new religious name, "Françoise de Sales" (in English, "Frances de Sales") on October 30, 1868.

Father Brisson later founded the Oblates of St. Francis de Sales in 1876), a congregation of priests and brothers in France. One of Father Brisson's maxims, his famous words:

The more one loves, the more one gives; the more one gives, the more one loves God.

The Oblate Sisters, daughters of Saint Léonie's order, taught at the French-speaking boarding school I attended in Châtel St. Denis, l'Institut St. François de Sales, near Vevey,

Switzerland. I was fifteen years old, a long way from home, scared out of my wits and plenty of tears.

Older by three years, my sister, Doris, first attended the school located in the French part of Switzerland during an era when parents were expected to put their daughters in a finishing school. Beate, eleven years younger, was lucky also to have spent one year at the exclusive boarding school.

This girls-only French-speaking school and, the nuns who taught there — who I have remained in touch with through all my American adult life — are the reason we will experience Rome. A trip for the soul, a trip of a lifetime.

A journey, my first story, would confirm I am a writer.

Monday, three days before our anticipated voyage to Rome, overcome with appreciation, I wrote a handwritten note to my mother, simply to thank her for sending me to that away-from-home school when I was a teenager. I tried to put an abundance of gratitude on paper, knowing my parents sacrificed much to be able to pay for such considered luxury.

Beate dreamed and agonized of meeting Lew and me in Rome, traveling from Zürich, Switzerland; however, one crucial problem, her fear of flying. With the anxiety of going anywhere, she was easily discouraged by the smallest difficulties.

For twenty years Beate has not traveled on an airplane. As a young woman, she had turned seriously ill, Meningitis, a gut-wrenching time of dependence on pills and — rehab. She returned home and moved back in 1984, to the old house where we all grew up. Our parents had remodeled the whole top floor for my baby sister.

In May of 1975, the wealthy house owner offered my father the purchase of the house on the busy main street. Later, my parents with their flourishing hair business remodeled and took over the two apartment's second-story floor, modernized it into one Swiss jumbo living space, adding a new bathroom, that once was a kitchen. A bathtub and a shower — what luxury — no more using the bathroom in the outside hallway, located near the stairs to the heavy wooden front entrance door.

A belief *we are rich* . . . appeared to have come true, a dream that started when we first received a color TV in our living room and a car, a green Opel, for Sunday drives only.

Beate, my little sister, whose diapers I changed when I was eleven, during her lengthy illness I prayed day-after-day to Léonie Aviat, Mother Françoise de Sales, the nun who would become a saint. She was beatified by Pope John Paul II in Rome (the first step to sainthood) in 1992. Beate, Doris, Lew, and I traveled to Rome, to participate in her road to sainthood. We experienced our first such religious ceremony on this simply spellbinding tour organized by the French Oblates, the sisters of St. Françoise de Sales Order.

Since that unforgettable journey to Rome together, Beate has been healthy — no medication or drugs — our small private miracle.

The day Beate, *Lumpi*, my sister's nickname, called Swissair — at last — finally to book a reservation for the flight to Rome, after days of back-and-forth, should-I-or-shouldn't-I, was **9/11/01** — one of the most horrendous and tragic days in American history that caused the world to shudder. That evening in Switzerland, with nine hours' time difference, Beate viewed images of horror from New York on TV in her tiny living room.

"A long-distance call from Europe," my boss yelled at our frantic beauty shop in downtown Scottsdale. He handed me the salon's phone. My sister's panic-stricken voice screamed at the precise moment the third plane crashed in Pennsylvania. My one ear listened to the skin-tightening shocker on the radio, my other ear *Lumpi's* desperate slurring words, *"Trunylle, was passiert z' Amerika?"* What is happening in America? She was crying.

A tense client in my chair and everyone at the salon held their breath, listening to frenzied words on the turned-up loudspeaker of the wall radio in the back corner — news that would change the world. Fear settled in everyone's face at this dreadful possibility of undeniable terrorist attacks, the terrifying results of human hatred.

My heart missed a beat as my trembling handheld onto the phone. A sense of powerlessness left me feeling faint. I reached for a chair, my knees simply too weak to stand, trying to picture my sister's state of horror. My only sensible thought: time to pray. I hoped not to pray for more than the Lord could give.

Chaotic days followed and the airports of the world were in disarray. After uncountable encouragements from my side of the Atlantic, Beate at long last decided to personally pick up her ticket to Rome. More stupefying news blasted on TV: Swissair declared bankruptcy and stopped all flights, indefinitely. Gasps of disbelief left my lips, the world and us dumbfounded.

My father must have turned in his grave. Not Swissair! News enough to put me in a state of apprehension. A plan shattered, again? How on earth will Beate be with Lew and me for this exceptional event in Rome? Will Delta flights to Rome keep flying?

Lew managed to find a seat on Alitalia, Zürich – Milan – Rome; however, another plane crashed in Italy, at the Milan airport. My blood turned cold with disbelief and anxious speculations at all the chilling events that would stop anybody from flying.

My galloping heart finally settled down. I grabbed the phone. With a small measure of hope, I called Switzerland, Sister Anna de Gonzague, superior at Villa Maria in Bern. The Villa, a unique residence for abused women, was run by the Oblates of St. Francis de Sales. Trembling, I hoped a call from far-away America would help the cause.

"Can you possibly accommodate one more person with your group by train?" I asked, ignoring the fact the advertised deadline for reservations had passed two weeks earlier.

After numerous phone conversations, Sr. Anna, de Gonzague reported, extremely joyful, "Yes."

She organized space for my little sister. Although, not Beate's choice, she responded with a bold *"Nein."* Afraid of conflict she struggled with a different worry in traveling — arriving a day earlier meant *one night in Rome without us.* Uncertain and scared of how and when to find Lew and me at the hectic Leonardo da Vinci International Airport, where we planned to meet up with our group from America, the Oblate Sisters de Sales from Mount Aviat Academy in Childs, Maryland. A travel agency in Chesapeake, Maryland, had organized the America — Rome trip.

Too much to worry about, my brain hurt from diverse thoughts. How in God's name would *Lumpi* decide? Grinding my fists against my temples didn't help.

Swissair back in business! Three weeks before our departure they called with words we had given up on, "The flight to Rome is back on schedule." The airline honored my sister's reserved seat, at a baffling lower price. A swirl of excited astonishment filled me, the kind that comes when God hands you a gift long after you stop hoping.

Monday before our long-planned trip, I had just finished my letter to Mom when jaw-dropping news blasted on TV — another plane crash in Queens, New York. In horror, I listened to the disturbing events. I held my hands over my ears and raised my eyes to heaven in an expression of utter bewilderment. I imagined my sister's anguish. I cursed the TV. She surely would hear the same broadcast blasting across her screen. Not from me.

How much more could Beate, or any of us, handle? What about the booked flights from Phoenix to Rome? Will Delta fly and take off on schedule? I tried to calm down, not scream. Would my sister honestly be strong and board a Swissair plane by herself? In a life with all the terrifying terrorist attacks flashing on the news and with flying anywhere questionable and problematic for travelers all over the world, never had I prayed with such intensity. Can the soon-to-be Saint Léonie Frances de Sales Aviat hear me? And God?

"Praising God amid a storm is the best way to weather it." —
Anonymous

❖ Thanksgiving Morning, 2001

In the back seat of a fancy town car on the way to the airport, on a typical blue-sky Arizona morning, my husband Lew and I glanced at each other in wonderment. After all the nervous speculations and gigantic hopes for this trip, from Phoenix to Atlanta, onto Rome, I marveled too often do we indeed get to go? Will we overcome the horrors of plane crashes, evil, and terror that have occupied everyone's mind worldwide? Lew reached for my hand and in a gesture with tenderness his alone he smiled his priceless grin — Lew's way of saying, *I told you so.* His relentless belief and optimism are to be admired more than he could ever know.

Our trip to Rome was a birthday gift from Lew; I turned sixty on October 18, 2001.

To travel on Thanksgiving Day, our first-kiss anniversary every year at 7 p.m., a fairy-tale kiss in 1968 that changed our lives into the life we live today, how exceptional. We celebrated high up in the clouds onboard Delta to Rome in Business Elite, hands linked near our hearts, holding each other's gaze, knowing there is nothing so gentle as the strong echo of our first kiss.

Severe security measures did not surprise anyone at Sky Harbor Airport in Phoenix. Lucky me selected to be patted down, strip-searched — *Thank you, Bin Laden.* We anticipated more of the same in Atlanta as we rushed to the international terminal. At the Delta Sky Club Lounge, I called Switzerland one last time to update Beate. My words, "our plane to Rome is on time," were buried under her wretched sounds over the phone.

"A big snowstorm has started." Beate's shaky voice shrieked.

"A what? In November?"

For a fraction of an instant, long enough for my heart to leap, a muted scream left my lips — one more thing to stop her?

Up in the air, close to heaven, I tried for my voice not to betray my emotions. During a predictable sleepless night, ten hours to Rome, my mind roamed. I prayed and agonized. Will Beate wake up at 3:45 a.m., ready to step into the taxi, reserved the day before? All alone to the airport at 5:00 in the morning?

I knew her habits too well, a tendency to change her mind at the last minute. I counted on my older brother Erwin, who resides on the second floor (still today), owner and savior of our parent's salon. Erwin's plan to drive *Lumpi* to the airport had altered dramatically when two days prior Mom turned ill — another gut-wrenching time. How could they leave Mom home alone?

All I knew to do was keep my fingers crossed, with Hail-Mary's clinging to my lips. As the sun rose in the distance in a cloudless sky I wondered, *Will we see Beate in Rome?*

"To worry is a sure sign we have forgotten to trust in God." — Unknown

❖ **Friday, 8:40 a.m. — We arrive in Rome**

Delta arrived — Beate's Swissair flight late because of the snowstorm. Elated, we learned Swissair touched down in Rome, Italy, a half-hour after our Delta-flight arrived from Atlanta, on a cloudless Friday morning — enough time for us to rush over to the Swissair gate. Miraculously perfect.

We dashed and waited. My mind racing, moments of hope had escalated to a state of staggering numbers. I watched anxiously and mystified as numerous people hurried through customs. With an apprehensive heart and feelings oh, — so — fearful, I searched intently for some sign of . . . did fear stop Beate?

My heart skipped, a swirl of jubilation in my throat, my unbelieving eyes intensified, possibly dreaming . . . Beate and I flew into each other's arms, two sisters never to let go. Through a sea of shimmering tears, we clung together, a time to invent a word. In Rome, together, for the upcoming, most meaningful days of our lives. Even the sun, after days of rain, was shining.

"Courage is fear that has said its prayers."— Dorothy Bernard

Time to search for Andrea, the US tour guide with the travel group from Philadelphia. I recognized Andrea immediately, a commanding lady with a voice that spelled comfort. I knew her not by sight but by frequent phone calls, asking and begging her to look for Beate, in case our plane from Atlanta arrived late. Expectant faith involves daring boldness.

In Andrea's ecstatic way she spotted the three of us in the crowd, she shouted,

"You found each other!"

The first group, radiating enthusiasm, had arrived in Rome. Some others from various parts of the world, a brief time later — planning at its finest.

Our private motor coach waited near the main entrance of the airport to drive our group to the Hotel Pineta, located on a high hill, overlooking Rome. I held onto Beate in astonishment, her face a celestial smile as stillness befell my soul, aware of dynamic feelings of the incredibly poetic scene around me.

My eyes shifted toward the sky, knowing we truly have a special friend in heaven, Mother Léonie Aviat, the saint-to-be. Simply, the Hand of God at work. Not after, nor ever again, have I identified nor felt the *Power of Prayer* as strongly as in that moment, at the Leonardo da Vinci Fiumicino Airport in Rome, Italy.

At the Hotel Pineta, surrounded by gorgeous grounds and flower gardens, we experienced our first glimpse of the dome of St. Peter's Basilica in the distance — another goosebump-moment! The two rooms assigned to the three of us were next door to each other on the fourth floor, with an overwhelming view of Rome, the eternal city. Humbling indeed.

At 2 p.m., everyone gathered for a city tour, four groups on four different-colored buses. Ours — the *Blue Bus*. Oops, blue? I ignored my dislike for blue.

We experienced an outstanding sight as we viewed the legendary Colosseum ahead of us in the late afternoon light. I watched Lew with delight, knowing this part of the tour had whet his appetite for what's to come and he would treasure forever, a result of his recent discovery of a family connection to the Roman Empire. Genealogy — his latest hobby.

At the Colosseum, we exited the bus and started walking. The cold north wind surprised us with a sky perfectly clear, streaked pink in the west. An eerie sense of history surrounded us, like going back in time, almost hearing the screams and shouts of thousands of spectators who witnessed the games. Laura, an Italian historian, a most expert guide, led this walking tour to the Palatine Hill and the Roman Forum of classical antiquity, Trajan's Column, the arches dedicated to the emperors Septimius Severus, Titus, and Constantine. Finally, we arrived at the Pantheon, the most impressive and best preserved of the early Roman buildings. Laura's knowledge of ancient Rome was tremendous and put Lew in history-heaven as we strolled around flooded with a powerful sense of the past.

The awareness of my sister's presence, her enthusiastic face, led me to feel a dramatic, majestic closeness to God, gratitude, and epic joy, knowing true happiness is only real when shared.

❖ Saturday, 8 a.m. — The Vatican

Another blue-sky sunshine day. The group on the Blue Bus was ready to leave for Vatican City for a morning visit at the Vatican Museums, to witness unparalleled artwork and — the Sistine Chapel — the Pope's chapel.

After lunch, time to shop. We found rosaries, postcards, and unusual Vatican stamps at a unique store close to St. Peter's Square. Next, we left for the Catacombs of St. Callisto. Lew could not wait to wander down below in narrow, history-filled tunnels. "Let me out." Lew's words echoed. A stunned group stared with feelings filled with mystery, where Christians were buried 2,000 years ago (100 – 300AD) in thousands of tombs. We all were thrilled to leave and see daylight — to escape the tunnels — a few managed to laugh at Lew's scary phrase.

At 3:30 p.m. the first High Mass at the magnificent Basilica of St. Paul Outside the Walls started right on schedule. Our eyes filled with awe inside this phenomenal church with

78

unequaled ancient Italian art. Where to look first? We discovered the best seats on the aisle. How fortunate — we could see *everything*. People full of excitement streamed in, including innumerable St. Francis de Sales nuns in their travel outfits, bishops, and countless priests from several parts of the world — and the lucky three of us together. Mass in honor of Soeur Aviat Françoise de Sales moved me to tears. Beate and Lew smiled. I pinched myself — goose-bumped again.

"Faith is not believing that God can – it is knowing that God will."
— Ben Stein

After the ceremony, surrounded by hundreds of spellbound people, in this majestic Basilica, I spotted a Swiss flag, most likely the group from Bern. We pressed forward through the giant crowd, holding on to each other. I shouted out, "Which one is Soeur Anna de Gonzague?" My goal for weeks was to find this gentle, ever-so-kind nun who had helped with the possibility of a seat for my sister on the Swiss tour by train. In my heart, I knew I must find and meet this most caring person, during all my desperate phone calls, for the chance to respectfully thank her.

"Over there," an unknown voice yelled.

Holding tight to Beate, with Lew nearby, I pushed my way to get close to Sr. Anna de Gonzague. Our eyes locked. "We are from Arizona," I hollered. In mere seconds, we fell into each other's arms, hugging like two long-lost friends. I will remember Sister Anna de Gonzague's heartfelt way for a long time, as well as her extreme happiness to see my sister with Lew and me.

She whispered in my ear, "Oh, I prayed plenty for Beate to find strength for her trip alone." My words of thanks expressed my belief in the *Power of Prayer*.

❖ Sunday, November 25, 2001 — Canonization and High Mass in St. Peter's Basilica

A shrill, early hotel wake-up call, to be ready for the 7 a.m. Blue Bus. Sleep-deprived Lew ordered room service. Sleepy Beate joined us.

"Jet lag is a way of life for lucky people," Lew clarified trying to convince himself. Amazed, we peeked in bewilderment at food enough for eight as a handsome, smiling Italian rolled in a large table and bellowed, "*Buongiorno*." Breakfast Italian-style at a hotel trying to make a difference.

In a panic, rushed because of our private morning buffet, we searched for the Blue Bus, only to hear words blasting through a horn, "The Blue Bus has broken down. In repair."

When, where? Valeria, our tour guide, nowhere to be seen. Our group separated with worries and panicky boarded any one of the other three buses, so as not to miss the Vatican ceremony. We were the last ones to find space. Elated, not yet aware how much this mishap would help us three later. For now, overjoyed to be off to St. Peter's Square where we would mingle with possibly a million people, the estimated size of the crowd for exceptional events.

Stepping off the bus, everyone was offered a blue and white silk scarf decorated with Léonie's favorite blue cornflowers and

Trudy and Beate, I nicknamed Lumpi, she calls me Trunylle.

inscribed with the name *Saint Léonie Aviat Françoise de Sales* in fancy writing. Written in five languages, "Let us work for the happiness of others."

My guilty reaction, again, Oh, no. *Blue*? Horror . . . blue won't match any of my outfits. Too Blessed to be stressed, I managed a smile. Excited we rushed to the famous St. Peter's Square and spotted hundreds — no, thousands — of people with that same scarf. Kids, men, women, and Lew. I touched my scarf around my neck — time to love blue. Never again will I look at blue without memories of Rome, the magnificent city, and the honor to be included in a once-in-a-lifetime occasion.

St. Peter's square buzzed with hordes of people. On this

| St. Giuseppe Marello | St. Maria Crescentia Höss | St. Paula Montal Fornés | St. Françoise de Sales Aviat |

cloudy morning, with rays of sunshine breaking through, three more saints were to be canonized: Bishop Guiseppe Marello of Italy, Maria Crescentia Höss of Germany, Paola Montal Fornés of Spain, and Léonie Aviat of France. Pride swelled in my heart to observe all the different-colored scarves: Yellow, red, green, and blue, as far as my eyes could see, to honor the saint from people's native countries. Stand-out banners displayed pictures of the four soon-to-be saints, high on the Basilica — two on each side of the Holy Father's famous balcony where millions of people continue to receive the Pope's blessings.

The three of us pressed our way through the crowd, without Valerie our missing tour guide. On our own, as on every occasion, Lew acted as if to know exactly what to do. With his cool, unhurried voice he directed Beate and me to keep walking, no matter what. Security was incredibly tight due to 9/11. After an austere time-consuming search, we raced in a mad dash, Beate and I close behind Lew. Nobody to wait for.

"Lucky for us," Lew mumbled. No Blue Bus people in sight, anywhere. We spotted a nun who acted important. Her hurried walk spelled knowledge of where to go. We followed her. I recognized the Aviat Order habit the nuns wore in the boarding school in Switzerland. Her compassion and sight of our scarves allowed us to go along as she listened to our broken-bus-no-tour-guide story.

A barricade stopped us. Ecstatic, we detected one of the criminally handsome Italian guards take down a rope that permitted us to climb the final stairs toward the basilica's entrance.

We hugged and thanked our caring, smiling mystery nun.

We never knew her name.

In total awe, we entered the majestic St. Peter's Basilica. With reactions too startling, we gazed at architecture and art in wonder. A high-ranking-looking person interrupted. In his low voice spoke words still ringing in my ears, "Take a seat on the left in the back." Lew, on a mission, ignored this well-dressed-in-black-with-tie man and kept walking. The two of us held on tight through a crowd of people; an inner force pulled this threesome toward the front. Beyond the middle of the cathedral, we noticed empty seats right by the aisle. Lew hollered, "Sit down."

No — Beate and I hesitated. Surely seats this marvelous were saved for someone other than us? Feeling vastly bold is exactly where we stayed for the most unprecedented, emotional, three-hour canonization ceremony of four new European saints.

Hundreds of worshipers filled the aisles on each side. At precisely 9:30 — a hush fell on the crowd — our Holy Father, John Paul II, entered St. Peter's. Excited anticipation ran through my body, a piercing sensation I was not prepared for that caused my heart to hiccup and simply filled me with enormous pleasure. The memory of that undeniable feeling may never fade as everyone waved their scarves in the air. Tears of unbelievable joy ran down, messing up my make-up.

At the altar, surrounded by VIPs and dignitaries of the Roman Catholic domain, thanks to our nerve-tingling seats, in a miraculous state we witnessed our Pope — His presence of dignity and strength — our Holiness celebrate Mass — Time stood still.

When the world's most powerful, the religious leader began his exit down the aisle, the crowd, my sister, and I climbed on top of the chairs. Even proper Lew, although, with a pinch above his eyes he gave me a look of concern — *What if you fall?* Speechless, I glanced at my non-Catholic husband as he too climbed on a chair, touched beyond words surpassing the ordinary, turning into the extraordinary. An explosion of gripping joy, I can't explain, but only felt in the depth of my soul as Pope John Paul II came close — His eyes and gentle wave directed right at the three of us — created an elevated moment I am still dizzy from, as if I were bodiless, like floating.

As we left renowned St. Peter's surrounded by people filled with a spiritual remembrance, we detected an oversized TV screen in the massive square. Tens of thousands of pilgrims never had a chance to get inside. We recognized our Blue Bus group viewing this exceptional ceremonial Mass on a screen in St. Peter's Square. Sorrowful indeed, to travel so far and be denied entrance into the Basilica. The three of us, full of profound appreciation glanced up to heaven with a glorified sigh.

We joined the group for a luncheon, paid for by the Oblates of St. Francis de Sales, outside Rome at Villa Borghese with its stunning grounds owned at one time by the legendary family. Later walking continued through the aged streets of Rome to one more basilica — St. Mary Major. That is Italy. In America, the tour bus most certainly would drop everyone off near the front door.

A new tour guide, Grazia, awaited us. Fascinated, we listened to the ancient history that pervades this very old basilica.

❖ Monday Morning — Private Audience

Our bags were packed, stored on the bus, for a late afternoon journey to Assisi. Nonetheless, now we were on the way, in the repaired Blue Bus, to the Vatican Auditorium. Another exceptional morning for a private audience with Pope John Paul II. Again St. Peter's Square filled with masses of people, the security as tight as on the previous day.

My eyes wandered to the sophisticated Pontifical Swiss Guards dressed as if from a different century in times long past. Swiss Soldiers have served in foreign European courts since the late fifteenth century. I ran, this time Lew and my sister followed me. My urgent need to get near the Swiss Guards stupefied me.

"*Grüezi.*" Saying hello in my Swiss German, I dared to ask, "*Wie gaht's?*" "How are you?" Some answered with a grin. Their smiles left me with feelings of national pride.

Once a Swiss, always a Swiss.

Close to the front in this captivating auditorium, we found textbook seats thanks to early arrival. Anxiously we waited, to behold our Holy Father one more time for an audience. A

Roman Catholic tradition, where His Holiness meets the pilgrims in a more intimate, privileged setting, to recognize accomplishments of the saints canonized the day before. Dressed all in white, being helped up the stairs, John Paul II took a seat in a grand chair assigned to him only. On each side, a Swiss Guard like a statue stood for his protection. The Pope's godliness faced the crowd. He spoke in four languages — Italian, Spanish, French, and German. "The future starts today, not tomorrow."

A dream-like stillness engulfed the massive congregation when the Holy Father blessed us one last time. Everyone held their unique scarves high up, waving fiercely. The ceremony ended with a final, thunderous hands-clapping, like an orchestra on cue, with such intensity of emotions — feelings with no name, tears falling in abundance.

On the way to a typical spaghetti/pizza Italian lunch, of course, on foot, we found the famous Piazza Nuova. Out of this world to experience a different part of ancient Rome by simply walking as we wandered through narrow, dark streets full of mysteries, truth, and myth, where people lived in old houses with bordered up windows.

Leisurely we strolled to the Chiesa Nuova for the Holy Mass at 3:30 p.m. — a Mass dedicated to now Saint Léonie Aviat held in this antique historical church where its magnificence is enhanced by history.

The motorcoach waited for the transfer to Assisi outside Rome. A two-hour drive, a long bus trip, not my favorite. The concern of getting carsick troubled me. Due to Italian rush-hour traffic, we arrived late at an old Italian inn in Assisi, sure enough, nauseated getting off the bus. Lew opened the door to our assigned room — all in blue — not believing my eyes, I admitted, how pretty. Mesmerized, blue forever reminds me of a trip that changed my thinking. Never have I liked blue, except for a blue ocean or a blue sky that spells sunshine.

❖ Tuesday — Morning in Assisi, — Evening in Perugia

We felt blessed to visit the ancient San Lorenzo Cathedral in Perugia for the final High Mass for Saint Mother Aviat, Françoise de Sales, where we had visited nine years previously after her beatification on September 27, 1992, in St. Peter's Square, Rome.

My dream was about to come true, to revisit this magical old town, Perugia, where Léonie Françesca di Sales Aviat died on January 10, 1914.

Léonie began her path to religious life in April 1866.

Privileged to be seated right on the aisle, again, I gazed up to the altar at one of the most affecting pictures of our new Santa Léonie, who had lived her life for the happiness of others. I identified one of the leading nuns in front getting up from her seat. She strolled down the aisle toward me. In shock, immediately, I recognized Swiss-born Soeur Thérèse Espérance with her regal air, the presence of God exuding her, my favorite nun from forty-six years ago at the French/Swiss boarding school. With sudden dryness in my mouth, a knot in my throat, I softly called her name. She turned and smiled, that gentle smile I never forgot.

Snippets of past times surfaced; I was transported back, to the first scary day after my parents left me at the Institute in Châtel St. Denis. Fear, a persistent companion in this French-speaking school for a kid far away from a German-speaking home. Feeling extremely homesick, after a night of fighting and choking on tears, the next morning I became a woman. My *first* period occurred.

"Why am I bleeding?" I cried.

Soeur Thérèse Espérance held me in her arms during that fearful vital moment for a young girl. Her words in *Schwyzer Dütsch* (Swiss German), "This happens to every girl your age," comforted me enormously. She smiled her unique, unforgettable smile, which would linger on through all my life in America.

She taught me to smile.

I hunted for notepaper in my cluttered bag and scribbled my name and a few lines in haste. "*Class of 1956 — I never forget, did you?*" I slipped the note to Sr. Thérèse Espérance as she walked by to reclaim her seat in the front row. Moments later, she reappeared. Hundreds of people around us, she halted briefly, still clutching my note, to talk to me. I experienced unbridled joy; abundant tears tumbled. For a long while, they would not stop.

At the Italian Inn earlier that morning, I had been awfully sick and threw up several times, possibly dehydrated. Devastated, I agonized over missing this significant last day. Later, feeling fairly better, we joined the bus tour to visit the eminent St. Francis of Assisi's phenomenal church. However, once we arrived, my nausea struck again with force. Lew and my sister holding me up had to return to the hotel. The tour guide called for a taxi. Raindrops started to fall — holy water from heaven?

Back to bed. At 2 p.m., finally, after lots of liquids, I recovered. Behind my closed, about-to-open eyes, I heard the whine in my voice: "We absolutely cannot miss Perugia, my favorite Italian town."

"Nor miss the final High Mass in that monumental Cathedral," I stuttered. Beate contacted the bell captain and in her broken Italian requested he please call for any transportation.

I knew this would be my last chance at that church service, to possibly find Soeur Thérèse Espérance, assistant to Mother Mère at the Mother House, in Troyes, France,

A dose of determination caused me to recuperate. Our gray-haired handsome driver, no speaking English, stopped at an Italian Pizzeria. Promptly we remembered their famed minestrone from our first time in Perugia and the convenient short walk to the famous medieval San Lorenzo Cathedral.

Some Things Are Simply Meant to Be.

Now, Sr. Thérèse Espérance, as big as life, stood in front of me. The sweetest nun who taught me to smile, no matter what. If you smile the world will smile with you. To smile is one fundamental thing in life. I stared with a silent *wow* — she remembered the girl from Tann. How could a religious sister ever truly know what an impact she had on a frightened kid from long ago — an influence that would last a lifetime?

My chance to tell her was now! Her compelling hug and smile left me humble and in forever awe.

Nine years earlier in St. Peter's Square during Mother Léonie's beatification, I had spotted Sr. Thérèse Espérance in the massive crowd, for a brief minute only. Her smiling hello and a royal wave of her hand as she rushed by left me sorrowful, not sure if she remembered simple me.

My husband Lew, as my favorite nun did, held the same belief throughout our magical marriage, the importance of a

86

smile. Every morning, before I'd leave early for work, he smiled — until I smiled back.

"A smile is a curve that sets everything straight." — Phyllis Diller

Driving out of the garage, trying not to speed, I watched Lew plenty of times out in the street in the dark, in the cold winter mornings. He would cross to the other side to stand under the streetlight so I could see him in the rear-view mirror until the bend in the road. He waved. I knew he smiled.

"A smile is the shortest distance between two people." — Victor Borg

❖ Wednesday, 4 a.m. — Going home.

Early wake-up call. Going home. A fresh brew of morning awaited and *au revoir* on everyone's mind. We boarded the bus at 5 a.m. to return to the airport in Rome. Everyone scattered in different directions, filled with memories of unmatched magnificence. Beate next to me acted strong and even managed to smile. I held her hand tightly and trusted this upcoming flight would be easier. *Lumpi* had no knowledge of another dreadful Crossair plane crash (Suisse) at the airport in Zürich. During our captivating stay in Rome, news flashed on our small TV late at night in our hotel room, leaving us distraught.

Nauseous again, I threw up on the bus into a paper bag, an oh-no moment, like acid on my skin. Too many stops and detours due to frenzied Italian traffic, as well as concern for my sister. With forty-five minutes to spare before Swissair's departure, our driver sped toward the terminal, listening to everybody's apprehensive speculations. An accident on the frantic morning rush-hour highway left despair on all our faces. I winced in pain — my paper bag ready.

With emotions flying high, our bye-byes rushed, I tried to believe that was a good thing. Lew and I watched Beate charge to the gate. I saw no fear — rather, its absence. She turned with a heavenly, unforeseen smile, waved, and blew a kiss with memories of the most fascinating five days. A tapestry of life's moments — indelibly imprinted in her mind forever.

High up in the air over the ocean, exhausted yet thankful for Delta Business-Elite, although, still throwing up, vomit on the floor — embarrassing on an airplane, what a relief to land in Atlanta. Finally, I began to feel more like myself; nevertheless, Lew and I slept soundly from Atlanta to Phoenix, missing meals.

Back home in Scottsdale, I rushed to dial a familiar number in Switzerland. My sister's voice sounded like music. Beate — home, safe. Thank You, Lord, for an unforgettable trip, a magical dream etched-in-stone.

"Memory is the only paradise from which we cannot be driven away." — Jean Paul Richter

My life-long day-to-day habit, prayers before coffee in the morning, includes Saint Léonie Aviat Frances de Sales.

The Power of Prayers. . . never-ending.

By the way . . .

Soeur Thérèse Espérance resided in Troyes, France at Maison Mère. Her name in the inbox on my computer brought jumbo smiles, each time. At **88** years old, in late 2019, she turned ill, for the worst. E-mails from the Mother House stopped. She died in Troyes, 7/10 2020. She left for heaven 2 days before her birthday.

Soeur Thérèse Espérance, in Troyes, France

We visited Maison Mère in 200**8**, greeted at the Troyes train station by this most-loved nun with her all-too-familiar smile. Wearing my French boarding school beret from long ago, my thoughtful Lew's idea, brought tears to her dear face in the French sunshine.

One invitation for this holy event in honor of Léonie Aviat's canonization as a saint in Rome Italy to my surprise arrived from the motherhouse of the Oblate Sisters of Saint Francis de Sales in Childs, Maryland. Sent to me by one of the teachers at Villa Aviat, Sister Christine Elisabeth, who we met during the beatification Rome trip in 1992. This nun is the younger real-life, look-alike sister of my beloved Soeur Thérèse Espérance. Both nuns were teachers and at one time taught at the institute, the all-girl school near Lausanne, Switzerland. A second invitation followed to former students from the Oblate Sisters in Switzerland, at that French-speaking school in Châtel St. Denis. All girls and students who ever lived and studied at the French school were invited.

Lew and I chose to join the American group for one reason — so Lew, the American, would understand the numerous tour guides speaking English throughout the trip. Although Beate's English. certainly shaky, yet good enough to join us and the American tour.

Beate, my tall, 'little' sister, at 21, in July of 1972, took the leap to come to America. She arrived in Los Angeles, while Lew and I still lived in Santa Monica. A Swiss family in Beverly Hills California, gave her employment, room, and board, to take care of their two-year-old boy for six months. Afterward, she toured to Arizona by Greyhound bus, to live with Lew and me for almost a year. A job at John Gardner's Tennis Ranch Resort, thanks to one of my clients' help, awaited her. Cleaning rooms.

One late morning, Beate called me at the salon during the morning rush. All excited she asked, "Who is Johnny Carson?" He had handed her a one-hundred-dollar bill for cleaning his fancy resort suite, leaving her in a trance.

In 1992, for Mother Léonie Aviat's beatification in Rome, we traveled with the group out of Châtel St. Denis, Switzerland, on a tour by bus. A one-week travel tour naturally spoken in French and Swiss German; no English, poor Lew. I tried to be the translator. Upon our Delta flight's arrival in Italy, in Rome, from Phoenix, Arizona, we joined the group and my two sisters, at a hotel, walking distance from St. Peter's.

On the extended bus ride back to Switzerland, we enjoyed Italy's countryside, plus the picturesque Italian part of Switzerland. An unforgettable visit to the old boarding school was included. Walking up the steep stairs I remembered too well, as the massive wooden front door opened. Feelings of nostalgia emerged like a blow to my chest, the fear of a door that might never reopen after my parents kissed their young girl goodbye. Yet, outstretched arms of smiling nuns were waiting in a massive, cold, stone hall; they taught me to be strong.

***

Lew is not Catholic. On June **8**, 1972 (**8** had now become our lucky number), we married in my home church in Tann,

 Switzerland, the small village where people lined the street and waved from open windows to get a glimpse of the bride with her American groom. Church bells rang for fifteen minutes at 1:45 p.m. Rain all morning caused me to cringe. They say rain is "good luck" at a wedding; how true. At one o'clock the sun emerged and stayed out for our memorable, about 3 blocks walk to church — yes, the wedding party on foot — from my parents' house for the 2 p.m. Mass and ceremony. My mom let everyone know, "I prayed tirelessly for blue sky." Sunshine (a Swiss gift) remained for the rest of the day.

Lew asked my brother Erwin to be best man and Beate, my never-wearing-makeup 'little' sister *Lumpi*, reigned as my maid of honor. Not married, to this day she lives in the old family house in Tann, on the top floor, with three cats and one dog.

The evening preceding our *I do* moment; Father Jacomet visited the family's home to meet the couple from Arizona. Mom had assured me I would love the young handsome priest from Grison, her home *Kanton* (state) who had agreed to marry us. Moms know best. Instantly we adored this debonair priest, who spoke some English. Enough to recite the wows for Lew (and his family) in English and German for everyone else.

On his way out, he squeezed my hands and whispered, "At Mass tomorrow I will give Lew communion," words of dramatic and enormous importance. I hardly believed my ears. I shook inside as if my heart had come loose. Never did I pray for such a blessing, nor dared to wish for. Unheard of growing up I never knew that to be possible. This was not the Catholic way — Catholic Sacraments for anyone? All I prayed for was not to feel alone and cry during communion. Mess up my eye makeup and false eyelashes?

At our wedding Mass, my tears would not stop for one awe-inspiring reason — Lew was granted communion — a most humbling wedding gift. An unexpected gift is the best kind. Perfect does not always look like you imagined.

"God's gifts put man's best dreams to shame." —
Elizabeth Barrett Browning

On our 25th wedding anniversary, we flew to Switzerland, the year when June **8**th mystically was on a Sunday. Up in the quaint Grison Mountain village of Domat Ems, Father Jacomet, a pastor now for years, the priest who married us in 1972 I had kept in touch with, (each time I signed: *the happiest couple in the world)*, held a private Mass for us only in his picturesque old-fashioned church filled with flowers and roses all in pink — a gift from Mom. (After regular scheduled Sunday Mass) We invited family and some of the same guests from twenty-five years ago — and *Tädi*, Dad, as big as life in our hearts, in spirit from heaven, the garden in the sky.

Domat Ems, GR; Catholic church; June **8**, 1997.

Again, Lew received communion. While back home in the US, for months, I knew in my heart Father Jacomet would . . . he did.

91

I thanked God from the depth of my heart for that special Sunday in June. *Some things are simply meant to be. . ..*

Our blessed marriage lives on. A belief something extraordinary is possible continues.

One more thing . . . or two . . .

Each year our travels home include a never-broken tradition, on the list of places to visit: Einsiedeln's Abbey, a Benedictine monastery with baroque architecture and art. The Shrine of Our Lady of Einsiedeln, dedicated to Saint Meinrad, a hermit, and the famous black Madonna, serve pilgrims from all over Europe, like Fatima and Lourdes. Known worldwide *Klosterkirche* was repainted recently, as it appeared originally in various pastel colors of rose, green and gold leaf.

After a substantial cleanup of black due to the smoke of millions of candles lit, the glorious colors now take worshipers' breaths away. Entering the old church of adoration, eyes look up and words escape: Oh, my God!

Lew convincingly believes and tells everyone Einsiedeln's

Abbey/church is more beautiful than St. Peter's in Rome, Italy. Seeing is believing. On our first trip together to Rome, as Lew gazed around and admired the surprisingly dark, filled with history impressive St. Peter's Cathedral, he declared, "Oh, but not as beautiful as Einsiedeln."

Our parents were married in Einsiedeln on April 18 in 1938 at the Saint Joseph's Altar, located on the left side of the Black Madonna Chapel of Grace, inside the grand church in Einsiedeln. St. Joseph, many years later, would become my favorite Saint to pray to, as he listened to my endless praying for *Mime* to travel across the ocean, to visit her daughter and Lew in

Scottsdale. She did — alone — at **80** years of age. Prayers answered — what a gift!

There, where it all began, a life together — Mother and Father's wedding-day ceremony and Mass at the renowned church in Einsiedeln, a young Pater Daniel performed a private Mass for the celebration of Lew and my 45th wedding anniversary June **8**[th], 2017, attended by family. Einsiedeln, a unique tourist/worshiper's village, 25,9 Kilometers from Tann, became one of *Mime*'s most cherished outings any weekends, any day, to visit the Maria *Kapelle,* the adored and famous chapel.

A tradition lives on.

Our parent's golden wedding anniversary in 19**88,** celebrating fifty years of marriage, started with a private Mass in our home church in Tann. By bus, (a huge one), decorated with flowers and ribbons, guests, mostly family, toured to an elegant restaurant, Chrug, with a spectacular view above Lake Zürich for lunch. (The same resort where we relished our late lunch on our wedding day in 1972.) Again, the same fancy bus transportation. The four of us siblings showered Mom and Dad with fifty gifts wrapped in gold. To name a few: special Madonna candles from Einsiedeln, Vicks VapoRub, (I still use our father's 'secret cure for colds and everything.) Gift certificates to the Klosterhof, a favorite restaurant, and flowers at the *Gärtnerei Meier,* (today a huge Garden Center well-known all over Switzerland.) Naturally much-loved cheese and a variety of favorite Suisse chocolates, etc.

Mami and *Tädi*'s wedding picture, enlarged and framed in

gold, shipped from Arizona, (which did not fit in the suitcase) graced the entrance to the room where the festivities took place with forty relatives.

Tädi passed away one and a half years later.

A favorite family picture of that exceptional occasion,
Mami and *Tädi*, each holding 25 pink sweetheart roses.

Parent's 25th anniversary, 1963 Meisterschwanden am See, Aargau

Flashback to late afternoon on our Civil wedding day in
Beverly Hills on April 2**8**, 1972. On the way home from work on

that out-of-the-ordinary day, Lew stopped to surprise me with 2 dozen pink sweetheart roses. The identical pink. Pink roses would become and remain my favorites throughout our marriage.

Pink roses — the symbol of eternal love in the Meyer/Wells family.

April 2**8,** 1972, after the ceremony at the home of the lady judge, my client, in Beverly Hills, who married us.

Trudy Wells-Meyer

A Rose for Mom

*"Life may not always give you what you want. May it always
give you what you need."* — Anonymous

Sitting in a pew, I watch all mothers rush up front, to the
    altar surrounded by flowers, a pastor's invitation,
        to receive a rose for being a Mom.
            Mother's Day — a Mom — signature of life.

My emotions in check not ever being a Mom,
    chronic illness of nostalgia, a time
        missed like a deadline we ignore,
            the gate to memories never closes.

A belief in God's will, my complex brain,
    no proud surrender,
        stop haunting me and come uninvited.
            God's plan, no child of mine? I wish I could be certain.

Mom up in the big garden in the sky called Heaven,
    closeness beyond magic, her startling,
        bragging words ringing in my ears
            words I could never believe came
                from my stern, oh, so strict Mom,

"My daughter can do anything." Years later I would come
    to understand from a tiny seed of such praise
        would emerge an exceptional will to cause
            my hardworking mom to be right.

Now, realizing that I am my own mother — in words, actions
    I once feared I think of all the no-no-no's growing up,
        war of words, reasons to leave . . . for America.
            Today — a distant memory.

My seldom smiling Mom, a child beaten by a drunken father,
    enough to make angels weep. Now I understand
        and hope my daily prayers will do someone,
            somewhere some good.

I see a rainbow in the clouds near the edge of Heaven.
Mom, this rose is for you . . . red for Love.
Mother's Day . . .
I was handed a rosebud moment.

Each year I try to escape an emptiness on Mother's Day, distinctively when I see a boy. After years of clinging on tightly to a lifeboat of an idea with no children — the astounding responsibility of bringing up kids — it may be hard for friends and family to grasp I have wanted a child all along. I believed one gets married and has children. Family . . . a circle of life?

Today I know steadfast if God had wanted us to have a child . . . Some things in life are simply not meant to be.

What will be will be . . . Que sera, sera.

"For those who trust in God, the safest place in the world is wherever He leads you." — Anonymous

By the way . . .

Mom passed away at **88** on August 9, 2003. Saturday evening in Switzerland, still morning in Scottsdale, Arizona. A bossy, in-a-hurry client sat in my chair at La Chérie salon as I received the call.

Beate, my *Lumpi*, mumbled, "*Mami* wants to speak with you." One final time, to say goodbye. The hectic salon noise of hair dryers, clients babbling, and, not allowing me to hear each word through the phone line added to my despair. I was devastated. Years to come I would try to recollect Mom's last phrases, knowing words have meanings. Words I did not hear kept haunting me. Still.

To experience fireworks in Rapperswil on the lake of Zürich, a yearly celebration, that Saturday evening Beate, the youngest, sat in the grass high up near the *Hasenstrick,* on the mountain named Bachtel. From previous years she knew she'd be able to see the spectacle of lights. Her heavy heart belonged to Mom who had turned for the worst at the Assisted Living Home.

Erwin, our brother, sat at Mother's side, he held her hand as he witnessed her last breath leaving this earth, the last journey with fireworks in the sky. How fitting to announce this strong woman's arrival at the gate of heaven. *Mime* died two hours after the distressing but profound call to *Nildi*, her nickname for her daughter in Arizona. (Only Mom, no one else, ever.)

Melancholy repeated like a distant train whistle. An eternal ache had started for someone so far away who lost a mother. I would come to comprehend, however; a Mom is with you at all times — in your heart — how close is that . . .

The belief in the power of prayer that *Mime* came at **80** years old will remain tremendously huge. Her visit now turned more valuable than ever and her presence in and around our home in every room more graphic, on the patio feeding the

ducks, staring at a hummingbird she claimed she only ever saw at the Zoo before. Thank you, God, and St. Josef.

The many moments we call life tell us what to wear to a funeral, what color — still black in Switzerland —, though no one ever teaches you how to feel.

Standing at the graveside, surrounded by the cemetery's gorgeous graves, breathtakingly decorated with fresh flowers on a cloudy, humid August morning, I was stunned by the countless people and familiar faces showing up for Mother's burial.

Willi, the boy upstairs who grew up with no father, now stood across the dirt hole. With his wife smiling he waved when he noticed Lew and me.

I squealed as memories emerged of a day when Mom handed me my first, my very own dress in 1953. I was twelve. A dress of many flowers and colors. Flowers I had never seen before. Ecstasy, a never-fading memory to feel such sophisticated bouclé fabric on my body; imprinted still — I could paint those flowers — in purple — pink — yellow. No hand-me-downs that day for a glorious wedding of a close family friend, Hedi's son.

Hedi, Willi's never-married mom, lived in the tiny top-floor apartment of the old house, above us, she took care of my brother and sisters growing up. Babysitting between her demanding job and being a single mom. Now Willi's smile let me pretend to be a child again and put me at the local church, years ago gliding into the pew like a lady, troubled sick to sit on this wondrous dress. Wrinkles on my dress?

Did Willi and Dorli know, his wife of many years now, their wedding day originated my love for flowers and gorgeousness in all things, especially clothes? Their day in hand of marriage shaped my life on how to soar and fly in spirit when dressed up. I learned during that joyful event how to feel beautiful. An obsession for beauty and elegance had started. *When I grow up, I will have beautiful clothes . . . and shoes.*

Thank you, *Mime.*

Choking in panic and raw grief, my cheeks suddenly wet, I put on sunglasses as memory worked to paint the past in vivid shades of *Mime* visiting us in

sunny Arizona. The first evening she enjoyed having dinner at a typical Western Cowboy restaurant without showing the likely foreseeable excitement. I blamed jet lag — it was the middle of the night in Switzerland.

The following day — on the agenda only the best — lunch at the Phoenician, a five-star hotel. With Mom's almost smile, in my silver Mercedes 500 SL now well-rested next to me babbling about how well she slept on her pillows which she packed and brought in one of her suitcases. A suitcase for pillows? Typical Mom.

I maneuvered slowly up the hill to the impressive entrance and stopped at valet parking. A handsome valet opened the door. Mom stared. A nervous voice asked in bewilderment,

"*Nildi,* you leave him your car?" She could hardly believe a young attendant drove off in my elegant sports car.

As we entered the world-famous hotel, *Mime* stopped in the middle of the huge lobby, leaning on her cane. In total awe she admired a view of the city, never having seen anything like it. Her head turned to every corner decorated with palms and tropical flowerpots. With words as stale as dry bread. She mumbled, "Why didn't we come here yesterday?" Classic Mom.

I would repeat those words, for years to come, still do, to friends we'd meet for a drink at this unique and classy hotel.

Emptiness and more tears my clouded eyes noticed Mother's German cousin, elegant like a queen in a wheelchair across the open, newly shoveled burial place. My nose watered like a bad cold. Nobody guessed *Tante* Erna to travel from the Black Forest, Aichhalden in Germany, a four-hour drive by car, where Grandpa Franz Günther grew up — our Mom's German Dad. Next to Erna stood Uncle Oskar, a younger brother and famous chef from Lugano, the Italian part of Switzerland. His head bent low to hide his emotions, his oldest daughter Beatrice holding him up.

During lunch, *das Leidmahl,* at the only hotel in the small village, I sat next to my favorite uncle. We visited him often when we came to Switzerland, in Davos and Lugano, in 'his' kitchen where his chef knowledge ruled the hotels, wherever he worked. To Lew's infinite surprise — a chef with the power of food.

I elbowed Oskar and said, "Do I have a story for you, about your sister during her Arizona visit."

Ash Wednesday, 1995, forever cast in stone, at noon *Mime* and I had attended Mass at Lady of Perpetual Help, my weekly church. On this day filled to the brim with parishioners standing in the back, all around — no seats left in the huge church. Long lines formed for the receiving of ashes, a yearly Catholic custom.

Mom stared at the astonishing crowd. "On a working day in the middle of the week?" She shook her head as her patience had begun to dwindle through the long service, still dealing with the Atlantic time change.

I had mentioned lunch after Mass at the all the rage Sugar Bowl close by. She loved and devoured American food — a grilled cheese sandwich. As I rummaged for the credit card, I asked the waitress, "Please, one meatloaf to go." I hoped they had one. Knowing how much in demand their tasty, homemade meatloaf sold by the bunches, available every day. Simply pay money and dinner is ready — how cool is that? Another experience that put *Mime* into an awestruck frenzy.

"Only in America," she muttered.

At 6 p.m. we sat down for dinner at the rectangular glass-top table in the bay window corner, where the view dazzled Mom. She gazed at palm trees, the golf course, and Camelback Mountain in the distance, shades of pink roses and intense colors of numerous bougainvillea in our garden near the lake,

Lew had come home from a long day at the office and to his surprise found Mom sitting in his spot, his corner to relax. She helped herself to meatloaf, fork in her hand in mid-air from the plate, when I hollered, "It's Ash Wednesday — fasting — abstinence from meat. 1 forgot!" Horrified, my guilt showed.

Mime shoved that meatloaf in her mouth, glancing at the kitchen clock, and stated, "It's Thursday in Switzerland."

"C*heibe guet, Trunilli*," (extremely good) she added in her distinctly nonchalant mom-way.

Her logic and dry wit I would come to never forget. I wiped my tears. Sedona appeared in my mind, our weekend trip. Lew had rented a luxury car during her stay, convincing us, "We need *Mime* to be comfortable driving from place to place,

especially long distances."

We spotted the chapel of the Holy Cross, as Lew drove around the turn, I knew so well exploding the magic of Sedona. I pointed shouting, "*Mime*, that is where I prayed for a husband."

Mom knew the story perfectly, her daughter *Trunilli* driving to Sedona for Sunday Mass, a two-hour drive, when she first arrived in Arizona. Threatening clouds in the distance put sunshine on our faces and our hearts in this magical place close to God.

The last day of Mother's distinctively fantastic ten-day Arizona visit, one more lunch invitation by a dear client at a private club with a superb city view, as she got in my silver sports car I scolded," Mom, you forgot your cane."

"I don't need it." Her words with conviction, as strong as I know Mom can be, sounded like a miracle . . . Praise the Lord!

Silence in the car, only the noise of rolling down the window, out of the corner of my eye I saw *Mime*'s head turned to the sunshine, blowing her hair, smelling the orange blossoms.

The best poems are not written — but lived.

We all try to find some sort of closure, something to ease our pain. Closure does not exist, but peace does and eventually turns into smiling memories.

Fixing Mom's hair at the salon during her Scottsdale holiday.

During teary *Auf Wiedersehen* scenes after one of our memorable home visits in the early eighties, at the Zürich airport, I watched *Mime* in a last-minute gesture take off the long cross necklace I never thought she'd part with. As she put that glistening silver cross around my neck, she proclaimed with a strong voice, no tears, "*Nildi*, may this cross always protect you." Words of protection for a lifetime — a bond indelible in the heart for a daughter in far-away Arizona. I wear this significant treasure with an inner peace only a mom can give. In life and death.

How utterly wrong to ever have doubted mother's love.

A favorite moment that gives a snapshot meaning for eternity in our Scottsdale TV/den/computer room in 1995

In September 2019, while in Coronado at our condo, my sister Beate sent old pictures she had found in an aged box with family records up in the attic. Staring at my phone, a trip down memory lane happened like a blow to my stomach — 3 kids, the number 3 as big as life. . . my older sister, my brother and youngest, me in the middle, matching — even socks and 3 buttons in white. Our Mother, the seamstress, designed and sewed those clothes . . . matching to perfection.

Up in years, a brain moment, a picture left me speechless. I clutched my heart in blissful shock. A lifetime-need to tirelessly match everything, (a friend calls an obsession), I learned and received from my *Mime*. A revelation swirled in my mind and soul, that shattered as well as elevated my spirits. I could almost hear the late-night sounds of a sewing machine; Sunday clothes were no hand-me-downs? *Mami* sewed and designed our matching outfits. How did I, could I go through life without connecting the dots? Never in mother's presence acknowledged or talked about this unique phenomenon that rules a daughters' days for years? Did our father, anybody, compliment her?

When I reminisce about how poor I thought we were at that age, what about the hidden love of a mother, my *Mime*.

Praise God for family records in the attic!

Prescott, Arizona — Where Christmas is

Where "Merry Christmas" sounds like an echo — where two simple words have the power to transport me back to childhood.

Every trip is another discovery.

On Friday, the first weekend in December 2006, Lew and I drove to Prescott, a small Arizona town known for its annual courthouse lighting ceremony — a first for us. I had listened a thousand times to clients at the salon telling a variety of stories about that wonderful place, especially about this yearly event on the first Saturday of the month in December. Each time had me dreaming — Someday. . .

To have time is a gift.

Retirement means having time to say "yes" to everything.

How could we have known in 2006 Christmas to be in the air in a way that would leave an imprint in our minds? "Merry Christmas" played such a role in those days during the holidays. According to the news on TV and the Internet, *Merry Christmas* could perhaps be scratched from the vocabulary and saying *it* in certain stores and establishments.

After we arrived in Prescott late that afternoon, we strolled through its captivating main street. At a charming downtown store all decked up for Christmas, I wished someone "Happy

Holidays" with a smile. The lady stopped and looked me right in the eyes with stern words, "None of that! *Merry Christmas!*" Her eyes and smile were radiant with joy.

"Happy Holidays" is meant for the whole month of December — Hanukkah, Christmas, New Year's — and is the right thing to say. However, let us *never* leave out "Merry Christmas."

A wish of ours for years to stay at the Hassayampa Inn, a hotel with a reputation for its different, unique style from the olden days, where the ordinary turns into the exceptional developed into all that and more. What a surprise to watch people all dressed up and ready for Christmas with their red sweaters and outfits glittering with sparkles, even for breakfast. A bent-over gentleman up in age wore green pants and a Christmas bowtie matching the green of his wife's elegant sweater jacket. I stopped and told them how attractive they both looked, all the while pointing to the matching outfits Lew and I wore, the color-coordinated red and black, mine with sparkles. His joyful "Merry Christmas" with a huge grin echoed in the hall and sounded from the heart.

Late evening when we walked into our old-fashioned with antique furniture hotel room, Lew turned on the small TV set with news blasting and a commentator going on and on about Crate and Barrel's idea of not wanting to say, "Merry Christmas." We smiled at each other with memories of a Christmas experience that left us in awe — virtually speechless — for one simple reason: the 52nd Courthouse Lighting Ceremony had started with the real, one and only, Christmas story.

A clear, loud, and commanding voice narrated the story, the one often forgotten during Christmastime and the holiday rush. The voice belonged to a county official standing on top of the numerous steps leading to the entrance of the courthouse. Innumerable Prescott children and students with their red Santa hats surrounded him, filling the cold steps. They sang the traditional Christmas songs with clear convincing voices, in time to fit the story. The deep voice in the dark night left me trembling as it stopped to lend room for the perfect song: "O Little Town of Bethlehem."

When "Silent Night" filled the air, I choked on the sudden lump in my throat. I burst into tears. Silent Night — *Stille Nacht* — Holy Night — *Heilige Nacht,* a song I had heard countless times but never had affected me quite like that. The warmest feeling inside my heart belonged to my dad in heaven as the sounds of his favorite song from long ago repeated — a time when music tells you how to feel. Snippets of the past flashed through my mind — a child again, in amazement of a Christmas tree — *Christbaum* translating Christ tree, lit candles, — real candles — a Swiss tradition. Some years our *Tannenbaum* with a forest scent held up to twenty-five lit candles perfectly placed on branches.

How and where did Mom and Dad hide the *Tannenbaum* (pine tree), in the cellar or the attic? How did the live tree, like the ones in the forest, get to our house? We found out much later, I was eleven. The *Christbaum* hid in the attic. Both parents decorated on Christmas Eve, after a busy day at the salon full of last-minute hair services for the holidays; the kids were asleep.

Santa Claus visited the homes of children on December 6th Saint Nikolas Day. No belief in Santa coming down the chimney, but an angel sent from heaven, from God to all children who were good throughout the year. A heavenly angel with a lit Christmas tree and gifts would fly in the sky, through a window intentionally left open for the Christmas miracle — His gifts came from above. Vivid still is the memory of wishing the living room window was on the side of the house where we 3 kids waited anxiously. I fretted Mom and Dad might forget and not open the window on a cold Christmas night. Sometimes it snowed.

When we were small, we never saw the fully decorated tree until Christmas Day. Each year after dinner on the 25th. Doris (the oldest), my brother, and I were ordered to clean up and wash dishes while we waited behind the locked kitchen door for Christmas splendor. Beyond nervous on an evening full of nail-biting moments, we would peek, and sneak looks out the window, shoving each other, "My turn!" We hoped to see the magic angel with the *Christbaum* and gifts flying in the air.

We waited impatiently behind the closed door for the sound of Mom's key to open, and feverishly listened for the miniature silver bell in Dad's hand to ring — a sign — it's time. A divine sound for kids in expectation-agony, a bell so clear allowing us to storm to the living room. At the wide-open door, we stopped and stared mystified at a *Christbaum* lit with many candles, magic brilliance. Dad still holding the silver bell stood tall with pride next to Mom, who sat on the faded couch, both smiling.

The three of us, lined up in a line like soldiers rooted to the floor in absolute magic wonderment, not speaking. No running to the gifts around the glowing Christmas tree on the wooden floor; our eyes however inspected anxiously from near the door.

Before receiving any gifts, each of us had to recite a poem we learned during the month of December, a Christmas poem we'd hunt for in magazines and books. I would agonize and practice for days, hoping Dad would like the one I picked, all the more as I stepped close to the magnificent tree holding his eyes. Being the youngest, my turn was last — the most dramatic Dad would say.

Poetry — its words still in the air and a tight hug from Dad when heaven on earth had arrived to find a package under the breathtaking *Tannenbaum*, decorated with chocolate ornaments beside countless shiny ones. Remembering is like poetry in motion . . . fairytale moments, blessed voices from my youth I see in candlelight. Always. No eyes ever saw the adored angel yet, Jesus — His blessing remained . . . and the spirit of Baby Jesus in a crib lined with hay in a cold barn in Bethlehem.

As Dad would turn on the old radio he hoped for his favorite "Silent Night" — *Stille Nacht* — Holy Night — *Heilige Nacht*. Every year we waited. When the melody filled our living room, everything stopped. Dad, with dreamy eyes, started to sing along in his strong baritone voice. Three kids joined in — Mom. The sounds of this from Austria, all over the world known song, completed the festivities at our humble home.

One Christmas, a tiny machine, a 45-single record player, replaced the anxious waiting; a gift for everyone under the tree. A blue, round 'thing' played that treasured song over and over, anytime.

In memory-heaven, with a throat that contained a stone, I tried to sing along with the last notes of "Silent Night" when an unforgettable voice at the top of the courthouse steps bellowed out, "Merry Christmas!" then shouted, "Jesus was born." The very instant the lights turned on — Christmas splendor-magic all around us. A crescendo of lights blazed on all the trees in the park around the courthouse square, a phenomenal moment on a very cold evening in early December. A reason why thousands of people gathered with suspenseful expectancy — all bundled up — awe-inspired, smiling and delighted to experience Christmas feelings. A crowd of possibly 10,000 voices roared back, "Merry Christmas!" An intense sensation I was not prepared for filled me with pleasure and gratitude — two magical words — leaving a huddled crowd in wonderment.

May we never forget the power of those two simple words.

Rewarded with wonder, people dressed in furs, scarves, and gloves — anything to keep warm — strolled around the courthouse lawn at a slow pace, admiring all the thousands of lights. No rushing away.

With eyes locked, I relished my husband's embrace and touch, knowing in this unique desert town close to Scottsdale, we had found our place to start and feel Christmas — once a year.

[December 2006, one week after our trip, a part of this story was published in the *Scottsdale Tribune* and *The Daily Courier* in Prescott, Arizona. I wrote the story driving home the morning we left Prescott.]

By the way . . .

Every December, from when we first married, still not used to Christmas lights on a cactus, Lew and I explored the various tree lots of Scottsdale for a perfect, fresh noble Christmas tree with branches far apart. "Perfect" took on a brand-new meaning — some years we hunted all day to find Mr. Right.

"The candles need placement of precision so as not to hit anything above to burn and start a fire," Lew would holler. He agonized.

Lighting candles on a tree never turned into one of his favorite Swiss traditions. We lit candles on Christmas Eve, again on Christmas Day, and on New Year's Eve, called *Sylvester* in Switzerland.

One Christmas, as I initiated to open one of many gifts from clients, wrapped in shiny red from Joanna, a weekly customer, I frowned at Lew's name. Surprised, I handed the mysterious package over. For Lew? From a customer? A fire extinguisher emerged from the huge box. Joanna knew from my salon stories about Lew's unending worries each Christmas.

The same lady, Christmas next, wrapped a firefighter hat in glittery holiday paper. A Kodak-moment.

Everybody worried.

A fire did occur in 2003, on Christmas morning, not because of candles on a tree, but because of a fancy candle left burning on the living room coffee table that fell and scorched the celadon-colored carpet.

Ultimately a chance for Lew' to use his fire extinguisher.

Time to give in. My childhood tradition had found its end. Electric Christmas lights now glow in our home all through December; the American way had entered our lives. Candles on a Christmas tree — now memories of the past.

Allegro apartment 31**8** Christmas, 1970

December 201**8** at our home at Heritage Village
Real candles on a Christmas tree . . . a memory only.

Christmas party, at Mahogany's owner Riccardo's house, in 19**88**

"Ask not what your father can do for you . . . ask what you can do for your father." — Anonymous

1995, in Watertown, WI, at the Wells home
Dad, Lew, and Gladys

"Love is patient . . . Love is kind." — 1 Corinthians 13:4-8

My American Family

Intuition . . . When it Matters

"Mistakes of the past become the wisdom of the future." —
Anonymous

Let's go and visit. Words on my mind far too long, words uttered too often, repeatedly. The year was 1995. No more delaying another Fourth of July weekend in Watertown, Wisconsin. Family members met every year at the home of my husband Lew's dad and his third wife, Gladys.

It was our first time. Finally.

During my romantic marriage of twenty-three years to a rare jewel of a husband, I relentlessly marveled at Lew's distance from his family. He refused to talk about them, the irreversible loss of the past. How I tried to understand my most caring, intelligent, with dark, Sonny-Bono-like-hair, aloof husband.

My degree from the school of life didn't include not talking to your father. Continuous wondering and worrying filled my days. Not knowing what to say, knowing to say nothing — what a huge void it created. Nonetheless, I lived with a measure of constant hope.

Almost every year, we traveled to my home, where I grew up and lived when I was young, to visit my huge family all over Switzerland. Those frequent trips undoubtedly caused me to be more aware of never visiting Lew's relatives, not even accepting an invitation to attend his father's third marriage to Gladys. My father-in-law Jeff, however, and his second wife Ruth had traveled to Switzerland to be a part of our June wedding in 1972.

Feeling guilty countless times, I did not have the heart to send a postcard from the home country, with its world-renowned, magnificent beauty. I imagined Lew's dad and all family simply would have felt bad. Deep in my heart, I hoped none of them would ever find out about our numerous trips across the Atlantic. With a sense of hope, I prayed and lived for the day to convince Lew to do the right thing — someday — *to go home.*

Lew grew up in an extremely strict household on an old farm, where after-school work waited for when he was a kid, a small boy. A gruesome tractor accident out on the field claimed his stern father's right-hand fingers, ending the family's grueling farm life. Jeff, one of eleven kids, had grown up on an isolated farmstead. Now a father himself, he tried to make a living for his family, his four children, any which way during those difficult days after the war.

He purchased a Shell gasoline station and relocated his family to Mauston. Lew's after-school hours were filled with demanding work until late at a buzzing garage on the main road, the only highway between Minneapolis-Saint Paul and Chicago. Back then, pumping gas included changing oil, cleaning the windshield and car windows, checking the tires — a consistent service to anyone who stopped for gas.

Lew's best buddy from school informed him where his dad went almost every day after Lew's arrival at the garage.

"Your dad is with my mom," his buddy mocked one frosty winter day, news that changed Lew's life — the hard truth, the hardest of all. A guessing game of shame started. A father who acted quite shameless filled Lew with disgust and despair.

This time his dad had gone too far. The sneaky afternoon visits transpired too often for a boy with unbelieving eyes and ears, trying to deny it. A son's heart went out to his mom. Hate for Dad grew; Lew stopped talking to his dad. Getting back at him, as an adult, Lew never called or visited.

The test of the morality of any parent is what it does to 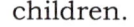 children.

Lew left home the evening of his high-school graduation. He asked no one. His mother watched him pack a few things in a hurry.

She shouted, "Where are you going?"

Lew did not answer; he didn't know. 3 of his buddies waited. Mom, who secretly understood, knew nothing would stop him. Her favorite son had lost all respect for his father.

Lew's half-understood promise of life did not include cheating on your wife — his mom — again and again. In his despair, Lew couldn't possibly know, on this life-changing evening, as he kissed his desolate mother farewell, how enormously intense her heart must have suffered.

Lew never returned to his childhood home. He spent a lifetime trying to forget. Sorrow which is never spoken is the heaviest load to bear. The image of his anguish causes me to close my eyes.

Except for one time. By bus to Mauston, while working in Chicago, Lew visited his weak mom at the old house. She had returned home from the hospital, fighting cancer. No cure. She passed away July 10th, 1969, the summer after Lew and I met.

To this day I hold a wish in my heart for a chance to brag and fill Lew's mother's ears, like when her son opens the car door, in our garage, with nobody around to see, only to melt his wife's heart every time we leave together. He still does, after 4**8** years of marriage. Oh, how I want to tell her stories of her considerate son, his unmatched sensitivity — something women seldom hope for . . . only in their dreams.

***

The mystery of no other family members visiting on this Fourth of July holiday weekend in 1995 found a way of sinking in completely on our flight back to Arizona. Mainly Lew's older brother Jeffrey, his Chinese wife Chen Chu. None of us understood their lame excuse for not showing up when Jeffrey called Dad's home with regret.

The day before our anticipated trip, simply a dream coming true for me, Jeffrey surprised Lew with a rare evening call to assure us of seeing everyone soon. From an occasional postcard and rare phone calls, we knew Chen Chu, Jeff Junior, kids Zandra and older son Geoffrey, had spent plenty of those American holiday family gatherings in Wisconsin, a two-hour drive from a suburb of Chicago. How well I know — my dreaming about Lew and me being a part of celebrating America's birthday with family had never stopped.

Destiny at work; the Hand of God guided this out-of-the-ordinary visit, pushing a father, in his autumn years, and a son toward the climax of their life — a time where a dad and son looked into each other's eyes as if it was their first time.

In a room with walls that had never seen or heard the son from Arizona, — Lew, the estranged son, — now sat at the old dining table next to his dad, closer than any of us and family had ever seen the two. He and his father were joking, laughing at each other, conversation at its highest. An unexpected alone time together, induced by a mysterious absence of other relatives.

I watched and stared with misty eyes of surprise and love. Forgotten was their awkward handshake upon our arrival at the front door that compelled me to wince. Several times I found myself looking at the two with a soundless prayer.

An exceptional occasion, a father and son united, a treasure to behold. Lew's surprising willingness to finally visit his dad, after our countless words — often harsh words turned into silence — now brought a faint smile of satisfaction to my face. It melted my heart. "Eventually" was now.

Where is the camera? I silently screamed. Witnessing the rarity of this event had me search with a swirl of eagerness and haste. *Hurry.* Time stood still at the sheer urgency of not being detected. *Act nonchalant . . .* click! What a Kodak moment, beyond the power of timing; simply the reason for this story.

The tiny house on the outskirts of town, in a friendly retirement community associated with nearby assistant living, where Dad and his adorable wife Gladys had moved years ago, was cozy and filled with a certain hush of anticipation only an estranged dad and long-lost son can create. Nostalgia filled the air; undeniably hard not to feel and experience a sense of loss, of years missed. My eyes filled with happy tears as I held my old-fashioned camera with trembling hands and clicked that rare picture that would become the center of a time-shared, a memory beyond description.

I spied on Gladys out of the corner of my eye, witnessing her astonished look and amazement at the miraculous scene of two people reunited. At that instant — clearer than ever — no matter how dark years and moments in the past, hope, and love are always possible.

As Jeff, my father-in-law stepped away from the table, he glanced at me and met my eyes with a ghost of a wink and a joyful smile. Gladys's beaming grin remained stuck on her face for hours.

What I discovered, on this hot and humid Fourth of July weekend in a small town in Wisconsin is, good does come out of hurt. Honest smiles and heartfelt hugs during an ultimately incomparable visit, by simply being there, brought light into the lives of Lew, his dad, Gladys, and me. That evening, as the four of us sat on wobbly chairs in an overgrown garden, feeling a part of this American holiday at a nearby park, together . . . the small fireworks display in the distance appeared huge.

Perfect does not always look like we imagine.

Our departing the next morning arrived only too soon. Packed and checked out of the motel where Lew's dad had suggested staying at, we drove to their home, one more time to encounter a simple breakfast together. On the way out I hugged my father-in-law, a dad who had caused so much heartache and grief. I whispered in his ear about his son's boundless dignity and strength, that he was the most caring person I had ever known, and about the sense of security Lew's love had given me.

My father-in-law's hold and physically powerful hug lasted an eternity. When he finally let go of me, his enticing smile did not hide his archangel-sized tears. Tears, a messenger of unspeakable love, grief, or joy? Tears speak more eloquently than a thousand tongues. His voice was above a whisper, "Thank you!"

I swallowed. The swelling lump in my throat got huge; my voice quivered, "Love is patient."

A united father and son, they grabbed to hold onto each other; a passionate goodbye embrace, to make up for a lifetime. Denying the sadness of the moment would be denying the magnificence despite it. Truly knee-buckling, if one can feel the beauty of a miracle, with eyes looking up to heaven with a silent *Thank You, God.*

At the bend in the road Lew slowed down, we turned one more time, smiling and waving with tears flowing. We blew one last kiss at a crying father waving fiercely. Lew's tears wouldn't stop.

Up high in the air on a bumpy flight from Milwaukee to Phoenix, Lew held my hand with familiar tenderness — not speaking, each pursuing private thoughts yet deeply connected.

He finally spoke, "Can you believe it was only the four of us?"

I nodded, not trusting myself to speak. I peeked out the tiny window at the edge of the universe, thinking of Lew's mom. Instead of joy for the reunion, the theft of the past kept creeping in. I found myself staring out at a momentary brilliance in the sky where the sinking sun rose through the clouds.

I could see 2 smiles — God and Lew's mom.

Upon our return home taking the miraculous film to Walgreens, written on top of my list of things to do, I knew the three days wait. After a long day at our hectic hair salon, nothing stopped me from picking up the developed pictures. A smiling girl behind the counter handed me the huge envelope. With haste, I ripped, searched, stopped, and gazed at one picture that bordered on magic, a picture of stop-my-heart importance. Tears rolled down my face. The intensity of my emotions startled the friendly lady behind the counter.

A father and son smiling at each other . . . for eternity. An elevated moment was no longer a dream. A goose-bump moment, looking at the two united after all those *alone* years in their hearts — never close before.

I drove home recklessly, with excitement guarding the Kodak pictures on my lap, only to realize Lew was not home yet, still at work for two more hours at his challenging job as an important project leader of a large company. His eyes were tired when he took a close look at that remarkable picture. His hands trembled. With eyes lit up and a cool, unhurried voice, he uttered, "*WOW*."

A howling sigh followed; a moment indelibly imprinted in my mind. Taking hold of this picture was like crossing over into another dimension, a leap through time.

In my heart I knew: *It is never too late — if you are lucky.*

One ordinary day in Watertown our Christmas gift arrived in September, a sweltering day still in Scottsdale, while the approach of cool weather and fall was in the air in Wisconsin. We will never know what a father experienced when he opened a carefully wrapped package with shiny paper meant to be the perfect Christmas gift. Nor will we know his words, his feelings as he looked at that gold-framed, enlarged picture: his far-away, lost-yet-found boy Lewis, his huge smile belonged to him only, on a hot July day. Dad, with a happy heart, possibly had tears of joy.

I forever will cherish the moment when lightning struck: "*Send the picture now.*" Why wait for Christmas? A sign from heaven; the timing will remain a mystery.

Intuition . . . when it matters.

A magnitude of timing . . . Lew's dad passed away in October 1995, three and a half weeks after the framed picture arrived. He is in that spot of grace for the rest of time knowing, when he looks down from the garden in the sky, time heals all.

Gladys, Jeff's wife of twenty years, passed on one year later. A retired schoolteacher when Jeff met the long-time widow at a church social. Love at first sight.

We attended the burial for a jewel of a lady loved by all. As we rummaged through some of Dad's belongings, we found that precious picture. I grabbed it and held it to my heart. Lew's worried look spelled: *Don't drop it.* I flashed a knowing smile.

The rare picture traveled back with us to Arizona. I found an exceptional place of display for everyone who enters our home to admire, a dad smiling at his son. Lew, with his priceless grin reminiscent of his father's, watched me hammer a nail into the wall, a gold nail matched the frame. His powerful embrace spelled closeness beyond. Holding tightly, I listened to the strong beating of my husband's heart.

May Dad and Lew's captivating picture in the entryway, the one that gave a father immense elation for a short little while, remind Lew day-to-day, as he walks by, to never forget a time when he experienced loss ended up in everlasting love.

A life story has moved from dusk to joy.

Lew had found the seed of gratitude.

Trudy Wells-Meyer

A Magnificent String of Firsts

"Emotional moments we don't seem to expect, countless times they surprise us, and how we can't believe when they happen — the times they happen are when we least expect them."

— Anonymous

Aunt Esther celebrating **100** years.

Esther Ruth Wells-Bagg grew up on a farm in Wisconsin. Her words during an interview with a newspaper reporter on her **100**th birthday:

"Growing up, my father always liked to be *first* to own anything new that came on the market. When I was eight years old, he purchased one of the *first* automobiles. I remember the experience of driving home with my father from town after he bought the car. As he tried to maneuver the car around some cows in the road, we got stuck in a ditch, and had to get someone with a horse to pull us out . . . What I remember most, for the next few years my papa would proudly show off the car to members of the church. When he asked if they wanted to see it, they would say, *What's an auto?*"

One month into Lew's retirement in 2005, on our *first* journey to Florida, knowing every trip is an added discovery, Aunt Esther at **98**½ was the *first* of six of Lew's elderly aunts on our bucket list to visit.

After a unique and unforgettable holiday in July, when we kissed Esther goodbye on a balmy Florida summer day, a promise surfaced: to revisit. We assured Aunt Esther we would not miss her **100**th birthday on November 16, 2006, only guessing what an outstanding celebration . . . clearly unknown, how special indeed.

Feelings for an occasion unfamiliar to many emerged: a **100-** years celebration, a *first* for us. At an age of sixty-five for Lew and me, one may wonder how many *firsts* are left.

My successful marriage with Lew, a life I could not have possibly dreamed of while growing up far across the ocean; consequently, I am a part of Lew's huge family: all seven aunts, sisters of Lew's father Jeff, have lived into their nineties.

Aunt Esther, the *first* to reach **100**, was one of those eternally healthy people. No matter whom you talked to, anyone who ever met Esther could not believe how young she appeared. On no medication, however, she did take vitamins and expressed misgivings about insurance, for never needing it after paying money every month for years. Lucky lady.

A widow for thirty years, she enjoyed meeting new friends, had God in her heart, and smiled at everybody. Esther exercised every day (not solely her idea) and loved a good meal of chicken, mashed potatoes, and gravy. A regal woman with sparkling eyes and skin you had to see to believe; a *first* for us to comprehend a lady at her age with such flawless skin.

The absence of wrinkles on a face so dear was the reason you stared when you met her. You could not help but touch that skin — they all did. Everyone wondered, "How? What vitamins???"

***

Monday, November 13, 2006, in the early morning our driver Les picked us up for the airport to fly to Florida, two days before Aunt Esther's **100ᵗʰ** birthday celebration. In the backseat, we looked at each other with wonder of things to come. I reminded Lew of Esther's words, she believed: *Happiness is a voyage — not a destination.* A picture-perfect, sunny Arizona day enhanced an abundance of *firsts,* a trip planned for months with anticipation and concerned speculations for this rare occasion to celebrate. The plan reality now, whereas we wondered how dear Aunt Esther would feel — anxious —confident? Healthy as ever?

In Orlando, we stopped for the night, where a rental car waited, a brand-new Cadillac in shiny silver, a magnificent car for an occasion out of the ordinary.

"That's what I call fancy. We'll take it," I shouted. A perfect vehicle to drive Lew's Aunt around in style, a *first* for her to ride in such a glamorous, classy car, clearly as Lew and I.

The following morning, we drove to Jupiter, a two-hour trip. Driving into this majestic entrance of the hotel, surrounded by the lushness of the famous Florida green, I will not forget how Lew's excitement grew; my facial expression changed to humbly staring. My husband, not close to his family for years and from the old school of life, rarely showed emotions, except for his odd quick to laugh at the wrong time.

His being-cool, even when the sky seems to fall, I often marveled over, and sometimes is more than I can handle. Aunt Esther remembered him as a quiet boy with trouble-avoiding eyes. Today was different — a delighted nephew, proud of his aunt turning **100**.

A *first* for Lew — a *first* for me to witness.

Again, we checked in at that outstanding beach resort, a vacation place right on the ocean Aunt Esther and Joan, her daughter, had recommended in July 2005. Esther's favorite place with a restaurant she loved; her choice each time when we invited her out during our first visit that summer in July. A hotel where the young valet who opens people's car doors for a living was fascinated by this royal-looking lady.

"No way," he uttered in his southern drawl when I told him her age.

Minutes later, after Lew had parked his car, we stood at the main door of the lobby to watch the scene of Aunt Esther's graceful way of stepping out of her daughter Joan's classy

Mercedes. Dressed elegantly with her wrinkle-free face, she gave a flirty wink of her eye to the bell captain as he helped her out of the car. I was in awe-delight.

Naturally, I announced, "Esther will turn **100** on Thursday."

I told everybody throughout our days in Florida — the hostess, the waitress, the busboy, people close by giving us looks full of curiosity. What a tremendous conversation starter.

After joyful-hello embraces, time for lunch; a unique experience for a lady up in years not used to looking at a menu anymore.

With words of dismay, she shook her head. "Why so many choices?"

The chef of this seaside restaurant surprised Esther with a small birthday cake with a candle. I pointed to it. "Aunt Esther, blow the candle out and make a wish."

She closed her eyes; in a voice unusually loud she spoke, "I want to hear."

Her new hearing aids were not to her liking, not working the way she wished they would or should. Esther's words: *waste of money*. Her ears and eyes had endured the predictable centenarian loss. A melancholic moment as Aunt Esther opened her misty eyes, the *first* touching instant during days to come with unprecedented memories.

That afternoon at 5 p.m. at the airport in West Palm Beach, one of the five living sisters, Aunt Isabel (age 94¾), and her daughter Beatrice arrived from Wisconsin. We drove to the nearby airport to pick them up. Rush hour in Florida traffic left us particularly edgy, though forgotten the minute we spotted the two: Beatrice, Lew's older cousin, and her mom in a wheelchair, smiling, showing tremendous relief to have arrived safely. Aunt Isabel looked around anxiously for her checked bag; she had no experience traveling from the cold to sunshine country, where tropical temperatures were absent. A *first* for Isabel and Beatrice to fly to Florida to attend a celebration for the ages — Isabel's older sister's miraculous **100th** birthday. The two sisters had not seen each other for ten years when all the sisters had come to Arizona for a family reunion where I finally met some of Lew's aunts for the first time.

With eyes that smiled, Aunt Isabel climbed into our fancy rental car and mumbled, "Oh, my!" Lew drove Mother and daughter to their hotel near ours. We stopped to have a bite to eat, where we engaged in non-stop talking. Too late unfortunately to go and see Esther at her new home. Two sisters exhausted. Traveling all day, the reason for one, and much birthday excitement for both.

We promised to pick up Aunt Isabel and her daughter the next morning, to visit Aunt Esther at the wonderful new assisted-living home where she had resided since June 29, 2003. She had lived in Tequesta, alone, in her apartment, until age 96½. How lucidly we remembered that first phone conversation after Esther's dramatic move, leaving her treasured long-time home. Lew, afraid to hear a distraught voice over the phone, but no. Eagerly she spilled words, yet sounded delighted.

"They are so nice, and the food is very good; my apartment is the biggest of anybody here, and oh, I can't find a thing."

What an attitude; words to that effect no need for concern.

"A happy person is not a person in a certain set of circumstances, but rather a person with a certain set of attitudes."— Hugh Downs

123

As the four of us arrived at 9 a.m. at Tequesta Terrace, a remarkably well-kept, beautiful residence, we witnessed two sisters reunited. What a Kodak-moment, a hug of all hugs and expressions of disbelief on Isabel and Esther's faces. Isabel touched her amazing-looking sister's glowing face in admiration.

Beatrice, Lew, and I watched mesmerized. Esther in her familiar way showed an air of immense dignity and strength, turning **100** in one more day. Dressed in a fancy Florida-pink blouse her daughter Joan had purchased for the occasion and shoes with a bow perfectly matching the pants and purse, she was ready to go out for breakfast. Aunt Esther, who claimed she had hardly ever been sick, walked as focused as any of us, (on a walker for balance). To see her go, motor on — the speed of it.

Esther's first glance at our rental car lit up her eyes. "That's what I call a car." She approved. We drove to the same splendid restaurant by the ocean, listening to conversations in the back seat of memories on the farm when Esther and Isabel were young.

"We worked as hard as our 3 brothers," the sisters commiserated.

Everyone shared a wonderful meal at a restaurant with a flair for elegance, where the classy hostess recognized us from July 2005 and with a broad smile seated our group by the window, at the finest table near the flower-filled garden.

Time to show the two sisters our exceptional room up on the fifth floor. The real reason we asked them up to our living-room-like quarters, besides the exceptional setting and breathtaking view of the sea, was for Esther and Isabel to have a quality talk — to be alone. Beatrice, Lew, and I went for a walk, a long walk to give two sisters time together, to reminisce about the good, yet, hard old days.

Another *first* arose the same afternoon at a Florida hotel parking lot, in a flashy rental car waiting for Tequesta's radio station to come on to wish Aunt Esther "Happy **100ᵗʰ** Birthday." When we stopped at the desk to pick up Esther that morning, we had introduced ourselves. With cheerful voices, the personnel peeked out of the office to notify us with excitement, "Esther's birthday will be announced on the radio."

To our dismay, we found the radio in our hotel room did not have clear reception. We rushed to our car, our one chance, and hope to hear Aaron Kohlman, host of a weekly Senior Lifestyle program at 3 p.m. — a *first* for him to wish anyone a special **100ᵗʰ** birthday over the air.

All dressed for the early evening party with family at Joan's home, we sat and waited. When those words emerged across the radio waves, in Aaron's strong voice, loud and clear, so did our tears. For a long time, they would not stop. Words by a stranger, compassionate words, belonged to our Aunt Esther.

Sitting in our dream car on a gorgeous Florida afternoon, palms swaying, our eyes locked as we held hands. Lew's ever-so-gentle touch spelled romance by the sea. Emotions went through us we did not know existed; another such time may never happen again. What a *first!* Words that invited to feel we forgot but not the joy of joys in our hearts.

After a short rest and salvaging my makeup, Lew and I picked up Aunt Isabel and Beatrice at their hotel for an eventful evening ahead of the actual birthday. We found Aunt Esther panic-stricken upon our arrival at her residence. Frantic about her outfit, a gift from her daughter Joan, an exquisite melon-color sweater for Mom's rare occasion.

Esther pointed to her pants with a frown. "I hate this color," she howled.

I tried to calm her down and offered to help. We rushed to the adjoining bedroom. I suggested possibly changing the beige pants to black. "Do you have nice black pants, Aunt Esther?"

"Yes." She squealed, "I knew beige is wrong."

I found an elegant black pair in her walk-in closet. Esther instantly sought after her dressy black shoes to match.

In the back of one of the old cabinet drawers Esther had pointed to, filled with jewelry, I found a brooch with matching earrings. Melon-colored and black — how perfect.

"Oh, yes." Esther with sparkling eyes got close to the

mirror with her priceless smile, trying to see. (She is legally blind.) I truly sensed she actually could see how stunning the combination of colors looked, not only by listening to me insisting and vowing how perfect indeed. I managed to move her hair into shape, with more style. A few touches — a welcomed difference. Esther was ready — let the party begin. We hurried back into her living room, where Lew, Isabel, and Beatrice patiently waited. Their unbelieving eyes gleamed and took notice of the birthday lady looking like a queen. Sister Isabel with joyful eyes approved.

A houseful of cheerful people, mostly family, waited at the home of Joan, Aunt Esther's only child, a realtor/owner of her successful business. A magnificent mansion, the kind one admires in *Architectural Digest,* and feels the need of dressing up with fashion sense to simply turn the pages. Thrilled to have chosen outfits with a hint of glamour for the rare affair, Lew and I felt respectable enough on this exquisite furniture.

Aunt Esther, like royalty, sat on a comfortable chair in a corner close to sister Isabel. Joan had assigned their seating so everybody could enjoy looking at the two.

A *first* to see balloons with the number **100**, a *first* to hold the most colorful napkins decorated with "Happy **100th** Birthday." My hands trembled; I could not stop an overpowering feeling of being there at all. Watching with misty eyes warmed my heart and induced my gratefulness for being a

part of such a history-making event.

After a marvelous buffet-style dinner, another *first:* number **100** on a fabulous cake with yellow roses, a cake too dazing to cut, surrounded by Esther's family, including Joan's four sons, their wives, and girlfriends. Paul, the ex-husband, stood tall in a corner; Aunt Esther's former son-in-law and the father of the four grown boys. (One son had died in a boating accident.) Grandchildren, great-grandchildren, and friends all gathered — laughter bound with unavoidable tears yet overjoyed everyone tried in a pushy fun way not to miss anything to take rare historic pictures.

Thursday, November 16, D–day! A *first* for the Wells family, to celebrate **100** years.

The terrific staff at Tequesta Terrace planned a luncheon for Aunt Esther at 11:45 attended by daughter Joan, sister Isabel, her daughter Beatrice, Esther's brother Jeff's son Lew, and Trudy.

This was the ultimate day for Aunt Esther. As she walked down the hallway, poised and elegant, toward the decorated room for special occasions, where residents lined up so as not to miss seeing Esther Bagg Wells on such a day, I saw tears in her eyes. Minutes before her sister Isabel had informed her, "We have to leave for the airport right after the celebration." Nonetheless, her tears had to be for other reasons. To reach a milestone like turning **100** left her touched, choked up.

Her words from earlier lingered still when Lew hugged his aunt to say hello: "I woke up this morning and said to myself, I can't believe I am **100** years old."

At 8:30 on that memorable morning, I jolted at the shrill phone in our hotel room.

"I need Trudy." Aunt Esther's frantic voice did not stop, "I need Trudy to come and help me dress."

A *first,* a Lady of **100** years asked for my help; her words sounded like music to my ears. Lew's favorite aunt had admired my passion for 'clothes with an attitude' ten years ago when we very first met and spent time together in Scottsdale.

"Don't worry. Aunt Esther, I'd love to help. I will be over as soon as Lew drops me off." I hung up and yelled, "Hurry, Lew, Aunt Esther needs me."

Anybody lucky enough to have met Aunt Esther knew the importance to look immaculate diligently, earrings and beads matching, pants and shoes the perfect color. Today was such a day when trying to look good might possibly bestow a headache. Esther's long-time hairstylist had come early, at 7:30, especially for her.

I became extremely nervous. "Lew, let's go!" I hoped my yelling would speed him up, "Your aunt needs me now."

Walking into Esther's home, her eyes ignited like turning on a light. I will never forget the short time alone I experienced with this amazing lady, good-humored, appreciative, and particularly thankful I showed up to help.

The previous day, we had searched for Esther's gold chain in the old dresser, upsetting her seriously at not being able to find her treasured jewelry with sentimental value. I regretted having mentioned too strongly, "You need a gold chain for this blouse with gold threads your daughter picked out at a trendy designer store. "

"Not to worry. Esther, I will bring you mine." I had managed to calm her down. "You will wear my gold jewelry."

Did she know I'd arrive with the necklace she had admired the day before — my favorite, a gift from Lew — with earrings to match, clip-on, the kind Aunt Esther wears and used?

Honored to be the selected one to assist, I put my chain around her neck, a final touch. Esther with trembling hands stroked the rope-like chain with tenderness. Her precious smile, her sense of stillness, triggered a bond between the two of us that remains everything and more.

"Great moments are born from great opportunities." — Herb Brooks

Esther relished a wonderful lunch, although she may not remember the food, her much-loved mashed potatoes. The instant we all had taken our seats, in a room immensely festive with flowers and balloons with the number **100** (a gift from the staff), the mayor of Tequesta and other city leaders arrived. *Happy **100**th Birthday,* Esther! The flashing of several newspaper cameras put the birthday lady in a state of utter disbelief. Her humble modesty and matchless sense of humor (a Wells thing) triggered a remarkable conversation with the mayor.

I on the other hand do remember excellent food, resembling a five-star hotel with an unforgettable touch. I gave this magnificent Home one more star, especially for their kindness and caring. An outstanding way to live, when and if you are lucky to age in a place, where continuing care is provided.

After the family meal, time for a celebration of **100** years.

Mother, birthday-girl, and only daughter Joan

On the second floor the staff and countless residents — some in wheelchairs, some with walkers — were waiting, and Aaron Kohlman from the radio station personally wished Esther *Happy* **100th** *Birthday.* More newspaper and television reporters appeared to celebrate a milestone day. Esther's incredible happiness is what everyone will remember.

Punch with strawberries floating for everybody was served, along with a dazzling cake with napkins, balloons with the grand number **100.** How can Lew and I ever again look at that number without thinking of this time, sublime in everything, knowing to be lucky to witness Aunt Esther's jubilant face?

Time to say goodbye arrived too fast, and two sisters united in a hug for the last time — literally. Hushed with waiting to watch a heartbreaking scene, Isabel and Esther let tears flow. Lew

129

struggled not to cry. I burst into tears.

Beatrice and her mom, visibly distraught, had to leave early to catch their flight to Milwaukee. We drove them to the airport, the excitement of exceptional memories lingering in our voices until we reached the gate to kiss Aunt Isabel goodbye. We stood waving fiercely to a mother and daughter who were visibly thrilled they had taken the time and effort to travel to Florida.

Aunt Isabel, in the last minutes of rushing to the gate, had put a 20-dollar bill in my hand. My first reaction: give it back! Her caring butterfly touch but firm goodbye hug let me embrace money from a lady who so appreciated the fact we were there to drive everywhere together.

On the way back to our hotel, Lew and I stopped at a soup and salad place. The bill added up to nineteen dollars and forty-five cents. We paid with Aunt Isabel's 20-dollar bill. It was the best soup. Back in the resort's room, in the drawer, I found a Florida sunset postcard, compliments of the hotel. With a spark of inspiration, I wrote to Aunt Isabel. I told her about that unusually wonderful soup and thanked her. Some things in life are only special if you can see and recognize the true meaning.

Late morning the next day, Friday, we called Aunt Esther, expecting her to be very tired. Her still excited voice chatted about a dream that had indeed happened, and she might never wake up from. A well-deserved rest day, for Esther, would not leave her chair, daydream only.

A *first* again occurred on Saturday, an abnormally cool but glorious Florida day. On the way to visit Aunt Esther, we searched for a grocery store. In haste, I expressed to Lew, "Let's call her, see if she needs anything." Her instant *yes* echoed through the phone: "I need soap." Tide, to be exact. Esther does her laundry daily in her small washer and dryer built into the closet. Her nightgown she wears once, in the morning, one a walker, back to the washer.

I asked, "What size?"

"Not too big," Esther replied.

"You mean small?"

She answered, "Not too small."

We managed to bring the wrong one. She wanted the one and only, the kind she has used for years, liquid soap with a handle easy to grab. Has anyone ever exchanged a medium box of Tide? A *first* for us; in Florida, they ask you for the reason for your return of a rejected purchase.

We positively had the best time telling the snarly lady behind the counter a reason she never had listened to, about our **100**-year-old Aunt Esther, who is legally blind and can't hear well, about her constantly smiling face and positive outlook, infectious character, something to see to believe. A lady who believed life does not always give you what you want, but it will give you what you need.

We found liquid soap.

In the afternoon Lew invited his cousin Joan for a late lunch. Her mom, still too exhausted, declined. Joan's idea to meet us at an old, typical Florida restaurant right on the water, with a lighthouse in the distance and a huge salad bar, brought a smile and love for the place instantly. We adored that lush Florida setting.

A short stop at Aunt Esther's followed. We brought cookies.

The visit next day, Sunday, we hoped Aunt Esther would be more rested. Lew brought his laptop computer for picture-showing time at the home for the old.

Esther, flabbergasted, with humongous eyes, asked "How can pictures be ready so fast for me to look at?"

"Already," she uttered in awe, as she stared with skepticism at a machine called a computer. Priceless pictures of the once-in-a-lifetime party were displayed in front of her nose — she had bent down to be as close as possible. Kodak moments replaced by a computer. With hesitation, Esther touched the screen, and selected a keyboard with one finger, "Whatever would I have done with *that thing* ages ago." She recalled the office typewriter.

In her younger days, Esther was a secretary to the administrator of a hospital in Oneonta, New York, for a number of years. Lew's matchless computer lesson remained another *first* for an aunt who simply did not appear to be **100.**

The same evening, too late for Aunt Esther to join us, Cousin Joan cooked dinner at her home, a fresh Florida fish for Lew he still talks about. As we visited her luxurious home one more time, with a spectacular view across the lake — we lucked out to relish a picture-perfect Florida sunset.

The cheerless Monday arrived

when we had to say goodbye. After everyday visits, sometimes twice a day, we would come to remember these hours as more significant due to Lew's genealogy knowledge. His favorite hobby let him talk with Esther about scraps of time, the good old days. Lew happily thanked her for real facts when she corrected him thanks to her remarkable memory.

When Aunt Esther touched his face to thank him for a visit that meant the world to her, I suppressed the lump in my throat. Tears welled up. When she hugged me one last time and professed, "What would I have done without you?", holding back tears was no longer possible.

Memories are, *praise God,* forever.

To know her is to love her.

As we walked down the hallway in this beautiful assisted-living home, Aunt Esther stood outside her door, waving ferociously. We blew kisses at the bend in the long corridor, the sound of the door closing left us desolate. To know how much joy we brought to a lady who knows what it means to turn **100** . . . a *first* for such wordless emotions.

We returned to Arizona content for there always is a telephone.

I now buy Tide liquid soap, with a handle easy to grab.

Esther Ruth Wells-Bagg remained the most gracious, gentle, positive, optimistic, buoyant, no-medication-taking, awe-inspiring, fun-loving lady we know.

"*We walk by Faith, Not by Sight.*" — Laura Bush

Words Aunt Esther lived by.

Esther Ruth spoke words from years of experience, reflecting on the necessary elements for longevity. My personal favorite: "*I believe in God, and I believe in always doing the right thing and remaining on the right path. It's important to remain unselfish and always willing to give, whether it is advice or telling people you love them. Life is about lifting people up.*"

***

Scottsdale, Arizona, July 19, 2007 — Sad news — **8** months after Aunt Esther turned **100**, she passed on to the big garden in the sky called heaven to be with God.

In early July 2007, ten days before Aunt Esther's passing, Lew and I spent time in Clifton Park, New York. We visited the Wells aunts — Esther's two younger sisters — Aunt Bessie and Blanche, during a time when the extended family celebrated Aunt Bessie's 97th birthday on July 9th.

Months prior Lew had planned a side trip, to Oneonta, New York, where Esther's family had lived years ago.

We drove down Valley View Street on a rainy dreary summer day, searching for the old house, where Esther grew up. Lew's sudden stop confirmed we had found number six, Esther's home. Pictures show a steady downpour did not stop us.

That same morning Aunt Esther had a stroke.

When we got back to our hotel room late afternoon, Lew turned on his computer and found the shocking news of Aunt Esther's stroke — on the screen. An e-mail from Florida, Cousin Joan, Esther's daughter, triggered off feelings too startling for words. I raised my eyes to heaven in a classic expression of wonder. At the time Aunt Esther had slipped away into a coma, we were with her in thoughts, there, at the place where she was young.

Some things are simply meant to be.

Aunt Esther never regained consciousness.

Esther had a strong belief in God. She had told me after she is gone, she'd be in heaven. Her words:

Heaven is . . . other people holding you in their hearts.

133

One more thing . . .

March **8**th, 2008, Joan and Paul remarried, after 35 years apart, except for family parties, school events, involving their five sons. While they remained friends all those years Paul had remarried, his second wife passed from cancer. Aunt Esther's daughter Joan had never remarried.

Following Ester's death, a class reunion invitation arrived, scheduled back in New York where Joan and Paul had grown up and met. They decided to attend together. At the airport, walking to the departure gate, Paul reached for Joan's hand . . . Joan's dazed look at her longtime friend and ex-husband, not leaving his eyes, guided her hand into his, to remain where it belonged.

We attended the esteemed wedding celebration at an elite Florida country club. Lew, the only Wells cousin Joan invited to the festivities.

Cancer took Paul's life on November **8**, 2010, after incredibly blissful months together. A guest house adjoining Joan's mansion was built especially for family to visit and stay with them.

We did. Several times. We broke our rule of not staying with anyone and lame excuse not wanting to be a bother. An exception to every rule turned magical, each time.

In February 2019, Joan's invitation to her stunning home had a special ring:" I could take you to lunch at Mara-A-Lago."

Joan's son, a successful real estate mogul, (Mom's business) is a member. He called for a reservation. Lunch at Mar-A-Lago, a pinch-me-moment as we walked in. Perfection extraordinaire and splendor surrounded us. To top it all off — a surprise dinner planned at Trump's National Golf Club the next evening left us enthusiastic, where members all dressed in their finest gather, (men with ties). What to wear left me dizzy. I should have packed one more outfit — I cursed the agony of traveling.

Lew (yes, he wore a tie) claims it was the most excellent food he ever tasted. I explicitly adored the ambiance and learned new boastful words, including awe-delight, for friends and family.

A mindboggling, classy *First.*

A Young Girl Trapped in an Old Body

For Aunt Bessie

"Each moment is a place you've never been." — Mark Strand

To live to 99 in the circle of life — moving in and out of
time, a circle of memories,
a milestone birthday, the exceptional kind.
At Dakota Sky Manor we celebrate life, Aunt Bessie's
profound regal air, her sense of humor, gigantic love for
laughter; infectious characteristics for us all.

Family from far listening to her chatter as divine
softness comes over her wrinkled face, to let us know
she is speaking of love, stories from her youth spill out
at a slow pace, showing her missing lower teeth.
Bessie stops at moments to catch her breath or
simply overwhelmed by memories like
random photographs: the stars seen from her tiny room,
dreamy eyes talking of Papa,
his rare almost smile, and Mama, oh, to pretend
to be a child again . . . as Bessie slumps
in a worn-out chair; home now — in a corner.

Bessie cuddles a bear with pink polka dots, Dolly,
her name for a stuffed toy bear,
that traveled from Arizona, not to ever be alone.
Aunt Bessie, a strong link in a growing family chain,
for Swiss-born me, from far across the sea —
some ties are simply meant to be.

Bessie talks about her long-passed brother, my husband
Lew's dad. I hope to hear something, anything,
to understand this thoughtful, brilliant genius, Bessie's
adored nephew, my love for thirty-eight blissful,
romantic years. My changed life forever — I had only
see Lew once and feel his gentle touch — the end of
the life I knew because of a kiss, as if now
responsible for the scene in front of me.
Bessie's soon-centenarian eyes not able to see, yet her
mind can, she whispers, *I see the way Lew looks at you.*

Today, magnificent flowers for a rare exceptional day,
one balloon with that magic number 99,
few get to live and see.
A nurse tries to ignore Bessie, her cry for help, for a
simple act of needing *to go:* "I can't lift you alone."
Horse shit, Bessie barks.
I begged yesterday . . . you want me to pee in my pants?

A quiver in her voice and extremely tilted head: *don't go.*
A promise, unbreakable by distance, nor time,
to come back and visit, again, anytime soon.
Bessie will know we carry her in our hearts, as she
grasps Dolly to hold tight — when she is alone.
Thank God, her twin daughters. Lew's cousins nearby
stop daily at the home for the old. A mother's lost son
for far too long, flies from Florida, a trip to the sun,
visits his Mom — led by his guilty emotion,
after life's family heartaches . . . new-found gratitude,
when it matters most.
The fact that after days of rain the sun decided to shine,
compels one to believe and smile: it's never too late,
when God's abundant love, peace, and healing . . .
His presence is with you.
The theft of the past, a distant memory.

A simple goodbye kiss seeming like nothing, yet

136

everything. Only too soon, I can feel Bessie's tears.
I smile without much joy, though still a smile.
The image of her anguish forces me to close my eyes —
oh, not to ever be left alone.

We feel the vital need to stop one more time, witness
immense joy in her eyes, again as if every minute
spent doing something else is wasted time.
Those moments repeat in my mind like a song,
impossible to forget as we fly west, back home.
I marvel, will someone, anyone, someday come and
see us? Will it matter at all at an age when we admit
staring at sunsets longer, humbly knowing contentment
is luxury — a gift — one of God's immeasurable
blessings and always remember:
True happiness is . . . to want what you have.

["A Young Girl Trapped in an Old Body," published in October 2017,
Goose River Press *Anthology 2017.*]

By the way . . .

At Aunt Bessie's funeral service in church upstate New
York in Clifton Park, one of her granddaughters read the poem,
"A Young Girl Trapped in an Old Body."

I wrote the poem at Jackson Lake Lodge located in the
Grand Teton National Park, one of my most treasured places in
America, two weeks after we had visited Aunt Bessie and
celebrated her 99th birthday at Maplewood Manor in Ballston
Spa.

Grand Tetons (Switzerland in America)

From our fabulous view room across the Moose Pond towered the majestic Tetons that remind me of Swiss mountains each time we travel in Wyoming; what a magical place to write.

I sent the poem in August 2009, not ignoring an eerie feeling: *Why wait? Send it now.*

Bessie's aged eyes, however, not good enough any longer to read; therefore, every time someone, anyone stopped at the nursing home to spend time with her, Bessie pleaded to please read the poem. Dawn, her daughter, told me this with a cracking voice, the day she called of Bessie's passing — four weeks later.

Daughter Donna and Dawn, twin sisters, had visited Mom almost day by day, taking turns. (Their homes are located not too far from the County Nursing Home.)

Aunt Bessie passed away on September 23rd, 2009.

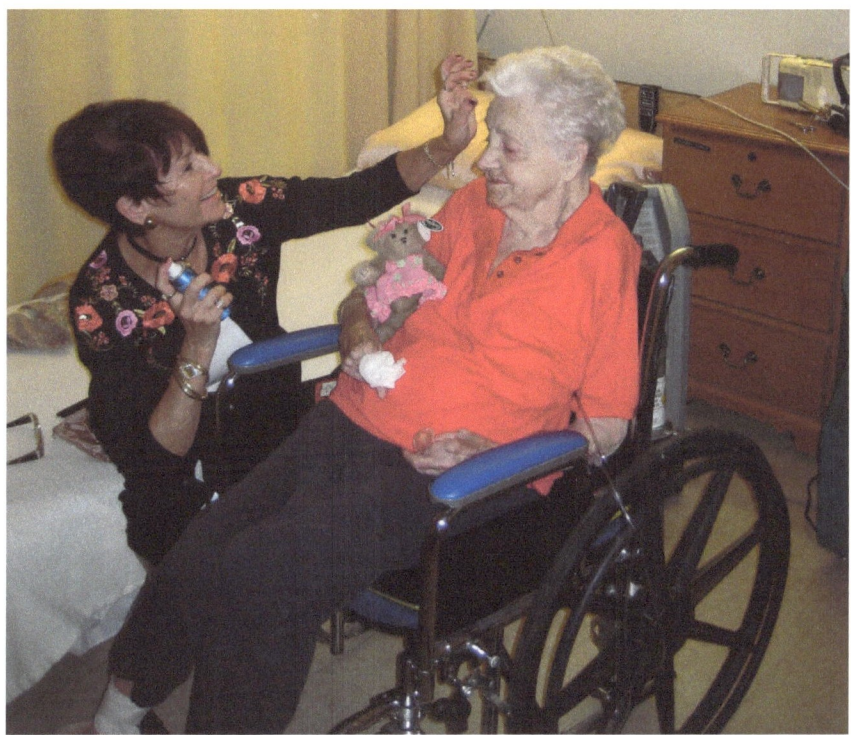

A precious time, Bessie smiling, holding Dolly from Arizona, before her 99th birthday party/celebration.

Oh, how Bessie loved my sparkly fun hats; (I had many colors.)

Trudy Wells-Meyer

What Possible Is . . .

"So long as one continues to be amazed one can delay growing old." — Anonymous

Isabel,
happy at Edgewater Haven, to be **100** years,
a mind so clear, a smile so dear, adored by caregivers.
Life is rich with sunshine in your heart.
Thinking of Aunt Isabel, I see flowers — irises,
azaleas and lilies, an infectious smile,
a glimpse of faith — eyes of joy,
her regal air reflecting gentleness everywhere.

Isabel
fell in her garden at 95 cutting grass with a
weed whacker, a momentous, life-changing slip.
A widow living alone moved into a newly built
dream house at 85 years old,
enjoying each day of days.
A lady with an extraordinary sense of stillness,
strength, unconscious grace, thinking of

those long-ago childhood mornings,
growing up on a Wisconsin farm,
a more innocent time. Winter days hard
and dreary, gray the color of the future,
remembrances from the past not necessarily as
they were, but where all that love began.

Isabel's
now-home is a small room, a wheelchair her
best and daily friend, pictures on walls and dresser,
endless days she claims speed by too fast.
People there from all walks of life, some with dementia —
they still know to smile. The question of time,
its elusiveness, as Isabel looks out to the gray,
sometimes blue Wisconsin River
across the street —
her eyes can see silence outside — safe inside.
Thoughts of Byron, a son far away in sizzling Arizona,
her oldest daughter living near; safe indeed.
Caregivers with happy eyes,
their hue of kindness warms the heart.

Isabel,
when she was young with hopes and desperate
feelings, her future a blaze of maybes,
harboring dreams of greatness, the size being
measured by her memories
as she pretends to be a child again.
Memories like random photographs, the smell of a
summer rainstorm, the million stars seen from
her cold tiny room.
Her sisters and brothers all gone — all ten of them.
Favorite sister Esther's 100th birthday, in Florida,
she attended at almost 95,
her aged hand holding old pictures close to her nose,
those centenarian eyes still able to see.

Isabel,
In age she understands . . . the fountain of youth
now her fountain of wisdom:
Contentment is one of your greatest blessings.
Experience, a brutal teacher, losing a daughter,
Janie only ten, to Polio. Now no longer anything to fear,
Isabel, no stranger to reach for the light . . . and pray.

Isabel's

face wrinkle-free, beauty as evident as in youth,
still using Oil of Olay, for anyone to stare at,
a sight of wonder for her visitors from the west.
Isabel's sophisticated, genius nephew with a degree
from the school of life, Isabel's brother Jeff's son,
my husband for 40 blissful years.
Not meant to be for us to attend a milestone day on
March 9th, 2012, to celebrate **100** years for a
most considerate, kind-hearted aunt.
A once in a lifetime birthday party at the care home
for the old, we had to miss.
Changed plans, as Lew declares such is life.

Isabel

knows about a momentous life-changing slip,
hers on grass, in Wisconsin, mine on black ice
one frosty January morning outside our condo
in the Rockies. I went down, heard the break,
twice, dislocating my foot.
At **100** years, a life of caring, Isabel's first words as we
surprised her later in July, one sunny Saturday
morning, soft-spoken words, their echoes
endless as she looked down at my leg,
How is your foot?
In disbelief I shouted: *Aunt Isabel, you remembered,*
left fascinated, we only anticipated a face of
surprise, as she stared at Lew and me,
hearing her words, immense joy that stems from
the unusual rather than the expected,
our long-lasting hug capturing the magic and depth
of a compassionate lady up in years.

Isabel

did not know we had arrived late the night before,
from Arizona, in Lew's hometown —
that we could not, would not wait for
the planned Monday morning visit.
Time is now . . . not knowing, one day this
memory of her regal poise and unexpected words
would be more precious to us than imagined.
What a privilege to write what I feel . . .

Isabel,
with a centenarian knowledge of life, a
lifetime to talk about, she knows time lasted
a little longer each day back then —
now her room holds her colors —
her timing, her heart. The journey is the reward.
A gentle wave of a hand that touched many,
to remain etched in stone, a prayer that
will carry me — get one thing right — that is Love.

*"What lies behind us and what lies before us are tiny matters —
compared to what lies within us."* — Ralph Waldo Emerson

["What Possible Is..." Goose River Press published a shorter version,
September 2015.]

By the way . . .

A visit in 2014 to our special aunt with smiling eyes, at age
102, her grace simply baffled us once again and verified: Be
kind, gentle, and smile. Everybody will remember you.

I brought Isabel a copy of her poem, on special paper with a distinctive font. As I glanced at her unmatched reaction, my heart chanted. Aunt Isabel adored her poem and held it close to her heart with a gesture too humble for words.

At Edgewater Haven with smiling Aunt Isabel

In the summer of 2015 Goose River Press published Aunt Isabel's poem. I could hardly wait to show her in person and hear the exciting news, for Isabel to witness her name in black and white in a real book. We had planned to attend Lew's 55-year class reunion in Mauston, Wisconsin the weekend of September 10th. Edgewater Haven was only one hour from our hotel at Wisconsin Dells. Our Thursday visit at the care home was first on our lengthy list of organized activities with relatives and friends, after a drawn-out drive from Steamboat, Colorado, where we spend the summer every year since we retired.

A notification from my editor and publisher shocked me into a tizzy: Goose River Press running late in printing, my ordered books were not shipped as promised. A late due date of delivery. *Oh no!*

I called my editor in Maine; my racing thoughts had found a way. I begged, "Is there any way to get a copy sent to the Hotel at the Dells in Wisconsin? Special delivery, possibly?"

My devastated voice babbling about visiting Aunt Isabel up in years must have touched my editor's heart. Dana's helpful words rang like music in my ears,

"I will send you my proof copy." Thank you.

At least I would have a not-perfect book, but a book nevertheless to present to Aunt Isabel, hoping her aged eyes were still able to read. The elation did not last long; a cell phone call from Isabel's daughter with devastating news — Aunt Isabel had turned for the worse after a sudden illness.

Aunt Isabel passed away on September 3rd, six days before our planned visit to the assisted-living home.

Lew immediately got on the phone and searched the internet. Labor Day weekend — to change our hotel reservation along with our three-day trip to Wisconsin turned out particularly stressful on such a popular holiday weekend. All we knew come hell or high water we would be at Aunt Isabel's burial and funeral service at her beloved church on September 8th, the day before our not-to-happen visit at Edgewater Haven.

Another such time when the number **8** had turned from lucky to significant, and foremost, momentous.

The book, a proof copy *Anthology 2015,* arrived at the hotel the evening before September 8th, in time to at least show Isabel's published poem to immediate family. Without a doubt, I knew this was more like what this unassuming lady would have wanted — to share the joy with her family and friends. Naturally, in my travel bag, I had extra copies of the poem, on special paper, just like the copy I had provided Aunt Isabel while visiting Wisconsin the last time. On the table at the church, where people attending the funeral signed in, daughter Beatrice displayed the poem, in case someone, anyone, showed interest.

For Christmas, I sent out a copy of *Anthology 2015* with that valued poem to Lew's family all over the US, including several I had never met before the funeral service. I could see Aunt Isabel's cherished smile in heaven with a nod and wink of an eye.

Aunt Isabel on her 100th birthday

"Beauty in age is art — in youth it is luck." — Unknown

Family Reunion — When Dreams Are Put to Shame

"Memory is the only paradise from which we cannot be driven away." — Jean Paul Richter

Explosions of color in Bretton Woods, a burst of sienna
scarlet at Mt. Washington Hotel's stunning grounds.
Fall's vibrant brilliance delivered by God.

Spectacular a word only, as Lew and I arrive; a first
in cold New Hampshire, a family reunion, a tradition
one of a kind, causes a word to come alive.

Jeffrey, Lew's stern from-Chicago brother, his lips utter
spectacular on our morning walk, intensifying feelings
of time not spent together, wishing words unsaid.

Aware of the irreversible loss of yesterday, unmatched
emotions, wars of words; now smiles with misty eyes,
gratefulness knowing no end.

Remembering a life with anger, as a sun-splintered
terrace of clouds turns darker; today, however, no
matter what — sunshine floods all our hearts.

Spectacular, a word bound by memories, only love
can bring God's healing from above, where love was
not meant to be. Love is patient — love is kind.

No more traditions without us — too far — no time, a
frenzied dash to make up time lost and vital need to
be a part of connecting echoes of the past.

Meeting the twins, now five years old,
Elise Alexandra's unconscious grace
and
Robert Thomas, close beside her,
to protect his twin at all times.

Elise Alexandra and Robert Thomas'
unique meeting of eyes —
togetherness —

classic twin-action, oddly luminous, as lit by
an invisible candle.

Colorado brown bears, stuffed animals the twins
named Happy and Barry traveled from Arizona into
their hearts, light up their eyes like turning on a light.

Elise's gentle touch, her head on my aged arm,
my heart missing a beat. No words, none needed as
I show love for Robert's train; his heart leaps into mine.

Perfect not always looking like we imagine, gone by so
quickly two days in my American life, in 2014 —
tears of joy — I smile because it happened.

Remember: **Spectacular** — thank God for fall's
unprecedented magnificence in New Hampshire, no
place I'd rather be. *Some things are simply meant to be.*

Love is **spectacular** — Family matters — what measure
of peace. Look at what you have left —
not what you have lost.

Mt. Washington resort Brettenwoods, October 2014

Coronado, California — Our Getaway

To Be Thankful . . . The Essence of Life

"A thankful heart is not only the greatest virtue but the parent of all other virtues." — Cicero

Thanksgiving Day, an all-American holiday, an extraordinary day, (not celebrated in my home country of Switzerland), is simply the US way to have such a distinctive day of thankfulness.

America, a huge country fortunate in never-ending ways, may need to be reminded: Be thankful day by day. . . not only once a year. *Every moment is gratitude.*

Why do people feel sorry for a couple — *alone* — on Thanksgiving?

Thanksgiving Day, one in a string of thrilling days for my husband Lew and me; we celebrate in our own unique way.

Turkey Day altered our lives forever, long ago when I kissed the man of my dreams. The year was 1968 in Phoenix Arizona, the time 7 p.m. at the Allegro, apartment 318 on the third floor. Nothing ever compared to that single moment that brought us together . . . a magical spell we both were under, sealed by a kiss, our first, a fairy-tale kiss changed everything.

It was Thanksgiving Day in America.

Truly happy people are thankful every day.

For years, on Thanksgiving, we walked to the elegant Hotel Del Coronado, near our condo, all dressed up to celebrate this treasured day. Traditions connect us to the past. We loved the ambiance and the food fit for a king.

Coronado, for years now, since 1976, has been one of our favorite places we call home — away from home, escaping the four seasons of the desert: 1: Almost summer, 2: Summer, 3: Still summer, 4: Christmas. The high-rise condo at the Coronado Shores, on the tenth floor in building **8** (of ten buildings) we purchased early in our marriage, at an age we doubted we could afford such luxury.

A model unit, designed by a Los Angeles decorator with flamboyant flair, we are lucky still to call ours. A view of the water as you walk into the bedroom reflects in the mirrors behind the bed as well as mirrors in the living room — one side reflects the bay, the other shows the ocean. At the kitchen counter, one can watch waves of the ocean in the mirror behind the couch.

I witness poetic brilliance and behold the sunrise early in

the morning in the mirror while sitting at my computer.

"It is not about where you are, it is about how you feel when you are there." — Anonymous

Coronado Shores is our 'love-nest get away' from our hectic life, called: *"Work hard . . . but don't forget to live."*

On Thanksgiving weekend 2005, we broke our tradition. As predictable we walked along the boardwalk, where countless times we watched the sight of seagulls, fog, crashing waves, and sunsets on the horizon to remind us of things past and yet to be, as a ship of nostalgia.

The place where we would eat all that food on turkey day changed, however, possibly due to constant higher prices at the Del for a Thanksgiving buffet that had everything and more.

Nevertheless, how can one eat *that much?* Overstuffed for hours. Or maybe it materialized the year before when we were appalled how innumerable people dressed down . . . a trend with no class. This was not a first at this five-star hotel famous all over the world, but undoubtedly more significant and upsetting. Once a year, couldn't *they* for one day ignore baggy, worn-out blue jeans, shirts like they were going to play golf, and tennis shoes?

What happened to respect for a special occasion and a sophisticated hotel?

I wrote to the management of the Del Coronado — not merely to complain but to express disappointment. Their prompt and unusually kind answer: A free Easter Brunch for two.

"Attitude: Life is ten percent what happens to you and ninety percent how you respond to it." — Lou Holtz

Time for changes. A miraculous Thanksgiving in 2005 — the year my husband retired; his day-after-day smiling face, a gift to see to believe. Time to walk the road of autumn's past.

Retirement is freedom.

I still cut hair, however, holding on to my *old life* and some of my longtime customers, now for over forty years, at a salon in old-town Scottsdale where I had worked several years.

Now a few days have changed into one day every six weeks.

To dress for our yearly Thanksgiving dinner at a Polynesian

 restaurant, with waterfront dining facing San Diego, our sense of effort was to be fun more than ever. As advertised, they served a spectacular Thanksgiving dinner. As we walked in, dressed in our colorful coordinated outfits, hopeful for a table near the window, I stared with unbelieving eyes. I swirled around. The décor, purple and turquoise green, hit my eyeballs — the restaurant décor in the colors of our clothes. In shocked delight, I hollered at my

151

husband, "No way!" Since I had decided what to wear a month before the *significant day,* when we were still in Arizona, long before we knew where we would end up eating a holiday feast.

During Turkey dinner, served with a purple orchid on each of our plates at a table surrounded by San Diego water and boats, my eyes found my husband's. I chuckled at his belly laugh. The orchid was the color of Lew's tie and the flowers in my skirt.

Couples that match stay together. (Lew and I are known to *always* color-coordinate when we go out.)

Lew's toast, gazing into my eyes in a way only he can, his glass touched my glass, "Happy first-kiss day."

A pinch-me perfect moment.

Red wine that afternoon, the most elite I ever tasted, as Lew was early — only two o'clock. Our tradition is to celebrate at 7 p.m. on Thanksgiving evening each year.

Heaven is . . . to know what happiness is.

Our awe-inspiring walk along the bay in Coronado, swinging our linked hands between us, concluded our new Thanksgiving dinner experience. The skyline of San Diego to our left, the dynamic Coronado Bridge in front of us, a clear blue sky. Serenity beyond comes from the heart. We know our love has been fed with admiration all our days together, solid like a fortress of love.

A small garden with the most gorgeous pansies, filled with enough California humidity, compelled us to stop and stare . . . yellow and purple. Loralee's colors. My husband's older sister had passed away in Chicago ten months earlier from cancer. Her favorite colors throughout her life — purple and yellow.

Lew slipped his arm around my waist, pulled me close, and squeezed my hand more firmly than usual. A touch with such significance, at a time when our locked eyes said it all: "*We are not alone.*" We laced our fingers, never to let go. To live the dream of miracles is to recognize the presence of God.

"*There are only two ways to live your life: one as though nothing is a miracle; or, as if everything is a miracle.*" — Albert Einstein

For all my family in Switzerland, every year, Thanksgiving Day is in September, the third Sunday: *Eidgenössischer Dank Buss und Bettag* celebrated not with going-all-out food like a feast — but prayer. Thanksgiving-time in America to this Swiss immigrant nonetheless turned out to be a favorite: *Off from work,* for three days, starting Wednesday evening on our flight to San Diego, once a year.

152

Coronado, California — Our Getaway

"Gratitude makes sense of our past, brings peace for today, and creates a vision for tomorrow." — Melody Beattie

By the way . . .

In September 2006, during one of our Coronado months where everything is California-perfect, we revisited that same restaurant for lunch. With incredulous eyes, more like a gape, we stared at

the décor. The colors had changed. For an instant, I thought I was dreaming. They had remodeled six months ago Carlos, the manager, informed us. I told him I'd send him a story. I did.

Such is life.

["To Be Thankful . . . The Essence of Life," an earlier, shorter version published in "Loving-Life-after-50", November 2006, in Arizona.]

One more thing . . .

Lew's famous words: "The IRS forces you to become rich", spoken the first time, left me with totally no-idea-what-he-is-talking-about. On Lew's mind, investing in real estate, was a constant due to allowed tax deductions on rental properties by the IRS in the seventies and eighties. Owning real estate would and did become like a business. Tax advantages the legal way.

My rich clients at the salon raved about Coronado Island in dreamy ways, as well as the old Hotel Del.

"You will think you are in a European Hotel."

Our first time at the Del, though not reminding me of a hotel in the home country since I never had stayed in such an elegant place, was spectacular. We found the boardwalk along the ocean next to seven Coronado Shores buildings, towering like a dream.

Jane Estes, a realtor, called and informed Lew of a resale studio condo. Jane, my customer for years, had transferred to the Shores, to Las Flores building 5 facing the bay. She knew of

153

Lew's interesting ideas of investing in real estate. Her call from Coronado one Thursday included an invite to stay with her, to see a unit on Saturday she knew had an Open House scheduled.

Never had we stayed overnight with anybody (my parents' house, yes). It was our first time. (Still today, we choose hotels and decline invitations to stay with friends or family).

Some Things Are Simply Meant to Be.

Friday evening, we flew to San Diego. Lew knew the models opened Saturday morning. At the Brigantine on Orange Avenue, Jane's regular hang-out, during dinner, Lew enlightened us of his plan. Jane's instant reaction, a call to the guy in charge, Ira, the salesman for building **8**. He met us at 10 a.m. sharp on Saturday when the models opened at El Encanto, Coronado Shores.

I had no idea of Lew's plan. None. Lew, however, for weeks knew of the Model's opening date and the builder's lease-back plan, for one year. Loan payment of model condo equaled rent for use, we'd pay the monthly maintenance fees. The resale unit, the reason we accepted Jane's invitation to sleep in her guestroom, so I thought, we never saw. Lew accepted the sleepover at a stranger's condo to merely check out the models of building **8**.

As we stood at the open door of the one-bedroom model on the 10th floor, a classy, posh decorator and crew still hanging the living room drapes and finishing last touches, I held my breath in shock of utter excitement. We walked in. I got exceedingly jittery as I gazed around not believing my eyes, the colors — style — modern — chrome — mirrors, a gray couch with lemon yellow pillows matching foil wallpaper with birds, a touch of black — a sight I would enjoy and love for years to come.

"We have to buy it," I squealed at Lew. His typical calm unnerved me to heights I did not understand. How can you stay calm and not rush so nobody else beats you to it? I learned that day Lew, the proud owner of #1001, remains composed no matter what.

Our motto had begun, I say *where* and Lew says *how*.

"Points of No Return"

"For it is not difference which immobilizes us most, but silence."
—Poet Audre Lorde

To know who you are . . . difficult to be clear about mystery,
　　trains of sadness rumble throughout the crossings
　　　　of his life, he carries a taste of his past.
　　　　　　A bridge that waits to be crossed.

Denial, like the color of rain.

Feelings hidden with no season — rare but constant —
　　in a field of light, its protection, ready, to share
　　　　visions of his heart and mind. Don't
　　　　　　let anyone tell you fear doesn't
　　　　　　　　have noise all its own.

"Points of No Return" . . . more like a time tunnel.

Travel through the dark is over, walking on the thin edge
　　of dusk, no longer soundless. Life does not
　　　　come looking for you, you must find it.
　　　　　　Nostalgia hits me over the head
　　　　　　　　with sounds of the ocean.

Let there be solace . . . comfort is luxury.

Manny sitting on the edge of a designer couch, "I am gay,"
　　gay not meaning *happy*. A measure of profound calm
　　　　like a Coronado California sunset,
　　　　　　an expected sigh of surprise
　　　　　　　　did not happen.

A glimpse into another world, a rainbow in his clouds.

I hear sounds of his breath, the weight of words, and hidden
　　meanings, tender as a love poem, an oil-painted
　　　　glow of relief, no more silence, a storm
　　　　　　with no noise, no wind.

Let the absent be present, as clear as reality.

155

Words illuminated by the setting sun, my words turn into
    outstretched arms. Transparency sheer as a mirror
        life compares to the moves of the daily tide.
            None of it in the end matters.

A winner in the game of life.

Words: *Points of No Return*, I came to understand one Coronado
    Thanksgiving Day. His mentality allowing to be strong
        in a place beyond knowing. Love your life —
            and it's many blessings.

Keep your face to the sunshine; each new day sings its own
song.

*"Nothing is so strong as gentleness, and nothing is as gentle as
real strength."* — St. Francis de Sales

Beach near the Hotel Del Coronado, California, November 1995

Holy Father, Pope Benedict XVI, 2008

What a moment when Pope Benedict XVI landed on American soil . . . as His plane got closer to where the President of the United States waited for His arrival (first time ever done by a President at Andrews Air Force Base.)

A swirl of excited anticipation was interrupted when the Pope stepped into view. His smiling face and arms waving to the crowd.

I jumped off my chair in our home in Coronado – tears of all kinds rolling down my face – I waved furiously . . . for a long time, my tears would not stop – an elevated moment I am still dizzy from.

At this moment, on this day it seemed to me clearer than ever: to believe — what a gift!

The Holy Father will hear those children's voices that greeted Him by singing: "Happy Birthday" long after His return to Rome. . . the voices of the future.

[The First Coming" article, published in the Arizona *Scottsdale Tribune,* April 18, 2008.]

During our month in Coronado, I wrote scribbled words, while watching TV, as the German-born Holy Father stepped on American soil. *Coming to America* the first time. Overwhelmed by his arrival in the US, I sent the Pope a copy of the published article with a handwritten letter of THANKS.

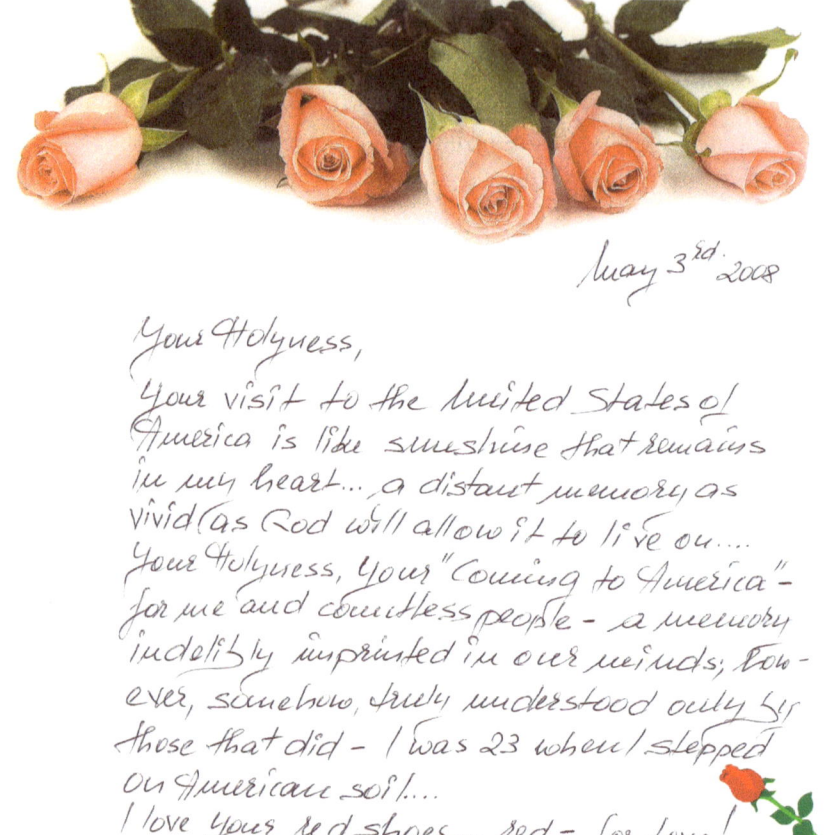

May 3rd 2008

Your Holyness,

Your visit to the United States of America is like sunshine that remains in my heart... a distant memory as vivid (as God will allow it to live on....

Your Holyness, your "Coming to America" - for me and countless people - a memory indelibly imprinted in our minds; however, somehow, truly understood only by those that did - I was 23 when I stepped on American soil....

I love your red shoes... red - for Love!

Included you will find a copy of a published article I wrote (I am a new writer) "What communication through the written word..."

From Arizona with Love   Trudy Wells
(Swiss born)

Ms. Trudy B. Wells
7843 E Via Marina
Scottsdale AZ 85258-2826

A letter from the Vatican in our mailbox . . . Does anyone know that feeling of finding an envelope with a Vatican stamp in a pile of mail, mostly bills? I danced around the kitchen with outstretched arms to heaven, holding an answer to my letter from the Holy Father. How startling was that? I wanted to dance for days.

SECRETARIAT OF STATE

FIRST SECTION · GENERAL AFFAIRS

From the Vatican, 14 June 2008

Dear Ms. Wells,

The Holy Father has asked me to acknowledge the kind letter which you sent to him following his Pastoral Visit to the United States. He very much appreciates the devoted sentiments which you expressed.

His Holiness will remember you in his prayers. As a pledge of joy and peace in the Lord he cordially imparts his Apostolic Blessing.

Yours sincerely,

Monsignor Gabriele Caccia
Assessor

Ms. Trudy B. Wells
7843 East Via Marina
Scottsdale, AZ 85258-2826

One of my forever daily morning prayers: *"In jedem Moment unseres Lebens sind wir von Gott Beschenkte." "In every moment of our lives we are gifted by God."* — Benedict XVI

Christ our hope

Benedictus PP XVI

Apostolic Journey to the United States 2008

April 15 - 21, 2008

The Holy Father's eminent words, *"Although life is uncertain, there is nothing uncertain about the destiny of every person. Go in the footsteps of Christ — He is your end — your way and your prize."*

Steamboat, Colorado — Our Switzerland

Paradise in White

Spellbinding snow, a dream quality, promises power,
uncertain power filled with an undeniable mystique
of fearfulness, fear of falling. Unknown territory,
a mountain's dips, unforeseen rocks.
Ecstasy is our prize.

Conquering elevation at our own speed, controllable speed
of two high-tech-boards on our feet, sudden danger for
skiers with brains, heavenly measures of speed,
a rattling, mysterious, sensuous world.

A memorable feeling stirred by the intimacy of two lovers,
leaving trails of S's in tracks of snow spread toward the
valley below, simply catching the sun's shadows — we stop —
an embrace that lasts beyond the hold.

Paradise in White . . . a unique grandeur for body and soul.

Seduction of a snow-covered mountain, feeling the eyes of
powerful pines in white upon us, cold slopes with the unknown,
what is around the corner, where daredevils crash on a
snowy highway of chaos; left breathless,

mostly smiling, happy in pain. Sounds of silence interrupted
by the sudden thud of snowboarders — a new-millennium-
sound
too loud for us up in years amidst the grand peaks —
the familiar echo of skis is what we cherish.

Blizzards of emotions, a top-of-the-world feeling, people in love
sharing dynamics of unprecedented views in the distance,
a silent valley below. Inches of snow on aspen fingers
swaying in the wind, a sight gone tomorrow.

Paradise in White . . . thrills on skis.

High in the silver-slick mountain landscapes, humbling with
its immensity, knowing nature letting go of any sadness.
How we wish the world could see what our soul

beholds on a clear-cold January day.

A multicolored *snow bow* presented in the sky, like a unique
rainbow beyond the clouds, a most awesome show given
freely to skiers huddled on chairlifts. Sun and frozen moisture
creating glitter afar — a sea of dancing diamonds.

Extraordinary to witness the unthinkable with the same eyes —
thrilling — as we descend, down slopes surrounded by
sparkle — the purity turning into calmness.
Love and unity at its brightest.

A glimpse of heaven, to live the dream of love —
our Paradise in White.

["Paradise in White," Loose Moose Publishing, *ABSOLOOSE* Volume 2,
Spring 201**8,** and Honorable Mention, The Writers Workshop Poetry
Contest, June 1**8**, 2011.]

Shared Moments on a Path of Gold

Walking is a feeling — a meeting of your mind — a celebration of life and close to God beyond.

Fall, one of the most dynamic seasons, a time when our love for walking expanded to a new high in Steamboat, Colorado, 2007; it was the last weekend in September. A mad dash of people rushed onto a gondola to be transported to the top of Mt. Werner one last time.

Much is written about experiencing those magnificent autumn colors, the dramatic display of nature's handiwork, a feast for the eyes and soul. This had to be that absolute perfect time — the sun was out, and the sky an impeccable blue, no clouds. Stepping out of the gondola into the open with my mouth open I looked at my husband with a silent *wow* on my lips.

I was transfixed. Immediately overtaken by an exceptional golden hue, my eyes stared. I was not prepared for such jaw-dropping sights, where leaves give autumn its special zap of orange, copper, red, and gold. Mesmerized, I stood at the top of the gondola stairs and leaned against the rail with feelings so startling I rubbed my eyes. Left speechless, I realized I was looking at an image I would hold onto for years to come. This timeless view and breathtaking landscape — what a measure of peace.

On this day God had simply used all His colors. With every step, every bend in the path, Lew and I beheld colors become more intense and powerful. What unprecedented magnificence! I could not help but feel amazement at the stillness, at the immeasurable quiet, aware only of an occasional fluttering of leaves glittering in the autumn sun.

We were first on the Nature Trail above Thunderhead; God, the mountain, and us. A range of times I found myself looking at all that humbling splendor with a silent prayer.

To witness the beauty of such brilliance brought abundant tears on our favorite two-hour hike down to the bottom of the mountain we had come to call our own after visiting Steamboat since we were single, owning a condo since 1978 near the slopes at *The WEST*.

For years, we came to ski only. One week. Today had to be the most stirring time, where the ordinary had turned into unseen powers, when appreciating nature lets go of despondency and embraces passion, and a simple act of counting and treasuring blessings becomes huge. When stillness happened inside me, aware of the dynamism of bedazzling things around us . . . a powerful feeling of love from above. The underrated beauty of fallen leaves on the narrow trail, autumn-colored leaves, sacred to walk on paths of gold. The word *beautiful* was simply too inadequate. Romance is . . . shared moments.

Transported to a place of serene splendor, I felt privileged and fortunate. My life flashed in front of my eyes, awakened by the heartfelt mystique of nature. I was flooded with a powerful sense of the past, of bygone memories. Closeness to my disciplinary dad transpired extremely strong and genuine; oh, how he would have loved to be here on this trail with us.

When I grew up in a modest village, in *Zürich Oberland,* Switzerland, Dad ordered us to walk — no choice, no car. Four kids, one brother, and two sisters, we had to walk everywhere, every Sunday to Mass dressed in our finest Sunday clothes. In the summer, barefoot to school. Much later, when my parents bought a car for pleasure only, Sunday drives were the in-thing. "*Are we rich?*" echoed in our minds. My half-understood promise of life did not include walking everywhere, although today I understand completely my dad's passion for walking . . . especially in the forest. I could see his face and unique, modest smile in the sky. An infinite bond sparked for dad on a path of gold down Mt. Werner.

As we continued to hike through the forest with the breeze rattling the leaves and sensed the eyes of the trees upon us, I knew, if once in the forest, it keeps calling you back. We listened to nature's music of the wild including its most endangered sound — silence. My dignified husband of thirty-five blissful years stopped. We hugged surrounded by this enthralling spell we both were under, knowing we truly saw beauty with the same eyes . . . the ultimate of closeness. Miracle of miracles to love so much and to be loved back more.

We met in the magical year of 196**8** when Lew dropped anchor in my eyes to pull me in forever. A time when we made each other's hearts sing when nothing compared to that single moment our wondrous love was sealed by a spellbound kiss on Thanksgiving Day, promising a love that would last. Always. Marriage is two lives joined by one love.

In early 1969, Motorola sent Lew out of town, to Chicago for months on business to earn extra money on one of his job-shopper deals. I missed him with curiously sharp anguish. In one of my everyday letters, I posed a delicate question. Anxious for a response, I asked Lew, "Why do you love me?"

His long-awaited answer arrived like a magic gift in my mailbox. I tried to understand why it had taken him so long. (He had no love for writing.) Lew's imposing words stunned me: "I could tell you I love you because you are beautiful, charming, because of your smile when it belongs to me only; however, the real reason I love you is because you see beauty with the same eyes as I do."

Romance of words . . . how could I have known then how much more a single phrase can mean now, as we grow *old*, retired, with more time together and truly content?

Happiness is a journey, not a destination.

"True happiness is . . . to want what you have." — Trudy Wells-Meyer

As we approached the bottom of Mt. Werner, the spectacular sights and gold colors faded some, although the feelings remained.

The next day, it rained — a steady downpour the entire day.

By the way . . .

In August 201**8** we put our Steamboat condo, home away from home since 197**8**, on the market. Sold — to the second couple that inspected #3402. Location, location, location.

Who needs three of everything anyway? Consoling us? Not exactly. (Although, we still could (would) come and visit — at the Steamboat Grand next door on the knoll, enjoying the view from a 5th-floor hotel/condo facing The West in the distance).

The WEST Condos, updated in 2010.

Hiking in the forests and trails of the Rocky Mountains had neared an end; one more mad dash that summer to enjoy the beauty of nature in the Steamboat Mountain world and our condo one last time with a smile and a tear. We hoped to return, witness our favorite season — fall when we ask ourselves: Why do leaves change colors every year? One simple answer: God — for everyone to enjoy and appreciate nature. Reflect! Stop, look, and listen!

"It's not what you look at that matters, it's what you see." — Henry David Thoreau

A favorite look of the outside at The WEST, summer 2007

Red-tailed Hawk . . . Messenger of Peace

"May you live all the days of your life." — Jonathan Swift

Twist of fate or the Hand of God? Destiny — I wish I could be
certain, or simply bad luck as one friend called it.
In the land of black ice, a momentous, life-changing slip
one frosty January morning in Rocky Mountain sunshine
outside the near-the-slopes condo.
No skiing with the weekend mob, laundry-day not to be.

As I tumbled back in slow motion, sounds of a break,
twice, both sides of my leg; a pile of laundry scattered in
snow on a breezy-clear Steamboat morning.
I saw their faces, unable to look; my foot dislocated 90° west,
the look of pain. Sounds of help, the speed of it, sirens,
like music when they are for you.
I thought of tears, beyond weeping I smiled without much joy,
but still a smile.

For weeks my imperative need to find the good in my
misfortune,
from my bed, I watched a bird as I lived upstairs in the prison
of my days, crutches near. A road I did not choose,
anticipating sorrow, a time to easily be discouraged,
bringing me back to a more innocent time.
I found the seed of gratitude.
Unexpected, irrational optimism comes from where?

In helpless surrender, I watched the immeasurable quiet,
on a snow-covered aspen branch, a breast-piercing
red-tailed hawk —
a dream-quality to see silence outside, snowflakes, a calm
world of frozen moments allowing my soul
to escape from pain, filling me with inner harmony.
Oddly luminous as lit by an invisible candle.
To know peace is to know God; nor after, nor ever
will I forget — a bird of peace.

Wounds eventually heal, scars remain, an event that won't
change history indelibly leaving a belief — something
is good about everything. Time to write.
When the nothing that is something surrounds you, when
your caregiver is Lew, my love around the corner,

food on a tray fit for a queen; a new chef was born.
Romance of broken bones.

Whatever tragedy I encountered, I sigh as baby steps
teach me to walk. Will the pain of spring give me
a true gift: hike again in the summer?
Looking upon the blue, no-snow sky I winced as if in pain,
the cold breeze unaware of the dark eyes of the future
silenced by snow — memories of one rare bird.

January 2012 as seen, from my bed, most mornings.

["Red-tailed Hawk . . . Messenger of Peace," published in August,
Goose River Press, *Anthology 2014*.]

By the way . . .

In July 2015 on our way to six weeks of Rocky-Mountain-air glory for our first long stay, as we drove into Steamboat on US 40 at the outskirts of town Lew hit the brakes. A red-tailed hawk, my hawk of peace, soared by in front of our car windshield . . . as if to say hello. Welcome to Steamboat!

The next morning the front page of the *Steamboat Pilot & Today* featured a write-up and picture, in color, of my messenger of peace huge in flight on US 40 reminding me of a spiritual time in my life, and bearable but drawn-out pain a part of it.

Fall 2012, September **8** we hiked Sunshine Trail high up on Mt. Werner, extra careful with my walking stick Lew had found in the forest I called my third leg, not to misstep. Still feeling vast pain in my broken ankle when my foot hit a rock, a thud got my attention, a rare noise scared me, knowing animals see us.

We never noticed the jumbo cinnamon bear — my eyes were glued to the top of an old tree on one branch with no

leaves. I yelled, "Lew, look." We gazed at a red-tailed hawk — protecting us — we learned later.

Across the mountain, on the busy nature trail, we detected a group of people standing still, looking in our direction constantly. For too long their bodies were not moving. What are they staring at? Nonetheless, being used to getting noticed and repeatedly complimented on our matching, color-coordinated clothes, as well as declared best-dressed couple on the mountain trails (by guys mostly) several times a season; we guessed this another such time. My mind wandered to a memorable phrase on a morning hike, my sparkly rhinestone matching cap adding to the look: "Couple of the day winner," bellowed out by a guy speeding by on a bicycle. Possibly Lew's white jeans on the mountain trail getting extra attention, a couple in red and white on this blue-sky day? Every bend of our trail, we saw the two couples, one guy, still in the same place, unmoving.

We caught up to the group of five. They had waited for us. With worried faces, shock, and alarm in their voices, they howled, "You did not see that massive bear behind you?" "No," I hollered. "Where?" Relief on everyone's mind and faces to see us safe. My question, "Did you see the red-tailed hawk?" got buried in everyone talking over each other and all the black bear excitement.

Thinking back, no doubt in my mind and happy heart, a red-tailed hawk, messenger of peace, my angel in disguise was close for our safety. We never panicked. We did not know.

On our final morning, the end of August 201**8**, as we drove away from Steamboat, our home away from home for all those years since 197**8**, at almost the same spot, on US 40, as the universe would have it, on my side of our car a red-tailed hawk sat on a post on the edge of the road, as close as to touch him. I waved . . . wings down, my *Messenger of Peace* looked lost. He came to say *goodbye*. I wept.

Memories of our hawk on Mt. Werner, on a picture we were not aware of, did not know he posed, until back at the condo as Lew downloaded the pictures of the day onto his computer. He shouted: "Look, who is in the picture. . ."

Some Things Are Simply Meant to Be. . .

What timing on Mt. Werner — my red-tailed hawk,
he posed with us — July 2013

Something Good about Everything

"For every setback, there is a comeback." — Anonymous

I learned:
> Walking — slipping on black ice is more dangerous
> than skiing.

I learned:
> Falling back in slow motion, one can hear the breaks,
> twice; sounds of pain.
>> Do not take loafers to ski country.

I learned:
> How to get out of laundry-day: slip on ice; a pile of
> laundry scatters in snow.

I learned:
> Help in Steamboat, Colorado arrives like a bullet train.
> Sirens, a melody in the snow,
>> sounds of music when they are for you.

I learned:
> People freak out beyond at your dislocated foot
> on black ice, facing 90° west. Scissors
>> are huge that cut your favorite jeans.

I learned:
> Two sticks called crutches become your best friends
> for 8½ weeks.

I learned:
    How to move to escape pain, in solitude —
        not to explain patience in one word,
            adore my husband's gentle kiss.

I learned:
    Friends give new meaning to generosity, a marvelous
        discovery and, disbelief.

I learned:
    A daily confining bedroom turns into a
        spring garden.

I learned:
    Hurt and pain — *Break a leg* — an attention-getter with
        its many faces.

I learned:
    To find a rainbow in my clouds on a path
        I did not choose.

I learned:
    To have time for a rare bird, a red-tailed hawk,
        on a snow-covered branch, my daily
            morning buddy; a messenger of peace.

I learned:
    Fifteen stair-steps in our Colorado condo, a prison
        upstairs, with sunshine, no trips to the
            refrigerator cause your pants to fall off.

I learned:
    To wash my hair on a stool with one leg hanging
        over the bathtub,
            glamour on vacation.

I learned:
    How to cope with disappointment and smile as though
        I invented it.

I learned:
    Promise of peace, receive communion on Sundays
        as Leah, a friend, brings God
            to my humble upstairs.

I learned:
    New magic moments, listening for Lew's steps,
        a tray of food fit for a queen.

I learned:
    I have a husband, who for weeks did not, would not
        go skiing without me.

I learned:
    To cry behind my hand at the wonder of a man
        who left his skis in paid storage
            to take care of me, his invalid.

I learned:

> Seeing stars beyond my sight; converted to optimism —
> time to write — healing is a matter
> of time but also opportunity.

I learned:

> Be happy wherever you are; find the music
> in your life. When last did I
> receive a lollypop?

I learned:

> To fly home on crutches; a wheelchair waiting
> at every airport.

I learned:

> To enjoy spring from the kitchen window,
> on a blue lake in Arizona.

I learned:

> Looking down with every step will keep you safe,
> knowing sunshine is above.

By the way . . .

Broken-leg-day struck on Martin Luther King weekend, January 21, 2012: Everything happens for a reason . . . the challenge in life is to find the reason.

Our Coronado balcony, facing the ocean, bay behind us, Easter 2012. My cast in daily demand, a question everywhere we went, "Where can I get a cast with pink butterflies?" (I used pink stickers, to match my hat.)

Trudy Wells-Meyer

Night of Broken Bones

"If life were easy, would there be music?" — Anonymous

How far can a hand go when pain is nothing he can see,
    only his love can feel. His gentle touch on my arm,
        my tummy, searching in the dark,
as I lay not moving, escape pain all night and day,
    a statue for weeks; my sense of glamour in a ditch.
        Reckless skiing by an 18-year-old flying like the wind.
Broken ribs, six the doctor said, a fractured collarbone,
    collapsed lung, three pieces broken off my left pelvic wing,
        iliac wing, the leg nearest to my love.
Lew's hand's journey stops near my heart, ending up in my
    hand, undeniably underrated — a touch of holding
        hands under sheets, a pursuit called love
of the simple kind. Sounds of his breath, his warm skin
    too far yet close, divine peace, unity of two souls,
        one in pain, one wishing pain gone
for his wife of 42 years. Agony, memories, twirling in his mind,
    a ski crash on Mt. Werner's famous Buddy's Run,
        collision on snow, in the cold, plowing into her —
as he watched his love fly up in the air, plummeting like a
    ragdoll on a groomed ski run, not letting her breathe —
        hearing her soft moans. Lifesavers on skis,
ski patrol guessing, rushing for what — oxygen?
    A torturous ride down the mountain on a toboggan
        I live to tell, ambulance waiting, blue sky above —
seeing stars beyond my sight — pain I can't see — but
    Lew is near. Oddly luminous, as if lit by an invisible candle,
        hoping for a rainbow in my clouds.
No snowflakes on my face in the morning, yet knowing
    unmatched love beyond.

(Ski accident on Martin Luther King Day, January 20, 2014.
Broken leg on black ice on Martin Luther King weekend 2012.
On crutches **8** weeks.)

["Night of Broken Bones," Loose Moose Publishing, Prescott, Arizona, *ABSOLOOSE* Volume 1, published October 2016.]

Roads of Gold . . . Going Gold

Much is written about fall's dramatic season,
an astonishing surge of colors.
Nothing sets the trees on fire of orange and gold quite like
the sun beaming down behind them.
Trees simply glow.

Pinch-me perfect hiking, joy beyond,
daily journeys filled with surprises around each bend.
A wow on my lips, a unique fluttering of my heart.
Trails with no name, *Roads of Gold . . .*
humming profound words like a melody.

A scenery that bankrupts the English language . . .
hard to ignore this magic season in an early-autumn haze,
a vivid display of nature's handiwork.
When God simply uses all His colors.
A quiet crescendo enveloping my world — silence —
nature's most endangered sound.

Trudy Wells-Meyer

Autumn leaves with their snap of color — orange, red, copper
an explosion of gold, a carpet of fallen leaves.
Today, sacred to walk on as I time-travel
back to a place, I lived years past —
no love for walking — no car.
A kid stomping on leaves with no knowledge of life.

To witness fall's humbling splendor
steps to *Roads of Gold* are worth our every breath.
Fallen leaves compel me to look up,
love for a season and its many treasures rises
each year, knowing God creates
Colorado's brilliant autumn glow —
Going Gold . . . Roads of Gold.

Sunshine Trail, hiking again . . . Fall 2012,

["Roads of Gold . . . Going Gold," published in *WestWard Quarterly*. I
received notice and a copy on my birthday, October 1**8**, 201**8**.]

Health

NORMAL . . . The Meaning of One Simple Word

"To live with fear for days is what makes elation seem a brand-new feeling." — Anonymous

The morning I walked into the place that hurts women for a living, for a mammogram I did not believe in getting, my thoughts were carefree, my face smiling. My overconfident mind planned to get it over fast; I hoped it would not take too much of my organized day ahead, Monday, my day off. My instincts had taken over. I no longer ignored my doctor's orders, neglected for too many years. I had called for an appointment. I momentarily disregarded my health-nut beliefs, which I held for years, knowing health is a choice — a story for another time.

No man will ever know what a woman goes through on the way to that controversial mammogram appointment: what a woman's mind does to her brain, wondering about all the possibilities that can happen to one of the female body parts — her breasts. To face possibly missing a most visual part of her body: can anyone truly relate to that? The pain of a mammogram, the squeezing hard and flattening of a breast — a machine that does not seem to know when to stop. It's like being attacked by a robot. What about having to grab your breast and lay on a shelf designed to accommodate your height, your size? All the while you listen to a nurse in charge, saying,

"Higher, more to the left." Over where? Anxious moments last too long, simply no fun.

I undressed to the waist, put on a flowered blue gown, and pulled it tight, trying to ignore my dislike for blue that changed in Rome, Italy. An exceptionally friendly young girl with smiling eyes showed me to the tiny, dark exam room. The dreaded picture-taking machine appeared huge. Nurse Wretched was waiting. A middle-aged, unsmiling, overweight woman with hair that matched her mood, an early Monday-morning-sour behavior like a weekend gone badly. In her irritated voice, she instructed me to put my breast — where, on what?

"You're sure, up there?" She had forgotten to lower that famous mammogram shelf where countless breasts have gone before mine.

"How long has your nipple been inverted?"

"My what?" I mumbled.

She repeated the question in a loud voice awake now.

"Sorry," I answered, "I don't make a habit of looking at my nipple. I am now to look at my nipples, what happened to check for a lump?" I know I sounded flustered because I was.

I could feel the smile fade on my face, her words sounded uncaring, "An inverted nipple is not a good sign."

An eerie silence filled the room as she continued the exam. Fearful speculations started to rise, abruptly interrupted after Wretched checked with a frown and looked at the pictures closely. It was my right breast.

Finally, with a quiver in my voice, I dared to ask, "What does an inverted nipple mean?"

Her harsh, business-like voice persisted like an echo for days,

"In general, 'something' is going on in there. . ." Her facial expression revealed **cancer,** as did my racing thoughts.

To cover an unfamiliar nervousness and near trembling, I put my hand on my heart. I took a deep breath. I told myself to breathe because this was one of those moments where I could easily stop. I tried to act nonchalant.

On the way out, I stopped at a buzzing desk with phones ringing too loud. Nurse Wretched, in her stern demeanor, shouted, "Your doctor will have the result today. She will read it tomorrow and let you know."

Why the urgency? I was too dazed to ask an important follow-up question.

With sinking feelings, I walked to my car. I raised my eyes to heaven in a classic expression of disbelief. I raced home. I could not wait to call my gynecologist's office, my doctor (a woman), to ask a question I never thought about or heard of "What does an inverted nipple mean?" I dialed with such haste I missed a number. I redialed, only to get a recording: Vacation had started, today for ten days. I must have looked downright ill. Now what? Scrambled thoughts flew around in my brain.

Who will read my test? And clearly, when?

Life slowed to a crawl as the minutes filled with worries. The texture of reality underwent a dramatic change. A fear known to all women enveloped me. It looked as if to be my turn. I called the emergency number provided on their vacation message, only to talk to another answering machine. I explained my problem with a voice not resemble my own, listened to by whom? No callback.

The cold, hard side of life tested my day-by-day smile. A huge cloud had formed. Lost in my thoughts, I listened to the sounds of silence, wondering if my life would ever be the same again. I silently cursed the gut feeling that had driven me to make an appointment for a mammogram; this had developed to be entirely the wrong time to stop ignoring my doctor's orders. In a few days, we were leaving for a most anticipated trip to Europe for three weeks.

Spring in Paris, the city of lights; it was May in Arizona.

Our amazing trip included visiting my family in Switzerland and a class reunion in the tiny hometown where I grew up. A trip planned with countless, prearranged dates and times to see friends and family in various Swiss cities. Traveling to the Italian Alps, Cusio, a long over-due invitation to visit my favorite Uncle Oskar in his high-up-in-the-mountain summer home.

Our return to Paris was first on our list. Paris, our honeymoon destination thirty-six years ago. After two days in the dream city, we planned to travel on the TGV, a high-speed train, to Zürich, Switzerland.

Cloud nine in a ditch . . . for now.

I called the office again, leaving the news of my supposedly huge problem on the emergency-number answering machine. Again, nobody called me back. Was my problem not severe enough for the courtesy of a callback for me to ask someone who knew something? Mentally exhausted, I left one last message on that detested recording. I moaned I would call from Paris as soon as they were back in the office, the only thing I could do with a ray of distant hope. I hung up with a bitter sigh, seeking warmth from a chill only I could feel. The sense of powerlessness made me feel faint.

In the days that followed a crucial morning of dreadful news, in my mind I tried to instant-replay every word the nurse had said, hoping I would find something, anything I may have missed, to make it all less serious. I explored the Internet intently for some information about an inverted nipple, fearful of what I might find. I talked to people, anybody. The one I wished I hadn't confided in was my neighbor. She blurted out in words too loud, "Oh yes, my mother-in-law had an inverted nipple. She would not go to the doctor for months. She died because of a tumor in her breast."

Did I stumble on the truth, only to wish I hadn't?

While I was packing and for days to come, I lived in the prison of my nights and days. On the flight to Zürich, Switzerland, changing planes in Atlanta, with nine long hours

179

across the Atlantic to worry about breast cancer, undeniably a restless night where sleep did not come. Though, high up in the air, close to God, the quiet in my heart was immeasurable.

In the early morning, I looked out at the magnificent sunrise over the Swiss Alps and stared at the momentary brilliance in the sky emerging through the clouds. I closed my eyes with a sob, blinking, not to miss this entire splendor in the sky. I will not forget the cold echoing calm, like the icy silence of the Alps in the distance embracing me. Several times I found myself looking up to heaven with hope that was more than a wish — it was a silent prayer.

The most unexpected moments in life compel one to appreciate anything — anything at all. Feeling close to despair, an amazing calmness transpired, almost like a surrender, a close-to-God feeling, knowing the future is in His hands. Always!

What will be will be . . .

"Yesterday is history . . . tomorrow is a mystery . . . today is a gift."— Bill Keane

The word **normal**, through a phone line from Arizona to Paris, the clearest sound, like an echo indelibly imprinted in my mind — it was dinnertime in France.

I shouted back, *"NORMAL?"*

The cheerful voice on the other side of the deep ocean, clear as a bell, repeated that glorious word. News of massive importance; for an instant, I could scarcely believe my ears. My jumping off the bed caused my husband concern, yet with hope in his eyes, I had heard what I wanted to hear. A piercing sensation I was not prepared for triggered my heart to leap and fill me with pleasure. I stared at Lew with a silent *wow* on my lips. Left speechless, I understood I would remember these startling feelings for the rest of my life.

Thank You, God, I prayed, filled with an abundance of gratitude. Oh, how the power of one word can pave the way to extreme jubilation — *normal* — a goose-bump moment in Paris. Such ecstasy, a feeling like music, as I danced around our fancy hotel room, arms stretched out toward heaven; it had taken mere seconds to feel free again. The Eiffel Tower in the distance never looked better. The word *happy* was simply too weak.

Lew's priceless grin got huge. He leaped off his chair and ran to me with outstretched arms. He held me tight. I listened to the strong beating of his heart . . . closeness beyond. How madly romantic. Happiness shared is truly real.

The clouds in Paris for days had turned to blue sky sunshine — literally.

Normal — *to* hear this glorious word is an elevated moment that still makes me giddy. A word only, translated into *the scare is over . . .*

Was it?

***

Five months later I had another test (mammogram) on the breast that worried me sick, as well as an examination by my doctor. The mystery of my inverted nipple is still not truly clear to me; however, I now do look at my nipples on a regular basis. When *out* I feel ecstatic — when *in* the wondering continues. My doctor and a mixture of well-educated people have told me it is a really good sign if the nipples do not stay in constantly.

Only time will tell.

Call for a mammogram!

By the way . . .

I struggled with weight all my life. For years I did everything to look "small" — well, smaller. Baggy clothes included wearing bras the wrong size. I didn't care if part of my breast did not fit into the bra. The underwire was cutting over the breasts, especially my right breast. My habit of never choosing fitted clothes didn't give away the secret of ultimate ignorance.

Now, finally, I changed the bra size; I didn't have to go shopping. I found five bigger bras, size D, hidden in the back of my underwear drawer, some still with price tags. I had worn a bra too small, stubbornly, believing to help me appear less huge; I was foolish for far too long. Imagine how countless women pay to enlarge their breasts. Crazy me spent a life intimidated, passed on by my mother's problem and dislike of her monstrous breasts.

Growing into a woman in Switzerland, I was sixteen when my mom took me along to the big city to a specialty store for bras, where they fit and measure you. I can still hear Mom: "They don't make your size." She also needed to be fitted; her bra gross and outer-space-like to a young teenager. While traveling to the exciting city was thrilling, it reminded me profoundly of being different from other girls my age. Large breasts were never on my list of things I wanted. Why would I want to look enormous?

The pressure of the bra may have caused the problem of my inverted nipple (my own belief). What a wake-up call of magnitude in 2008 for a woman who naively did not want to look fat. The future will tell. Now I am old and wear a bra that fits.

Mistakes of the past do become the wisdom of the future.

["NORMAL . . . The Meaning of One Simple Word" was published in the Goose River Press *Anthology 2016,* in October, and received an Honorable Mention, in the 2013 Betty Simmons Short Story Contest, in California.]

A Friend Who Wanted Me to Live

"The human body at peace with itself is more precious than the rarest gem. Cherish your body; it is yours this one time only." —
Lama Tsong Khapa

Health is a choice . . .

The world deserves to know good nutrition saves lives. Health is your fundamental wealth.

I am determined to share the healthy-days factor through my Swiss-born eyes, knowing health matters — health is a choice. Communication through the written word is miraculous, and I hope my words are not simply floating around and taking up space on a page. May my writing, possibly arrogant words to some readers, help someone, somewhere. May awareness be possible in a small way through my daily example.

We will never see the light unless we make the effort to flip the switch. A fresh start: a healthful, nonviolent diet, called a way of life of vegetables, fruits, whole grains, nuts, and seeds — a meatless diet — is approved by major health advocacy organizations and health authorities.

"Delay is the deadliest form of denial." — C. Northcote Parkinson

At this time in my life, it seems imperative and clear as reality my feeling good is of undeniable importance to share with whoever may read my story, as my own life reaches a new high for a fat kid in former times.

Be patient. Learn willpower.

I recognized my life was run by people who think up diets for a living; I blamed them if again and again I was not successful. After countless shimmers of light and newfound energy I now experience daily, my gratitude belongs nonetheless to Judy's generosity of spirit in her teachings and her husband Gene. Two friends taught and educated me on how to live — showing me a healthy way of life. Eat right!

Are there words for gratitude? A humble *thank-you* — how simply inadequate. This energetic, healthy couple is a constant spark of inspiration and a strong link in a growing chain of fruits and vegetable knowledge.

"Truly great friends are hard to find — difficult to leave and impossible to forget." — G. Randolf

183

Gratefulness of tremendous proportions belongs to my stunning-in-all-counts lifelong friend Judy, with a smile that sets everything straight, her golden blonde, finger-combed hair and effortless way of looking elegant, and to her husband Gene, with his forceful way of telling you what possible is. Way back in 1976, the couple's health vision was not widespread — not yet; nevertheless, Gene's teachings constant but seldom welcomed — *Fruits — Vegetables — Seeds, and Nuts.*

I listened to both doling out advice not once . . . more like a thousand times. Names of vegetables I had never heard of and words as foreign as learning a new language. Alfalfa sprout sandwiches? Grass on bread? How could anybody live eating like that? The sounds of certain fruit and vegetable words flew over my head, out of my mind, to be ignored for a long time.

Gene as a young man lived with breathing problems like asthma; the question *Why* had him thinking. He set out to study up nutrition relentlessly. Years later, Gene's findings and studies earned him a degree in Naturopathic Medicine, the title of Nutrition Doctor — simply a hobby, not his profession. In his free hours of a successful, money-making life in land development and real estate, Gene searched for knowledge that paid off immensely — a healthy lifestyle of happiness and feeling good.

"You never know what feeling good means until you know the difference." — Anonymous

Sasha, the couple's Pomeranian with a thick and glossy coat and a curling tail — a vegetarian dog with **no** bad breath in a world without meat, a dog began to awaken my curiosity. Pay attention had started. Sasha never consumed meat all her dog life; bananas were Sasha's favorite. I hated bananas.

A ski weekend in Park City with the Phoenix Ski Club changed my life — an altering event in the early eighties. My whatever shrug turned into ears that listened on a blue-sky ski day. Typically, I hoped to start with a favorite meal for breakfast: French toast and corned beef hash knowing I would worry about the calories later. Not to happen on this specific, sunny, ski-heaven Saturday with predictable lift lines around the block, the end not in sight. Gene, the best skier I had ever seen speeding down a range of runs over the years showing off his dare-devil skillful skiing, acted as our private ski instructor. His words that morning, still today, echo in my ears:

"Let's skip breakfast to beat the lift lines. We can eat a banana on the gondola. You will ski better without a heavy breakfast. More energy — fruits are more energy." He laughed as if to say, w*ait until you find out.*

I'd remember these unquestionably clear words for the rest of my life. As we stepped onto the gondola, with visible resignation I snatched a banana out of Gene's hand, struggling with the certainty of getting nothing weighed against the possibility of getting something. How could I know, on this precise morning, my skiing on the famous slopes of Park City would turn out to be as sensational as any skier hopes for — impressive until today, because of a banana? Fruit is food? Too hard for me to believe in those days. Whereas my body light as a feather with no heavy breakfast weighing me down, I skied exceptionally and full of irrational optimism compared to any other weekend.

"We learn to do something by doing it." — John Holt

Today, my ritual is a banana first thing every morning, persistently. Energy is what I am looking for — fruits are energy, a drug-like experience. Gone from my mind are French toast and all other breakfast goodies, but not from my memory. I try to start the day right and reflect on the power of these words: *"If you eat right not only do you feel better — you will look better."*

When Gene met Judy in the early seventies, Judy's love for steaks, known to all her longtime friends, is a sight I cannot get out of my mind. On any given weekend night out together, I observed Judy attack her steak, and finish with her two hands — not only her steak — she grabbed my leftovers.

Judy, the Vegan, will admit in utter misery, "I did what? I can't believe today how I abused my body. Me?"

In friendship silence, I try not to remind my friend. Now memories only.

Growing up in Switzerland, my overweight chubby body guaranteed unhappy days. Memories drift into my head and carry me back to my young adult years as effectively as any time machine. My American way of life never forgets how I spent those days in self-loathing and self-consciousness. The lack of confidence and self-doubt ruled my teenage life. I pretended disinterest. *Hello, reality.* I was consumed with an overweight complex, being fat and ugly.

I learned how to cover up and hide my bulges. I had a knack for knowing how to dress; my uncanny sense of style

185

proved to be a tremendous help. *Thanks, Mom.* I found ways to look *slender*; people acted surprised when I admitted my true size. Yet how I hated the creeping everyday weight gain.

Chocolate-fanatic, my longing for sweets spelled bliss for short moments only; candies made my eyes bulge. To want something so badly a once-poor youngster never forgets. During a time after World War II when food was in short supply, hungry often, unforgettable is my obsession to buy chocolates as soon as I had earned money, I worked for in my parents' hair salon.

To overcome cravings remained my life. My erratic attempts to eat less still torment me. My life consisted of diet pills — the drug generation had arrived, curbing appetites. I learned to count and watch calories. Fifty pounds overweight . . . when I met Lew, the love of my life, how did he ever look at me twice?

In those magical days of new love, a new rage for losing weight emerged in Arizona in the late sixties. Perfect timing. I started to believe in counting calories. A diet where a doctor gave shots daily, the in-thing, oh so popular. I showed up each morning early at the downtown Scottsdale doctor's office, including a number of my clients. A race between women. Who will appear slim sooner?

I won. I had desperately searched for help and energy of any kind. Yet shots, to count on the assured energy level, as looking better transpired with every pound dropped? No doubt, a scary and getting hooked experience, the drug generation here to stay: no hunger, no cravings, cleaning the kitchen floor at midnight.

I thought I knew it all. I learned from the best: my flabby want-to-be-skinny customers and my mom, never slender (except in her younger years) her constant concern and trying with sight but no vision. I gaze at pictures from those long-ago days and think, *If advertising were needed, I'd qualify.*

Mrs. Wilkins, at the salon every Friday at 10:30 like clockwork, I confided in this elegant, sophisticated, and happily married client. I immensely appreciated her advice about my new love-flame and admirer, Lew. During one of her weekly hair visits, I dared to ask, "How does one know when you are in love?"

Her swift answer: "When you lose weight." I did. I was in love.

Nonetheless, my not-always-understood promise of life did not include any knowledge of eating to live — the healthy way. Today I understand: *Diet* is a four-letter word. I had tried plenty.

A twist of fate, or simply the Hand of God transpired the day I met Judy and Gene at the Phoenix Ski Club in sizzling, glorious, Arizona. A life-shifting time in my life started. Gene and Judy gave me a flicker of motivation that took years to understand and change my attitude. I learned the hard way, with detours: *You are what you eat.* A simple choice between health and illness — literally.

"Give your body a break — abuse means sick." Gene's dramatic words sounded like an echo. "It's all so simple . . . just not simple to do." Staying healthy is a skill.

We humans, are we too complicated to let living to be simple?

Gene's unpretentious words, with more influence than any others, imprinted in my brain, "If you eat fruits, you will have more energy — also, lose weight — not gain weight."

"All glory comes from daring to begin" — Eugene F. Ware

I learned to eat cantaloupe — daily — at one of the most prestigious hair salons where I worked for twenty-two years. I kept an attractive plastic container at my station — I ate one piece at a time — easy to reach with a stunning silver fork, a Christmas gift from one of my classy clients. No offensive chewing, effortless eating since cantaloupe melted in my mouth as I arranged hair with flair. My extremely busy schedule did not allow a lunch break of any kind.

Husband Lew, with his organized-by-nature, compulsive attitude, cut the cantaloupe for me each evening. Three small jars of bite-size melon pieces, so perfect my customers marveled over. With a hint of jealousy, one cool, unblinking loyal lady snarled, "If you had to cut *them* (cantaloupe pieces), you would not eat them."

Lew, the melon-cutter, had a demanding Government job, a most prominent position, but nothing stopped him from preparing cantaloupe for his successful wife.

Love is . . . have it all.

One buzzing Friday morning at the upscale Mahogany salon, one of my cherished customers, who had moved to California, rushed in, ecstatic to find me at the same corner after all those years. She gushed a cheery hello. We hugged like long-lost friends. She let go of me in the middle of our embrace and shrieked, "You are still munching cantaloupe?" She stared at my half-filled bowl. It had been twelve years since I last cut her hair.

Her words reminded me of one day before one of our long-planned trips to Switzerland, going home — an enormously busy day as if I were not ever coming back. Late morning Eileen, my esteemed assistant, loved by everyone, whizzed to fetch my second heaping-full container of cantaloupe from the refrigerator. In her haste, she missed the counter as she rushed to put the jar at its usual place. Oh, noooo — cantaloupe flying to the floor.

My scream woke up everybody at the salon. I shouted, "Eileen, wash them! Move . . ." Sounding too stern, I knew full well I couldn't conquer this monster-day without my energy food. Disbelieving eyes of waiting clients glared at Eileen, still in shock, pick up piece after piece from the hairy floor. Everyone wondered how I could or would I continue to eat that melon mess. I did.

Eating cantaloupe, still? Yes — a regularly asked question, on the contrary, I added mangos — melons of any kind. (Never had heard of melons while in little Switzerland).

I take pleasure in explaining tirelessly how healthy cantaloupe is with all its vitamins.

The dynamics of my world indeed had come to be different, with a smiling face, an everyday proof of healthy and joyful living. Willpower paying off. Filled with wonder and amazement at my accomplishment, the infinite delight of looking better; yet, feeling better is a huge bonus. Priorities rule our lives, all the more now in my busy retired life. Habit, however, can be a wonderful thing.

Give birth to your dreams — you too can do it. Two reasons to eat healthier and eat right: To look better *is* to feel better. The journey is the reward. A steady shimmer of light happens when you realize how much energy you gain facing daily demands and working hard. Discover this yourself on your own body. Come to know firsthand the miracle and nutrition factor of fruits, vegetables, seeds, and nuts. Be kind to your body.

Drink water! A must, absent from my life for too long. The idea, *Water is for poor people* planted in my brain for decades; water simply didn't taste good enough. My parents ordered us kids to drink water, no choice at a time when soda was a treat beyond a dream; a war child during World War II doesn't forget when my family sacrificed and lived without much. My husband, however, taught me to drink water. Shaking my head in bewilderment, I grimaced and stared as he gulped water seemingly all the time. Years later I'd learn.

Most of us, above all older people, do not drink enough pure water. *"Water is the fountain of youth."*

Today I chuckle. Struggling to reach for water is a distant memory. What truly matters is what is *good for your body.* Consumption of water, a fundamental nutrient for all is a vital necessity, beneficial for your digestive system. Lots of times I have repeated Gene's, lingering words, the nutrition doctor's famous words *"The inside needs a bath too."*

Ultimately, I believe water curbs appetite. I squeeze some lemon juice in a delicate Waterford crystal glass (adds glamour), allowing water to taste more satisfactory. No more wishing I had something else. Remember the energy one develops from merely drinking water, as well as a much better mood. Find out!

"The groundwork of all happiness is health." — James Leigh Hunt

"Fat and ugly attacks" still happen — health no-no's repeatedly don't stop me from eating the wrong things, like cheese — wheat — bread tastes fabulous. Swiss chocolate is still my favorite. Stop haunting me!

As the Arizona sun high in the cloudless desert sky shines almost every day, I try hard to get ahold of anything healthy. My sweet tooth is stilled by my identifiable personal mix of walnuts, dates, unsweetened coconut chips, currants or raisins, sunflower seeds, and pumpkin seeds — a mountain of healthy delight.

Hunger, which I basically call a *desire to eat,* makes you reach for precisely anything; but if not in the kitchen, you will not eat it. Be proud of what you store in your refrigerator and reach determinedly for the right food.

They say you must eat to live, not live to eat. An eating addiction is not healthy. The fat-acceptance movement is not something to participate in. Sadly, willpower isn't always enough.

Find someone to do it with — share. Studies show lonely people are less healthy. How I bear in mind the emotional solace in eating. When I first arrived in the United States, alone — homesick — I'd hunt for Sara Lee's German chocolate cake. I drove to the store at ten at night, nauseous the next day, although not only in my stomach. Giving in left me miserable.

Everything in moderation.

You may think no one listens, but *they* hear you; my aloof husband did. No more red meat, a giant step. A Teriyaki steak at our favorite restaurant left us violently ill. A first wake-up call.

Lew watches his weight, on the scales every morning, a sure way to find the road to health. *Praise the Lord.*

I recall an old saying: *Food speaks to your soul.* I often wonder if we endured beforehand the way we feel after overeating we might not do it. Life is a trade-off.

Put up a sign. *"After 5 p.m. is what puts on weight."* A diet doctor's statement from long ago I never forgot. Don't eat late — chew well — slowly. Well-eaten food results in fewer problems with the digestive tract later in life.

Good fortune is a result of careful planning.

Our friends, Judy and Gene are never sick, no catching nagging colds, and their tireless health education and support encourage me and countless others. Words to live by, raw food — green and leafy vegetables — live food (not cooked) — no fast or processed foods — no dairy products — wheat — or meat.

Absence of meat was relatively easy for me to achieve, not a major or favorite part of any meal as a child growing up. Plus, I have my recollections of walking by the butcher shop close to home on the way to school each morning. Kids being kids, we patted the cows and calves tied up outside, huddled in a corner waiting to be slaughtered. We had names for our morning pets as their eyes followed us until the bend in the road.

The corner of the slaughterhouse, a vacant space in the afternoon when we returned after school. My brother's one shriek still buzzes in my ears, pointing to the open door: "Look at the poor animals all bloody hanging on a monster hook."

A picture cast in stone. As children, we woke up to the meaning of slaughter.

Judy, a vegan for years, calls me one of her best students and lets friends know, to anyone she brags about me. Can my caring friend guess how difficult to follow her advice can be? How agony, faith, and belief ruled my days to be a student Judy can be proud of? I came to understand years later from Judy's tiny seed of such praise emerged a flowering of my hopes and dreams that guide me still: feeling and looking better. This goal, a long-lasting achievement, will ultimately define me — already has.

"Happiness lies in the joy of achievement and the thrill of creative effort." — Franklin D. Roosevelt

Unfold your own dream and take control of your destiny by improving your nutrition and lifestyle. Climb your mountain. The Internet is essentially a giant billboard; read books, listen to speakers who promise good health and healthy living. This isn't about separating you from your money; it's about investing in a healthy future.

Do not be satisfied with stories about how things have gone for others. *Live your own story.* Remember: A winner never quits — a quitter never wins. The challenge is in the moment — the time is now. Not tomorrow.

"Live as if you were to die tomorrow . . . learn as if you were to live forever." — Gandhi

You will find yourself easily discouraged by the smallest difficulties, like not having sugar and salt within your reach. Read the ingredients. It's alarming how much salt and sugar exist in too many foods. Cut down on wheat, dairy products, and red meat — they carry the risk of cancer. Your body will love you. Learn the difference, and what not to do; guilt can be your friend when you sneak food you shouldn't.

For every setback, there is a comeback.

Don't dwell on missteps, don't give up on your sense of effort, and forgive yourself. Ice cream does taste better than cantaloupe. The loveliest thing about failure: without you'd never know how delicious success tastes. (Non-dairy ice cream is available).

Acknowledge all healthy choices you make each day — self-esteem will be the reward. To love yourself is to live your best life. Lack of self-esteem is the root of most of our problems. Praise yourself for each small accomplishment. Enthusiasm is contagious. Cherish your body; it is yours this one time only; you are a priority. Welcome the sense of attempt.

Life is not a rehearsal . . . live your best life.

May you look back and comprehend life's true success is, getting up each morning and realizing you have a very good life — no aches!

Feeling good is only defined by knowing the difference. Search, and you will find out. Develop willpower.

The secret of life is Balance. No one's last words ever were, "I wish I'd eaten more celery sticks."

Day-to-day, I live to feel a surge of courage, the power of intention, knowing my path curves in the right direction, dealing with being far from perfect, and aware of what I have yet to learn. I have a huge advantage: if in doubt, I ask. I call Judy. Strong people allow others to help them.

You too can change your destiny by improving your habits, I did. Every so often I cannot believe I did.

Death by food is a slow death. Chronic illnesses can be prevented by healthy lifestyle behavior. Everybody is going to die — not everybody lives. Life is a gift; it is health that is real wealth — not silver and gold.

I dedicate this story to my friends for life, Judy and Gene: My gratitude is endless for their infinite amount of help as I pursue the being-skinny-and-healthy dream. I dare to live today.

Judy, a friend, expected everything of me and wants me to live.

Gene passed away at age 93 of heart failure, during early Covid, alone, the night of his transfer to the Rehab Place. Judy not allowed in, how cruel . . . in 2020, on March 14 — on my mom's birthday.

"Friendship is a promise made in the heart; unbreakable by distance — unchangeable by time." — Malik Macone

Health is the biggest blessing of all. Health is everything. Health is a choice.

Salon Memories

Truly Trudy

Gloria Thomas-Welch, an exceedingly pretty, stunningly dressed lady, I noticed her watching me doing hair, continually, while getting a manicure in 196**8** at Coiffure International, Carsten's salon. Gloria had followed her manicurist to our salon on 5th Avenue in Scottsdale. She sent me smiles once a week. Stares and nods of her head resulted in booking an appointment for her hair. She became my weekly client with a standing appointment every Thursday and followed me to every (**8**) salon location I worked at around town. For forty years.

Truly Trudy

Trudy the darling who's always the same,
So sweet and soft spoken, with no little fame.
Her clients adore her, stay loyal and true,
Her talents so great, no other will do —

Her artistic way when working with hair
Has caused many strangers to just stop and stare.
They ask who it is who does hair with such style,
"She's a Swiss Miss named Trudy," I say with a smile.

Merry Christmas sweet Trudy, and to true love, dear Lou
May God bless you most richly, the whole New Year through.

From one in your
Fan Club for 22 years,
Fondly,
Gloria

193

Woefully, Gloria passed away during one of our bucket-list travels out of the country. Julia, her daughter, my client when she had the nerve to part with a few inches of her stunning long hair, notified me later on of Gloria's final resting place. Paradise Memorial Gardens, our final burial plot Lew and I chose together — prearranged together. Gloria's grave — same spot, a few plots down from us, same shade tree — close to a pond with geese, ducks, and birds. Such a peaceful place amidst the bustle of Shea Boulevard.

Arizona-perfect sunrises and sunsets — a final view for eternity — will surround us when the day arrives.

"People are like stained-glass windows. They sparkle and shine when the sun is out, but when the darkness sets in, their true beauty is revealed only if their light is from within." — Elizabeth Kübler Ross, — Swiss Author

One of many astounding sunsets in Scottsdale, Arizona

You Must Have Been a Beautiful Baby

"Denying the sadness of the world would be denying the magnificence of the beauty that exists in spite of it." — Aryn Kyle

What does a husband feel when hair flies off his adored wife's head as she sits in a barber's chair, his barber for years, who uses a buzzer with its mosquito hum to destroy a dream haircut in one agonizing instant? A stylish cut, given stares and compliments from countless women everywhere. His stomach turns. Fearing for his wife, he holds his breath with a face of crushing sadness, Ready to erupt a volcano stirs inside a husband's soul. His eyes stare at the floor, covered with blonde hair that means the world to his woman, his princess of forty harmonious years. His heartbeat franticly tries to match hers; to live such a monster moment is an experience shared by few.

In no time, a buzzer takes off a most eye-catching shade of blonde hair — hair with a high price tag, revitalized and paid for monthly. A shade achieved by Cara's favorite hair expert, miraculously matching her hair color when Jonas and Cara met in the magical spring of 1951. When Jonas first set eyes on Cara, a natural blonde, his date for the prom fifty-six years ago.

The cold, hard side of life tests Jonas's love and smiley face as he watches Cara's trembling — unstoppable at the switch of the buzzer. In helpless terror, Cara turns in the huge chair that almost swallows her slender body. Cara's sense of glamour deflated, not knowing what to say — knowing to say nothing — ready to scream. A husband and wife's eyes meet through a sea of shimmering tears as hair falls on the old worn tile — a giant moment in a wife's instant bald-head state.

Jonas's face, like a mirror, utters magical words, an echo from across the room to break the eerie silence:

"You must have been a beautiful baby."

The power of words grew huge in a world without hair. A miracle, no less — something so ruined could shine. A life-altering event, the romance of it . . . What a sight into a husband's soul one sizzling Arizona morning, as Jonas was forced to watch helplessly. The big C — Cancer — had called for his love.

No more bad hair days in Cara's life?

At a doctor's office in Mayo Clinic, located on the outskirts of Scottsdale, in the still blooming desert one cloudless day in May 1991, a husband and wife sat close to each other with worried faces. An oncologist, successful for twenty-five years, announced devastating news: lung cancer. Cancer hit their carefree life. (Later in the doctor's career, when he became a cancer victim himself, he found out what survival in actuality means and feels like.)

A desperate embrace of two people in shock was interrupted when a nurse with untidy, no-care hair walked into the freezing, typical Arizona-over-air-conditioned room. Cara and Jonas let go of each other to sit proper and listened to the know-it-all nurse's unfeeling words:

"Shave your hair! It will be easier than watching it fall daily."

One ghastly opinion, spoken by a nurse who unmistakably encountered countless patients dealing with cancer. However, how cruel to shave off anyone's hair, the pride, and glory of a woman's existence. Are there women who don't care? Not to this hairdresser's knowledge. Unimaginable and an undeniable act of self-destruction for a lady like Cara, with a unique air of elegance and glamour. A woman who understood the language of couture advised and helped by her private professional shopper.

***

Cara's panicky phone call to her much-loved hairstylist, one busy Friday morning at her esteemed salon, will remain in my mind forever.

"Trudy, will you shave my hair off?" The quiver in Cara's voice was like a whisper.

"Whaaaat"? I silently squealed. "Mrs. Jenkins, you want me to do what?" Words like a slur, with sinking disbelief I winced as if in pain. Overwhelming hurt surged for one of my favorite customers. Shave off her beloved, attention-getting hair — Cara's exceptional look, which she called a masterpiece created for her only, different from all other women? How could I say no to one of my long-time clients in obvious agonizing pain?

Cara's horror-stricken voice saddened me immensely. If I could have cleared my mind of Cara's words and wished them gone, then perhaps I could convince myself they had not been spoken but they had.

Breath catching in my throat I hesitated. On the edge of decision, I think I shouted,

"Noooo! I don't think I can."

I closed my eyes at the image of Cara's anguish dealing with the battle of cancer. I listened to her depressing news; my knees had gone weak.

"My husband's barber will," Cara yelled.

I grasped for my heart as if to hold it not to burst. Did it skip a beat? *How can words hurt and help at the same time?* It was of serious importance and abundantly clear I had to help somehow. With a measure of hope, a sudden thought had entered my mind. In mere seconds, I knew what to do. I tried to breathe; it was one of those moments where I could easily stop. I trembled as I mumbled,

"I will help you find the perfect wig."

Feeling a sense of relief, I now was crying behind my hand when Cara uttered words, I never thought I'd hear:

"I'll go to Jonas's barber. He listens. He will shave my hair."

Click. The phone went dead.

My stomach felt like turning. I tried to compose myself. From numerous cancer-stricken clients, I knew about the unbearable methods to deal with this devastating illness. The ultimate agony is the no-hair problem: long hair does not look like cancer. No eyebrows left, hair ending up in hands, mostly in the shower, like a monster appearing to scare you. A picture with no frame. Nonetheless, I also knew sometimes doctors were wrong, and some women's hair never fell out during chemotherapy. All depended on the needed strength of treatments.

With a potent mixture of sadness, I convinced myself, a one-minute shave of a modern hairstyle desired by innumerable women, was not in my job description. Seeking the joys of hair, I returned to the lady waiting in my chair, whose natural curls somehow shown more beautiful than before that desperate call.

Years ago, when Mrs. Jenkins first set foot into the fancy Mahogany salon in downtown Scottsdale, my racing thoughts of my busy schedule left me with anxious speculations. *Another new customer? Can I handle one more?* Knowing pressure is a privilege, I glanced at this sophisticated woman with a regal air look around and gasp at the number of clients waiting. I hoped she'd get scared off.

Cara ignored my worries. At each appointment, she brought a book and patiently waited her turn. On one of her visits, she carried a huge book. With my comb I pointed to it, shaking my head:

"It won't take that long." She smiled; in a way, a busy hairdresser does not forget.

Cara Jenkins' monthly visits included gossiping about her affluent circle of friends and family and bragging about her husband Jonas. Laughter and interaction with countless customers and can-you-top-this stories between women at the hairdresser's; hearing is believing. The smells of salon products and hair dyes possibly caused everybody to become lightheaded, yakking, and babbling even more.

Cara loved the new talk of the town Mahogany salon, a free-standing, imposing building with the unfamiliar layout of a sunken hair-dryer area in the middle of the huge rectangular room. Live plants, the rage of that era, decorated the corners and specific spaces. What a display of elegance; yet its cozy appearance gave a feeling of home to a salon written up in *National Hair Magazine* because of its uniqueness, serving men and women. *Unisex*, a new buzzword in the seventies. My day-to-day hair-heaven, back in the corner, consisted of two stations, (like Dad) a brand-new leather couch, and three fashionable, comfy chairs along the wall for my customers to wait and be spoiled by my assistant Eileen and Arlene later.

Mrs. Jenkins' instant trust let me accomplish her individual look. For years, we both received and experienced compliments, at times beyond comfort.

Cara lived the power of hair. Hair is a feeling.

This lady easily was a stylist's dream customer, without the usual orders: not too short, cover my ears, leave the back long. Her one wish: no bangs. She adored one style that made me famous, a distinctive look, a bouffant, no-helmet-like hairdo with flair. Hair flipping away from the face undeniably added youth to any visage.

Cara kept her hair looking remarkable between visits, a walking advertisement. I marveled at her knowledge of style and clear desire for classy dressing with utmost care. She regularly got stared at and admired by clients at our hectic high-class salon.

In the life of hair designers, numerous times we feel the agony of unreasonable, never-making-sense wishes from demanding clients. They point to pictures when all I can think or reply,

"I am a beautician, not a magician."

Yet with Cara's look, the magic of cutting emerged, often my own eyes hardly believed the capability of hair to astonish customers.

I lived for creating the perfect style for my clientele. I believed customers did not pay me for hair I cut off — they paid me for the hair I left on. My motto: *I don't cut hair to be short; I cut hair to look good.* Indelibly imprinted in my head are the words of one of my customers of thirty-three years. At my retirement party, a lunch at the Chart House given by my clients, in a note she wrote, *"Trudy, you gave us what we didn't know we wanted."*

The dynamics of hair and bad hair days reclaimed Cara's daily life. Pockets of paradise ignited a cloudy Arizona sky with ecstatic news: cancer-free. Free of lung cancer for twenty years now, a statistical miracle. No more feeling powerless. No more wig days like a hat reaching her nose infrequent gusts of desert winds. Gone were the days of a hairy hat never allowing Cara to feel beautiful. The wig to cover her baldness during those difficult months simply rendered Cara apathetic and feel naked behind lifeless hair. Nevertheless, she admitted I managed to style her rag-wig to be striking.

Nonetheless, Cara found a magical seed of gratitude in a barbershop one roasting Arizona morning. Words Cara would remember for the rest of her life: *You must have been a beautiful baby.* In Cara's darkest losing-her-hair moments, the power of words triggered a profound closeness to the man she proudly bragged about to anybody who would listen, "Jonas asks me every morning what I would like for dinner."

A cooking husband? Jonas cooked daily for his wife after he retired. Through books, the Internet (a billboard of knowledge), and with the help of friends, Jonas and Cara learned about healthy cooking and eating. He admits, "We woke up. We now check and appreciate the value of nutrition."

Staying healthy is a skill.

Cara and Jonas believe the world deserves to know, good nutrition can and does save lives. *Health is a choice! Simply eat better — make healthy choices.*

Love is known to have no boundaries. What a treasure. A couple now for sixty years, parents to one daughter who lives close by, they look at each other with eyes of immense love in life for better and for worse, a marriage filled with a glow of maybes when they were young.

Cara learned the rough and turbulent way; prayers carried her and Jonas. Nothing fuels a life quite like hope with the presence of God. How we live in our heads more than any place — aware of that more when things don't go well. What matters is the way we choose to remember how a whole life can come crashing down in a single moment, in June one blistering Scottsdale day. We live for changes — how do we handle them?

Jonas and Cara now live up north. They traded the big-city life for the cool country, the Arizona woods where their dream house became reality — a long-time desire of the Jenkins. They truly live a life thankful for all things, unpretentious things. Now gazing at sunsets, a little longer, when the sun turns an unusually deep color, like an overripe orange falling from the tree to become part of the earth, in a sky the colors of old China dishes. More than ever, they feel the wisdom that sees the ordinary with amazement. Contentment is one of their utmost blessings.

This twosome knows comfort is luxury.

God with His heavenly source of unseen power fills the life of a marriage, joined through tragedy and helpless moments of terror. A couple lifted from a spiraling freefall filled with hours of doctor visits and sleepless nights. Cara and Jonas learned health is their fundamental wealth.

One more thing. . .

Cara passed away on November 29th, 2019, at 86 years old.

In October, by divine chance, we detected Cara eating lunch with her husband, daughter, and other family members at LIV Generations, a newly opened Senior Living community apartment residence. Thoughts of our old-age future, Lew's and mine, on our minds for some time had found a way of creeping in. We walked around with the classy lady tour director we had made an appointment with to show us the facilities. Startled Lew spotted the Jenkins name on a door as we entered a hallway, where assisted living is provided. We were told Cara and Jonas had moved there in July, four months ago.

Some things are simply meant to be.

It would be the last time I'd hug this now frail lady with a stringy ponytail tied with a red bow on the neck of her head, who was mystified to see me and Lew, as we interrupted her lunch. Cara's voice still as commanding as ever, annoyed at the food on her plate, barking at the waitress for everyone to cringe and feeling awkward; we did not stay long. Cara's day, not her best, she was in pain. I managed to whisper in her ear as I hugged her goodbye, "Cara, you beat cancer for many years."

"Yes, I did." She shouted.

Last words I would remember her by.

We attended the funeral in December, her favorite month of the year. How fitting, since our dinners at the Hassayampa Inn in Prescott, while they lived up there, repeatedly happened on the first Friday in December, for several years, the weekend of the Courthouse Lighting ceremony.

Every time we saw each other included some hair snipping in the restaurant Ladies Lounge, or at her home. I would bring the gold-plated scissors Cara adored. Shears I had found and brought back from a visit at my much-loved hair supply store one summer in Switzerland. Each time I cut Cara's hair with that elegant tool put a terrific smile on her face.

Scissors, that matched the jewelry on my fingers.

["You Must Have Been a Beautiful Baby," published in Goose River Press *Anthology 2018* in October.]

Trudy Wells-Meyer

Song of Life

*"One word or a pleasing smile is often enough to raise up a
saddened and wounded soul."* —
Thérèse of Liseux

Sunlight fills her face, her smile and outstretched hand,
singing in the wind her heart she'd offer to anyone,
a blessing to value this Colorado lady who does
not know the meaning of not loving.

Love and you shall be loved.

They say joy is a choice; this remarkable lady who believes in
the good of mankind, she sees stars beyond her sight.
Oh, how I have come to love her joyful embrace
of life, in a growing collection of memories.

A woman young at heart.

Her kindness, a blue-sky Tsunami towering over everyone,
words and smiles touch shoppers in the mall, — the salon —
anytime.
Dallas her name finds the music in her world like a bridge
in the sky, a winner in the game of life.

A lady clear of mystery.

Wrinkles don't age, not smiling does — bony hands and loving
pink, always a beauty of design walking in like royalty, except
her limp curls all but cover her head, a cry for help,
a pleading stare I felt on the back of my neck.

Elegant is her middle name.

A resigned bad-hair day would bloom once again, her giant
smile to match, how high her hair should be, how I tried
to hide my cringe, *yes — higher — please.*
Closer to God, she'd say.

As if it wasn't already.

Every Wednesday she went to the mall, parading her hair, shop
at her favorite store, long-ago-fashion we'd see once a week,
heads turning, her taste impeccable, clothes and jewelry,
that would become mine, — *hand-me-downs* with style,

I still wear with pride.

The tide of time has caught up, bygones of yesterday, no more
winter trips for Arizona sun but, twice a year brings us back
to Grand Junction, her home, to find her smile — a smile,
the shortest distance between friends.

The lady with a smile for everyone.

Memories, the colors of the desert in the spring, a display of
stars, as a pharmacist's wife, a cocktail of wisdom and
knowledge,
to stay healthy I call, hear a smile in her voice,
love from afar, a miracle cure on the way.

Kindness delivered surrounded by love.

A belief in the presence of God, she keeps on sailing within the
sun, smiles for everyone, the fullness of her joy like a glass
of warm spiced wine for the soul ignites feelings
hidden from too many out in the cold.

Where love was never not meant to be.

A hush of surprise, thank God for a daily click on a machine,
called a computer, only one e-mail away. Dressed in one of her
gifts with class — I love them all, I write these words,
for a rare jewel, a lady who believes feeling good —

Starts with looking good.

A smile to follow me to the end of time, illuminated by the
setting sun, her way most likely to cheer up someone's day,
and before sleep, to make a memory,
God wants to keep.

May love guide your life, spread joy, and kindness . . . Smile.

Dallas, the lady of joy, every day for three weeks during my broken-leg ordeal, while locked up in the upstairs bedroom, sent a snail-mail card. To know joy is to give joy. . .

Boat House restaurant, Yampa River, September 9, 2011, Art's birthday

A two-day visit with Dallas and her companion Art in Steamboat Springs, to celebrate a milestone birthday. When Art saw the Yampa River, he turned extremely nostalgic. He pointed to certain rocks and with amazing certainty, he uttered, "I remember those stones right at the water's edge. I fished here with my father when I was a teenager."

Art, a widower from Mesa, Arizona, where Dallas and her husband's winter home was located, neighbors for years playing cards regularly. A foursome enjoying dinner parties and fun at the golf course.

Art called Dallas after his wife Jeanette had passed. Dallas, a widow for some time, started to write notes and letters to Art. He kept calling.

Life is beautiful and gave the two 'lovebirds' four stimulating years together.

["Song of Life" published in October in the 18th Goose River Press *Anthology 2020*.]

The Power of Giving

"Love and you shall be loved." — Ralph Waldo Emerson

"Why do hairstylists who charge me outrageous prices, and I give them a tip, expect a gift from me at Christmas? Enough is enough."

This quote, in the daily Arizona newspaper during the holiday season, lit a spark of writer's inspiration for my story.

I am one of those expensive, Swiss-born hairstylists. Tremendously fortunate and privileged throughout the years with a hard-working career in several hectic, high-class salons in America, I collected countless thoughtful gifts at Christmas time — they are a perpetual treasure to me. Some gifts are truly beyond belief, like Waterford crystal from Ireland (unknown to me at the time) — a collection of crystal glasses. Weekly coifed, permed, and regularly colored Shirley Murley, an inspiring lady with a caring heart to burst and constant giving, gave me the crystal for Christmas and my October birthdays. She incredibly let me select from the luxurious range of patterns: I chose Alana. In addition, every year Lew included in her generous giving: one Christmas a coffee machine for his office.

Retired now, in a world without hairdos and hair worries, which I have to admit I miss at times, what I remember most is how much those remarkable gifts humbled me.

One gift will remain indelibly engraved in my heart, from a lady with an air of glamour and New York elegance, Angela Carrington. She was my customer once a week for over thirty years in an era when women did not shampoo their hair themselves. A stunning lady, tall, demanding and stern, yet with a sense of grace and a face with crushing gloominess. As a client, she commanded attention the minute she walked in. Mrs. Carrington, a widow for years, with most piercing eyes knew the pain of losing a loved one, her daughter, to suicide. Sorrow never spoken is the heaviest load to bear.

Angela's overbearing way, as she gossiped about her wealthy circle of friends to other waiting clients, and her senseless, constant complaining and total lack of ability to tell her stylist what she essentially wanted to be done with her hair, were at times simply unbearable. I endured a once-a-week search for a wave that only looked good without her pushy New York directions. Angela did not let me forget New York is where people know more than anywhere else.

205

"Put the wave higher."

I did.

"Lower on my forehead," she smirked.

I did.

"No, higher."

When I'd say black, she said white. I'd say white because I knew she would say white.

"No — black." No winning, ever.

Her huge dislike of waiting for her turn left me extremely edgy. Irritated too often, my insecurity showed the minute I saw her waltzing in. Another wave-lecture. I still recall resisting the urge numerous times to yell, throw my comb, rip out her rollers and tell her to go somewhere else. Mostly, I tried to improve my not-so-perfect smile and listen to my husband's advice: "Why don't you try to be nice to her?"

Angela Carrington never tipped me. She'd say: "You are rich enough." However, my longtime, favorite assistant Arlene received a surprisingly generous tip on each of her visits, as did any of the assistants who worked for me during those thirty years.

Never a Christmas gift. When Mrs. Carrington walked in during the holiday season, staring at all the fancy wrapped presents my clients had left for me — small, big, all sizes piled on and around my two busy stations — I can still hear her demeaning voice: "What are you going to do with *it* all? You probably can't use any of *it.*"

Those powerful words left me feeling disheartened, sad and shaking my head.

One late morning on Christmas Eve, five months before I retired from my booming American salon life, Angela arrived for her weekly wave-bouffant hairdo. She carried a package in her hand wrapped with care, more dazzling than all the other gifts. I almost dropped my valued scissors — the client in my chair — her hair slipped out of my hand.

In total disbelief, I flashed a smile of surprise. I stared at Angela's rare smile as she placed the precious gift in the back of the pile. I swallowed. A sudden lump had formed in my throat trying my best to act indifferent. Tears I was not prepared for filled me with unknown pleasure. My eyes watered like a nasty cold.

Rushing over to Angela, I hesitated and stopped. She stretched out her arms . . . we hugged. A hug that felt endless with no words exchanged, a moment of such intense connection, experiencing rare emotions. To see and hear Angela's tears let mine fall and join in.

Christmas truly at its best. Memories are forever. An unexpected gift is the finest kind.

Wondering what caused the change of heart reminds me of a quote:

"*You cannot do a kindness too soon, for you never know how soon it will be too late.*" — Ralph Waldo Emerson

Delighted it happened is the memory I will treasure.

What was in the package may not matter. Nevertheless, a client's treasured hug and rare almost-smile, a moment in time where a customer and a hairstylist shared an unmatched bond, is carved in stone — will last forever.

***

That spring in 2005, at an elaborate, yearly Charity Cancer Ball in Arizona, I showed off that thoughtful, exceptional gift given by a woman who knew style and class: a dazzling black, jeweled flower pin on my neck, fastened to a black choker I had owned for years and found in a drawer.

A sparkling, black-jeweled flower pin was a first.

During my life of doing hair with flair and famous for my unique love of flowers, frequently I pinned a silk flower to my outfit, a perfect match with whatever I wore. The talk of the town, a hairdresser who believed in dressing for success.

One such day, a monthly client could not believe how dressed up I was. She flung herself in my chair with a smirk, "You look like you are going to a wedding."

She chuckled at my answer.

"If I don't look good, how can you expect me to make you look good?"

I sent Angela that stunning picture, captured by a professional photographer at the fancy ball. I tried to imagine her smile, as I hoped her grief and torment would leave her eyes like the moon with its glint lets stars disappear. In my heart, I knew for one unique moment Angela encountered happiness. Her prompt response in an e-mail, and rare words of praise I longed to hear for so long, I will cherish, always. Never, in our thirty years together at the salon, had I received any praise from her. As Lew would console me: "Yet, she comes back every week. . ."

Our war of words had stopped. Angela Carrington's buried kindness had awakened.

Receiving is extremely special . . . **Giving** is what warms your heart.

Do not learn to love too late.

Three months later, one blistering Saturday in June, I came home from a whoppingly busy day at the salon. I noticed a stack of new business cards on the kitchen bar/counter, near my favorite chair. Lew, my computer-savvy mastermind husband (I could not imagine a life without his thoughtfulness) created the cards on his computer. He had hunted for the picture from the Cancer Ball with the outstanding, jeweled flower pin, Angela's gift.

How to remember a special gift . . . always.

By the way . . .

Angela and I e-mailed every so often; her name in my inbox brought joy. Angela turned 96 in 2016.

Mrs. Carrington was the bossy client in my chair on that grief-stricken hot summer August Saturday in 2003. Mom's last phone call to say goodbye from across the ocean at the beauty shop that morning I broke down in hysteric collapse — unstoppable crying. The day Mom died; I learned Angela had a heart with rare yet forever cherished compassion on display.

["The Power of Giving" essay won third place at the Appalachian Heritage Writer's Symposium, May 2017.]

Not Choosing . . . Is That Still a Choice?

"Happiness is not the absence of problems but the ability to deal with them." — Charles de Montesquieu

She walked on the thin edge of dusk
when death flaps in like a wounded angel.
A long sigh of exasperation as though there was no hope.
Trains of sadness rumble through the crossings
like a mural's life.
Karlee's appearance — a disfigured mouth — noticed more
when she spoke.
Did anyone know — guess — her tide of disillusion and
despair?
Nobody heard her fear, her profound solitude — loneliness.
                    No light above her dark.

Karlee, a night nurse — no dinners, no dates, no dancing,
my client every other month,
early am, right after work,
a long night shift, on the way home to sleep.
Her golden hair without dependence on chemicals,
women pay for regularly,
a haircut triggered a rare smile each time,
                    head held high for a little while.

One hectic salon morning, her appointment at 6:30 am,
I phoned the day before,
tried to leave a message, *"No need to rush."*
She walked in at 6, thirty minutes early.
I shouted, "Karlee, you don't have an answering machine?"
Her words echoed, still, always,
"No! I don't want to come home and find no one called."
Lonely — a mysterious unmapped zone, as clear as reality,
spelled profound sadness.
If only I had seen her darkness,
                    to help see the light.

The life of Karlee disappeared from light but not from memory.
In her garage they found her — dead — windows closed.
Her separate world, a dent in time,
a hot calm August night, too late — in husky silence
desperate for breath,
did she try to claw her way out? To what . . . nothing.
Shock, stiff with grief limits to the unbearable,
I could see her not smiling, its hidden meaning,
she had the look of tears never shed,
                              profound unbroken solitude.

I stood and caught my breath before shivering at the news.
The tremendous fragility of a human heart,
eyes empty of tears descending into darkness.
Not choosing, is that still a choice . . .
Not choosing — is a choice.

The Ring

*"The road to heaven and the human heart is amazingly short
when priceless diamonds from the past are involved."* —
Anonymous

As I arrived at the downtown Scottsdale mortuary, the home of final goodbyes and viewings, where countless sad hearts had gone before, hesitating, I opened the door with a hefty hand. The body of my Arizona Mom, Margo Becket, was ready for me to add the final touch; my first time to style hair on a deceased person.

I still can feel my slow, timid steps toward the casket near the back wall, feeling safe from a distance. Unknown emotions surrounded me for what I might encounter. I stood in front of Margo's rich, opulent casket, experiencing the opposite of what I had visualized; I found out "perfect" does not always look like we imagine.

I gasped in disbelief as I stared at Margo's peaceful face, with the rare smile I had loved for years. All gussied up to be seen in heaven, she showed pain no longer. The word *beautiful* was simply too weak. However, one thing remained, to fix flat hair and perform my magic with her favorite hairstyle — an act of love.

A sense of gratitude surfaced being here with my dead client, whom I had known for more than thirty years. This was my parting gift, a promise for Margo to look regal one last time for eternity. A lump rose in the back of my throat as I gazed at her favorite ivory and gold dress, which I helped pick out for a fancy black-tie wedding sixteen years ago. Her cherished pearls and earrings were glowing in the light, and her smile expressed, *I look good.*

On her folded hands, her most treasured diamond ring, a spectacular anniversary gift from Stewart, was missing. I had never seen her without. Thoughts of her promise swirled in my brain; words exchanged on countless Fridays at the beauty shop:

"You fix my hair when I die — the ring is yours."

With unsure hesitation, I touched her lifeless hair. Curls were needed for sure. I tried to achieve the style countless women admired constantly, I got demoralized. My hands shook when I discovered her head slightly raised on a piece of wood, on a wood pillow, glued on the back of the skull and stapled. I had chills. Where did Margo's hair go? Her forehead was never that big; it had been pulled up high for the skin to look tight.

Her beauty wrecked but still evident, I realized only the front and top mattered for styling. My characteristic routine of whipping hair into instant glamour did not happen.

Give her bangs! A new look to parade in heaven, yet I felt guilty. Margo had never desired a different style.

***

With a mad nobility and regal elegance, demanding and stern, Margo Maria Becket knew what she wanted. She possessed an odd, recognizable voice, a loud voice — shrieky almost. Margo was my weekly client for years, my Arizona Mom, a widow with an extreme sense of style somehow more noticeable in a desert town, where fanatical casualness lets people dress down and blame the heat. In Arizona, a flip-flop state — I mean sandals — they show up half-naked at the supermarket, at restaurants — anywhere, anytime. Margo's fierce intention to look one's best each day matched my own.

Her shy smile had an awkward time surfacing. Yet when it did, still today, I can see it shine.

Mrs. Becket entered the new, fancy Mahogany hair salon one Friday afternoon to ultimately check me out and interview me.

That same morning, Margo had her hair done up north at a slow-paced, less busy Scottsdale salon. My ex-assistant Maxine, the kindest person I know, had shampooed her hair. Sadly, with a heavy heart, I had let Maxine go because she was sick with daily pains and could not keep up with my schedule, nor handle the pressure of pleasing as many clients as I demanded of her each day. As she listened to Margo Becket's weekly complaining, mostly about her dislike of the number of stylists who tried but couldn't fix her hair, Maxine whispered in her soap-filled ears, "Go and see Trudy downtown, at Mahogany's."

Margo yelled, "Who?"

Mrs. Becket searched for a salon named Mahogany on Indian School Road. The same afternoon she entered and commanded attention not only by her appearance but by a voice that could scare a fish.

"Where is Trudy?" Her voice echoed to the back corner of our buzzing salon, where my hair-heaven was located.

On a frantic Friday, Ricardo, my boss and salon owner, walked Mrs. Becket to my bustling corner to introduce us. This lady, who displayed the language of couture, caused me to look up, stop cutting hair, and nearly forget the client in my chair. Margo's bashful almost smile surprised me; however, I stared in astonishment at the gorgeous jewelry layered around her neck and ears and at the way she held her hands, showing off four rings. A dazzling, jumbo-sized diamond ring on her index finger triggered my heart to hiccup.

My full schedule left me with head-scratching speculations: *Another new weekly customer?* I watched her look around and put her hand with the eye-catching ring on her mouth as if to say, *No way.* She gasped at my waiting clients. I knew waiting would scare her off.

Wrong. Margo Becket's newfound hairstylist passed the interview, answering questions that sounded distressed. She pleaded and whined about hair never short enough — too long in the wrong places — the color never blonde enough.

"Trudy, can you fit me in, once a week, and work with me?" shrieked the classy lady with hopeful eyes.

"I can try. I cut hair to look good, not to be short," I answered, flashing a smile. I wished I could whip her hair into place right then since I knew instantly which style would look good on this hairdresser-hating, unhappy person.

On the way out, this stunning woman with bad hair made a standing appointment for every Friday — simply unheard-of — a decision without experiencing and knowing how I would style her hair.

Margo Becket turned out to be a dream client. No complaints about her hair or waiting her turn. She adored one style, my unique, signature look that added youth to her visage, hair flipping away above her left eye, a backcombed but not helmet-like hairdo with a twist of blonde glamour.

They called her "sexy grandma."

Our upscale salon became Mrs. Becket's weekly home. For twenty-eight years her outing to the beauty shop, at 12:30 every Friday, included listening to her valued Swiss-born hairstylist Trudy, gibbering about her exceedingly happy marriage. It reminded Margo, widowed for many years, of her own past life. Her unique smile would appear, and with faraway eyes, she would ask about Lew, Trudy's brilliant, with a degree from the school of life, genius-husband.

Margo loved to compare Lew with Stewart, her long-time husband who had passed away of complications from a heart attack long ago. Her smile grew titanic as she transported

213

herself back to her heavenly life, listening to how Trudy could not imagine a day without Lew touching her face.

Over and over Margo would ask about the gentleman who had become my world. Lew, like Stewart, was one of those men whose presence attracted notice at any gathering, anywhere. Lew radiated a positive, constant smile, a distinctive tilting of his head as he fitted his cigarette far back next to the knuckles, not ordinarily used or seen. "Just like my Stewart," Margo would sigh with dreamy eyes.

She relived her life weekly at the beauty shop.

Mrs. Becket in awe of my blissful, whirl-wind life and remarkable career, her questions most Fridays were the same, about my love life. She endlessly compared my stories with hers about her beloved Stewart — a privileged life, no doubt. Memories, like random photographs, filled her mind as she touched and caressed the amazing diamond ring on her right index finger, a spectacular dome setting studded with glittering jewels.

I stared at the blinding beauty once a week. Everybody did. The ring was a seventeenth-anniversary gift with seventeen giant diamonds. Frequently I had listened to that romantic instant when Margo's Stewart presented his wife with the magical surprise. Proudly she wore the precious ring every day, such as on her daily walk to feed the ducks at a pond close to home. Some Fridays she handed me the magnificent rock to wear while I combed her hair. The first time, I hardly believed how perfectly the ring fit on my index finger.

I joked, "Margo, now watch your hair turn out even more chic." I felt the stares of my waiting customers. All through my days at any salon in different parts of America, I was known for my love of jewelry. Six rings on my hands: a norm, notably matching my outfits.

"*How can she work with all those rings?*" Customers whispered and mumbled.

When Mrs. Becket entered, reliably on time like clockwork, she paraded in her elegant way with hair still in place after one week of not washing it. (Those were the days.) Curious clients stared and admired her at our hectic, high-class salon.

Ardis, another long-time weekly client, a divorcée who had "landed" a new millionaire husband she met on a plane to Denver, sat in my chair one such Friday. Her rare sense of humor provided hilarious moments, weekly entertainment for most clients. Ardis, ready to leave and be seen with her high-styled hair, watched Margo join the Friday gang.

Ardis snapped, "What the f*** are you doing here? Your hair looks terrific!"

"Well, I sleep alone," Margo shouted. The whole salon giggled.

Nothing could stop or spoil Margo's Friday at the chatty beauty shop. Her escape to the hair salon turned into fun and enjoyment, and ultimately glamorous again when she left. Margo sat patiently on one of the side chairs along the wall, repeatedly the end one so as not to seem brash while waiting her turn. Often, with a ghost of a wink directed at me, she'd say in unusually soft-spoken words, "When I come here, I don't plan anything else." With a *thank-you* on my silent lips, I gave her a heartfelt nod with love for her eyes only.

My Arizona Mom helped me bear my hectic schedule; wise words remain unforgettable: "Your talent is a gift from God; what you make of it is your gift to God."

If judged by the hair-world on how many clients waited at one time — I had to be the winner. Margo taught me pressure is a privilege, to enjoy my gift of making women happy.

I lived to find the perfect hairstyle for each one.

Now retired, I reminisce about the days during my artistic American hair life, times when I was jolted with the force of my identifiable creativity. Somehow, I knew what to do straight away and how to handle hair with ease, the ever-glowing crown of women, my fussy male clientele included. (Endless watching Mom and Dad as a kid for years — incomparable learning.)

The dynamics of my world reflected each day on my cheerful face. Hair is power. Not to say I did not know rejection. The more hopefully I anticipated the start of a client-stylist relationship, the more painful at the end, with no call-back and cancellations for reasons seldom known or understood.

***

After twenty-two years, Mahogany salon closed its doors. The building situated in the way of the main street to be widened, resulted in money to attain for the overjoyed owner Riccardo. My clients and I relocated to a new, gorgeous salon, a job offer with lots of space at an ex-jewelry store with soft ceiling lighting, a bonus for customers' skin and hair to appear more striking.

A promise that started one memorable Friday is simply the reason for this story. Roy Becket, Margo's younger son from Chicago, had come to visit. In mother's fancy car, he drove her to the front entrance, for the usual weekly appointment. I was flipping my Arizona Mom's hair into shape and style when Roy walked in to pick her up for a late lunch.

In her shrill voice, she commanded, "Roy, come here!" She pointed to the exquisite ring on her aged hand. "When I am dead and leave this world, I want you to give this ring to Trudy. She promised to continually wear it at the beauty shop when she creates magic with her clients' hair."

Her words echoed around the sophisticated salon on this unusually noiseless Friday. Clients gasped.

***

Retirement didn't stop me from doing Margo's hair. I went

to her home. No longer every Friday. We met on whatever day when Lew and I were in Scottsdale. Our continuous traveling required unique planning at times. My trips to the assisted-living rehab center, where Margo resided for weeks because of a critical fall, turned into inspiring fun at their tiny in-house salon. I paraded her like a queen in a wheelchair down the long corridor so she could show off her hair to many of the elderly residents. Some of the ladies' hopeful eyes and whispers, *Can you do my hair?* still, haunt me.

Roy, the big-town Chicago son, took care of his mother after falls happened too often, caused by age and excessive medication. The first fall in her bathroom broke her jaw. Later, in her small kitchen, she lay for hours with nobody to find her — nobody to call 9-1-1. A broken hip led to other extreme problems. More medication? Why so much? How do pills know where to go once swallowed — to the left, to the right, where? A pill cocktail in your stomach?

Margo remained bound to a wheelchair, leaving her angry and hopeless. Roy moved in with Mom.

My final trip to fix hair at her home, in the fancy dining room, will linger in my heart. On this specific day in 200**8** —

ironically, a Friday — Margo's frail state calm; pain gone, maybe? Her yelling and screaming had stopped. The shrill voice was mercifully silenced. I sensed an aura. *It's time.* She held my hand with a touch of love so strong for a weak, skinny lady, a parting gift I would cherish for a long time. Still, now I can feel a vital need to hug Margo longer than usual, to not let go.

At the bend outside the entry door, I turned. I smiled without much joy, but still a smile. Roy had pushed her wheelchair to the open door. I waved, blowing a kiss at my Arizona Mom with perfect hair, to revert to bed and sleep — an instant flattened mess in the back no doubt. As I walked down the balcony corridor to the elevator of the Beckets' condo complex, I experienced a chill only I could feel, as if knowing it was the last time. Everything suddenly was still. Not even the birds were singing.

***

A deafening cell phone ringing interrupted the newfound pride in my retired, like-a-vacation life, cutting roses in our incredibly splendid garden. I listened to Margo's devoted son Roy; his voice dejected with news of Mom's death. I leaned back against the wrought-iron rail, the brilliant glittering lake behind me, Camelback Mountain in the distance, while my soil-covered handheld the phone. I rubbed my eyes with the other. Roy's deliberate words echoed in my ears: "Mom has gone to heaven."

In that instant, my eyes stopped on a single yellow rose — the only yellow in the middle of a choice of pink ones. Yellow — Margo's favorite color. I trembled. I must have looked downright ill. I shivered at this heart-stopping moment of importance, as one breathtaking yellow rose let me see Margo as big as life. Like the opening of a floodgate, I wept. Timing in life — the mystery — oh, I wondered often why I had purchased and planted a yellow rose bush amidst varieties of pink, my favorites. Now I knew.

"When is the funeral?" I stammered.

I could feel Roy's tears and hear them as he whispered in a voice not sounding like his. I hardly had the heart to inform Roy of our upcoming month-long trip, arranged and planned long ago, leaving the morning of the funeral. Such is life.

His sorrow and personal sense of tragedy touched me deeply as I told him about staring at this single yellow rose in bloom in our garden, knowing full well Roy knew what yellow roses meant to his mom. I cried uncontrollably — knowing grief has many faces.

Nevertheless, I knew immediately what to do, and the full realization struck with such force I threw a chair over with the shock of it. *I must go to fix Margo's hair.* I rushed into the house to search for the mortuary's phone number. A promise came alive — a promise I never thought I would have to keep — her wish for her hair to look perfect when she arrives in heaven.

"You know you have to fix my hair when I die." Margo's often-spoken words had found a way to haunt me. After an exceptionally successful career where customers lined up, one may wonder why I had never, in all those years, performed any hairdo service at a mortuary. I believed I couldn't.

"Let's hope God will call you home on Friday afternoon after you had your hair done." My hesitant, unconvinced answer left Margo frowning each time.

She passed away on a Friday, early in the morning.

I winced as if in pain. I could not clear my mind of Margo's words. Wishing them gone did not convince me they had never been spoken — they had. With a deep breath, I dialed the number of the mortuary. A tremendously kind voice set me at ease. We arranged a time on Monday, the day before the funeral, the day before our long trip.

***

I silently prayed as I labored on her final goodbye hairstyle with three-day-old dead hair in my hands, foreign to my touch. Hair I had known and had added glamor to for more than thirty years, now let me down — I felt like a failure — yet my final hairdo for Margo ended up a new look for eternity. I simply hoped her days in heaven turned into fun, parading her new hairstyle, good enough to last forever.

Roy, who had promised to meet me at the mortuary, his eyes watching me from the back of the room, added to my anxiety. He had come up behind me, "Mom looks beautiful."

He joined my tears. His words helped tremendously.

"The ring is missing. Margo, without her ring?" I mumbled.

Roy answered with a voice above a whisper, "It's yours now." He choked up. "Mom wanted you to have her favorite ring. A promise is a promise."

Startling feelings emerged as my thoughts traveled to that Friday when the promise had started, for me to have the admired ring. When I agreed to fix Margo's hair one final time at the mortuary, to travel in style to the big garden in the sky.

The desire to give this dynamic gem to her hairstylist, not written in Margo's will, became an issue with the Beckets' huge estate. The son, as the executor, had to convince the lawyers. His brother, who never visited his mom, the estranged son, had to be contacted. He couldn't have cared less.

After our extended travel, I found a most heartfelt thank-you note from Roy between bills and junk mail held by the post office. He wrote to please let him know instantly when we returned to town. To get together, so he could hand me his mother's promise, the ring.

We met at a small bistro Margo had liked, near the Beckets' home, now Roy's winter home. We drove up at the same time. I waved enthusiastically as he stepped out of the car, a skinny, tiny cigar in his mouth. Was he nervous? I didn't know he still smoked.

I rushed to his parked car. He opened the trunk and bent down to reach for a golden box with shaking hands. When he looked up and saw me, he stared with a face of mortifying sadness. He pointed to my outfit: my dressy sweater in shimmering gold with a matching silk flower, identical in color to the golden box and the ring.

"Mom's color," he whispered. Margo's favorite, the elegant gold color which she had worn on plenty of Fridays.

I had dressed in her honor. Roy sobbed.

Repeatedly, still, I feel that exquisite moment of lift-off — in my hands a golden box glistening in the sunlight. A swirl of anticipation gained altitude, soaring higher and higher. A promise had become real. With eyes transfixed at the brilliance of the diamonds in the Arizona sunshine, in a busy parking lot, my hands trembled. Yet the moment when I put the ring on my finger, the spell broke. I knew full well a perfect fit.

My knees buckled. Unsurpassed nostalgia and tears turned into sobs. Fridays of the past flashed before my eyes — Margo's joy-filled face had watched me put that jewel on my finger — now the ring was mine. A sense of closeness to a lady who claimed to be my Arizona Mom, up in the spot of grace for the rest of time, filled my heart. Closeness expressed in a ring of unprecedented magnificence — a ring, the sign of eternity. How exceptional when a client and hairstylist share a bond lasting a lifetime.

The value of all those diamonds is not measured by their size but by the love given to a girl from far across the sea . . . *Some ties are simply meant to be.* Grief turned into intimacy as if a treasure had been transported to the pocket of my heart. The road to heaven is paved with memories. I could see Margo smile.

Don't cry because it's over; smile because it happened.

During our lunch together, when that dome of diamonds had become mine, Roy asked, "When will you work the next time?"

"Tomorrow!" I shouted too loud. It had been six weeks since my last working days. My exciting retirement still included several longtime clients at the same salon, (some for more than forty years).

Roy answered with haste, "You know mother wants you to wear the ring each time you work." Without a doubt, he knew of Mom's wish for me to show the jewel to the ladies at the salon.

The gate between thoughts and words opened and let out feelings of awe over the miracle of perfect timing. Our joyful tears for 'Mom' merged with sorrowful yet delightful memories.

That exquisite gift, an act of love, I wear with a proud heart. Always will.

"Death leaves a heartache no one can heal. Love leaves a memory no one can steal." — Richard Puz

["The Ring," one of the winning stories in a national short story contest at Living Springs Publishers, Centennial, Colorado, published in September 2019: *Stories Through the Ages Baby Boomers Plus 2019.*]

Dollars from Heaven

"A belief is not merely an idea the mind possesses . . . a belief is an idea that possesses the mind." — Robert Oxton Bolton

The first dollar appeared at Alicia's mom's favorite restaurant on the way to a gathering of relatives and friends. Near the entrance into the Sugar Bowl Alicia's uncomprehending eyes stared in shock. As she grabbed the dollar in haste, she almost threw out her back. She held the dollar to her heart. With tears in her eyes, she remembered the words her mom had spoken more than once: "I will send you d*ollars from heaven."*

A heart-stopping, goose-bump moment. It was the day of Dorothy's funeral.

"My mom is in heaven," Alicia bawled. Her heart floated with joy for days, mixed with tears.

In the two years since that dismal day in August 2004, when Dorothy passed away, a unique and exquisite treasure box on a shelf above the fireplace at Alicia's family home now holds 67 dollars.

Alicia, my friend, and hair client for many years chuckled and shook her head the first time she listened to the words *dollars from heaven* spoken by her mom Dorothy when she was admitted at the hospital, ill for some time, and barely able to walk in.

Alicia held on tight to her frail mother as they stepped onto a huge elevator. Alicia looked down and noticed a dollar on the floor. She yelled, "Mom, look, a dollar." As she bent to pick it up, she heard her mom's bizarre words, "I will send you *dollars from heaven."*

Alicia's surprised expression affirmed, "*What?*"

Ignoring a phrase that sounded totally out of the ordinary, they walked to the window, where Mrs. Dalton was admitted.

Days later, Alicia stood at the despised hospital bed holding her mother's weak hand in a way only a devoted daughter can, the naked fear of losing Mom in her eyes. As usual, Mother knew how to reach her only daughter to laugh and smile. Again, with a whisper, she mumbled, "When I am gone, I will send you *dollars from heaven."* Words sounding exceptionally foreign to a daughter in pain, not understanding, and Alicia's perpetually smiling face had turned into a frown.

Her happy-person appearance and uncanny constant smile underwent a time-out. She teared up as if she had a bad cold.

***

June sputtered into July, sizzling hot when Alicia found a dollar bill in a parking lot, near her car. Another dollar surfaced nearby on a sweaty, sunny Arizona day on the hot cement; it took mere seconds to remember her mother's words. Alicia paused and shivered as she picked up two precious dollars. For a while, she forgot where the heck her car keys were.

It happened again and again. Each time shocked Alicia into astonished silence, with a quick look around her for someone, anyone, who might claim the money.

Later still, a five-dollar bill. Her daughter Hailey symbolically stepped on outside a grocery store on Mother's Day. Alicia dumbfounded picked up that bill like a treasure. With shaking hands, she raised her eyes to heaven in a classic expression of disbelief.

"Happy Mother's Day to you, too, Mom."

Alicia, after sixteen years of marriage, became a mom. Long gone from her mind were thoughts of ever having a child of her own. At thirty-eight, she had experienced early menopause.

Alicia cannot get pregnant. Three doctors told her so numerous times over the years. The day her daughter Hailey was born, they called her a miracle child. A midlife miracle. An unpredicted gift of the best kind. Alicia's mother — Dorothy, a grandma, finally.

***

Rain, a rare occurrence in the desert, one January morning, while walking with some of the moms in the neighborhood after dropping the children off at the school bus stop, Alicia's eyes found a puddle of water amid many. Her uncomprehending eyes gazed at a ten-dollar bill, floating. With weak knees, Alicia bent down and grabbed it, ignoring the wetness as she ran home. It had stopped raining. She reached the house waving the soaking bill and howled, "It's from Mom."

Her husband Ryan, off from work, stood by the garage door. They both gazed up to heaven — it was Ryan's birthday.

***

222

In October, over a year after Mom's passing, another ten-dollar bill surfaced in front of Alicia's incredulous eyes in a crowded shopping center. Alicia directly stepped on while getting out of her fancy Jaguar sports car. Another birthday gift from heaven? Alicia had turned forty-seven; she was in a state of bafflement and absolute wonderment. *Thank you, Mom.*

In late September of the following year, one glorious going-to-the-beach day in Coronado, California, where Lew and I spent three weeks at our condo near the sounds of the ocean, the phone rang. Alicia's happier-than-ever voice sounded like cheering: "My mom sent me 20 dollars."

My flabbergasted reaction had everything to do with the fact only a few days previously I had finished writing the "Dollars from Heaven" story for my friend Alicia, a gift for her upcoming October birthday. The story was written on pretty paper bordered with purple flowers — lilacs — her mother's favorite. Alicia's unexpected call changed everything.

Rewrite — is what writers do.

Where Alicia found the 20 dollars is more surprising yet: one Tuesday, in a parking lot all the way in the back so her husband's new Jeep would have an ever-so-perfect parking space. (What men do with their new cars.) Alicia, Ryan, and Hailey were on the way to an early dinner. Nonetheless, what startling timing of another magical find during a challenging time for Alicia involving her job, her place of work for almost two years. Her boss had promised Alicia a raise. Words only, however, she found out when her commission got cut, which added up to less pay.

Most upsetting for Alicia was the way she found out. Lies were involved, never an easy thing to handle. A slap in the face would have been less hurtful. She searched for answers, Ryan wanted her to quit. Yet Alicia loved the classy gift and accessory store at the Biltmore that let her use her creativity for the ritzy, high-end clientele. The situation was virtually impossible for a woman who has a tough time with changes of any kind. She still loved her perms from the eighties. Wash and wear — curly forever — since the day she walked into Mahogany salon one hour early for her first appointment. Hair parted in the middle, long, no style, but a contagious smile for everyone as she sat on the couch and waited her turn on this franticly busy Thursday afternoon in 1982.

When Alicia saw the 20-dollar bill on that balmy Arizona evening, the surprise still as enormous as in previous times, only filled with more joy, especially the amount, she thought of her meeting the next morning at 9 before the store opened, to talk to her boss about the future of her job. As she embraced the bill with her trembling hands, holding it to her heart in a special kind of close-to-her-mom way, she could hear mother's voice: *"I will send you dollars from heaven."*

A sign from above, during a decision-making kind-of-time?

Her husband and friends translated finding that money to: "There are other places where you can earn more money."

Alicia stayed at her job . . . and eventually got a huge raise.

The belief in *dollars from heaven* lives on, a gorgeous, eye-catching treasure box is filling up.

By the way . . .

On Alicia's birthday in 201**8**, I received an e-mail with a picture. On her every morning walk, Alicia found pennies. One hundred and thirty-six. I responded with a simple question: "What happened to dollars?"

Alicia found more dollars that year: one twenty-dollar bill, two five-dollar bills, and seven ones.

Magical realism in everyday life continues.

["Dollars from Heaven": *FATE Magazine* published a short version in its May-June issue, 2009.]

Friendship — A Harmony of Hearts

"Wherever you are, it is your friends who make your world." —
William James

One of Rona's gifts, matching flower pins

Rona is her name. For years I did not know it is short for Ronaleah — stunning, dynamic Rona, in looks, actions, and skillfulness to take charge of whatever the situation calls for. Ronaleah, a name with a flair for the uncommon.

Her way — years later I still marvel over.

In 1986, one late summer day Rona entered Mahogany salon where I had worked for years. Five other new hairstylists had shown up earlier on that Tuesday; like an invasion. As a united team, they had all walked out of Cimarron, (the in-place in Scottsdale) located down the street near our remarkably busy salon. Rumors of a salon on the verge of closing had become reality. All stylists at Mahogany acted disturbed — concerned of possibly losing their space? Faces showed fear of change. I worried about my corner, chairs, and waiting area possibly in jeopardy. How can this bunch of extra hairdressers fit in an all-of-a-sudden seemingly small area? What was the boss thinking? Classic owner.

225

Mid-morning Rona arrived — gorgeous and charismatic. Royalty would have nothing on her splendid presence, dressed in style in the latest fashion. Shiny black hair pulled back tightly left my eyes staring. I wondered, real, or color-dependent? Her face had a smile igniting the salon. However, it was *her way,* how she held her head and hands, that demanded attention. I stopped cutting hair. Our eyes locked. When Ricardo, the owner introduced us, in an instant I knew this was someone exceptional.

A few weeks into the most chaotic, farfetched, and remarkable time at any salon I had ever worked at. Stylists' worries turned into laughter, teamwork, and happiness shared by all. The not-having-enough-shampoo-chairs problem handled by smiles and understanding. Clients experienced a noteworthy time in a crowded salon.

Hair is power! Beauty — what a weapon!

Rona stood out, doing hair with flair, and the way she spoiled her clients frankly something to learn from and behold. She also had her own assistant Jenna, just like I did. In her spare time, I'd catch Rona gaping at all the customers lined up in *my corner* waiting for me. In an era of standing hair appointments, clients came back weekly for more of the same, some twice a week.

I watched Rona observe and knew she was counting the dollars all those roller-sets must bring in as she listened to new clients tell how they found Trudy: "Oh, I stopped this lady I didn't know, at the mall and asked, *"Who does your hair?"*

One of Rona's favorite encounters happened as she stood close by and eavesdropped. A weekly Friday client, with thinning fine hair, Mrs. Nobel's boisterous voice proclaimed: "Trudy, you should not charge me full price for my haircut. It only took you five minutes." My prompt answer never had her repeat the question again. "You are not paying me for the five minutes it takes me to cut your hair, you are paying me for the thirty years I learned to do it in five minutes — called experience."

The first time Rona shouted, "Trudy, do you need Jenna to do a shampoo for you?" Words like a melody — I could not believe my ears. I nodded with a cheerful yes. Rona believed in sharing. Arlene, my energetic helper up in years, the best and for the longest I ever had, was tied up with a perm with extra time needed. Rona was watching. I could not possibly express in words how I welcomed and appreciated Rona and Jenna's helpful hands coming to my rescue. Though Rona knew — I believed in expressing thanks to the fullest and naturally, extra tips for Jenna.

Admiration between friends is an immeasurable gift; we may never know who admired whom more.

What a sad day when Rona left Mahogany to follow a dream of opening her swanky salon. One year into Rona's role as an over-the-top-happy salon owner, our receptionist called me to the phone. A lady from Napa Valley asked to speak to Trudy. Rona had given her my name and Mahogany's telephone number. Mrs. Kunde, from Santa Clara, California, had already called a range of beauty shops in search of a shampoo and set. No luck.

Roller-sets were a thing of the past, although not for all women who did not wash their own hair. Blow-dry-hair-only had taken over the hair-world after Dorothy Hammill skated at the Olympics. Her signature wedge haircut falling in place became all-the-rage, a number-one conversation at beauty shops in America. The importance of a haircut emerged as if never significant ever before. A new look was born — a new way of styling hair.

Rollers-in-hair were not in Rona's job description, nor for anyone at her salon. Rona remembered the ladies I spoiled with hairdos, looks with a panache that got attention and stares. She had told Anna Kunde, "Call Mahogany's."

"Is this Trudy, the 'Roller Queen?" (Rona's name for me stuck for years.) I listened to an unknown voice while she explained Rona had granted her my name. Mrs. Kunde called for a hair-set every time she visited her second home in Scottsdale.

My customers adored my new title, 'Roller Queen' specifically one chubby, short Jewish lady. She showed up at 6 a.m. every Friday, tired and sleeping under the hairdryer every week. One such morning as I finished her hair I asked, "Fran, why don't you come later, or in the afternoon?"

In shock, she answered, "Are you kidding me? I want my hair to look good all day. I want my money's worth."

With hair 'in my blood from growing up in Switzerland, watching Mom and Dad, both popular and in-demand, my love for hair grew by leaps and bounds during my American salon-life, away from competing with Mom and Erwin, the older brother. I wished my parents could see me now with all my customers. I never forgot that wobbly stool — a kid too short to reach the shampoo bowl — my after-school time, — salon-work.

A distinct memory is the sound of money as I jingled the earned coins in my apron pocket. Clients' words echoed in my ears: "Trudy is going to make such a good hairdresser someday."

***

Rona and I left for San Francisco to attend one of the prime yearly hair shows in the West. My husband could not believe I would go without him. Countless people and numerous friends would bet against that happening anytime. In all our married years since 1972, our togetherness and closeness bordered on wonderment for many who knew the inseparable couple, Lew and Trudy.

It was the last time.

The Southwest flight from San Francisco was late; the same plane turned around to take us back to the windy city; extremely late due to a huge storm somewhere. Lew tried to remain cool. His cigarette smoking had changed to smoking a pipe (since 1974) that kept him busy stuffing it with tobacco. I

loved how the walnut tobacco aroma filled the air and Lew looked too nonchalant for words.

I still see Lew waving goodbye — a worried look of despair on a face only someone in love can show.

The minute Rona sat down in the plane she buckled up, strapped herself in, and stretched out into a comfortable position, like at home. She fell asleep immediately.

I watched in awe the sleep I came to envy during a scary flight. I started praying. The pilot's voice, a couple of times, tried to assure the passengers of "making it" through this enormous storm. The shaking and bumping continued all the way to San Francisco. I promised God, myself, and Lew in my heart, I would never again fly without him — ever — if we arrived alive.

Rona woke up at the time when I must have been blue with fear, and with her smiling face she screeched, "Are we there yet?" The mystery of someone sleeping through a plane ride like that — that's Rona, different from any of us — or someone merely tired?

Walking off the aircraft, my legs still weak, Rona yelled out, "San Francisco, here we are." Let the good times roll.

We checked into the Hyatt Hotel; in astonishment, we marveled at the imposing view and lights of San Francisco on the 18th floor as we walked into the fabulous room, we shared for 2 nights. Ecstatic calls to our sweethearts back home were first on a hotel landline. (Practical cell phones, not as yet)

Rona's words flabbergasted me, "Let's go for a walk and look for a Catholic church nearby, to know where to attend Mass in the early morning, before the hair show." Rona is Catholic? Stunned, her words sounded like a song to my Catholic ears. She knew of my strict Catholic upbringing and my wedding-day story about Lew, — my non-Catholic husband.

On Sunday morning in early March, in the quiet streets of the windy city of San Francisco, both of us bundled up, we entered a sacred old church we had found the night before. Some memories in life remain — this is one of them. How little did I know a trip with Rona would turn out to be spiritual?

On this memorable, chilly morning in downtown San Francisco, a treasured bond started that would last a lifetime, our first Mass together, with many more in years to come. To date Rona and I, when we are in town, meet Fridays for Mass and breakfast. (2020 changed to Mondays)

In a massive convention center where a spectacular hair-extravaganza was about to begin, hairstylists from everywhere arrived to watch and learn about the beauty and salon industry that will never be outsourced to another country. The bad-hair-days will allow clients to pick up the phone right here in America.

Countless hairdressers knew Rona, some obnoxiously pushy for my taste. Nonetheless, even here she managed to be the center of attention as someone in her element, frankly, astounding to watch. Rona in preceding years had done shows on stage teachings about current trends. *Her way* stood out in San Francisco at a stellar show, surrounded by masses of flamboyant hair designers dressed exceptionally well, looking stunning. Any fashion show paled next to this.

Over the years we'd see each other, although never often enough. When we did, each meeting turned into a time to treasure.

Rona sold her small beauty shop to open another, bigger salon on the first floor of a well-known hotel. Enormously proud, she hoped I would join her staff and come work with her — for her. Nagging guilt for not taking the leap remained. Number one reason: not enough space compared to what I enjoyed at Mahogany salon for twenty-two years. Two chairs (I had asked for) in the corner, with my private waiting area, near an exit door to the parking lot. The use of three more stations near the shampoo chairs named the color-corner. Ricardo loved the idea I presented when he had the high-class salon built. 3 — for-color-only stations — were installed for his busy stylists.

Rona's words about my space: "To see is to believe it."

Success has to be earned — success will follow commitment; it starts in the heart and caring for others.

I know unmistakably, I was born to do this.

Believe good fortune is a result of careful planning.

"Begin somewhere; you cannot build a reputation on what you intend to do." — James Russell Lowell

Sadly, the not-working-for-Rona decision put a certain strain on our relationship. Can two friends genuinely work together — in the long run? Against odds — as if it already had — business does not mix with pleasure.

One cloudy December morning, months had gone by, Rona called and shouted, "I met my Lew."

An overjoyed phone call with her cheery voice blurted out, "I met Mr. Wonderful." Rona referred and comparing to my husband. She simply believed our marriage to be a dream come true and my Lew to be the best . . . How true.

In a wildly romantic wedding on a cloudless desert valley fall day in a park, predictably Rona as a bride strikingly gorgeous. Yet, her new husband stupefied guests. He ultimately was smaller than the giant I imagined him to be. He did not turn out to be *a Lew*. Her marriage remains a shattered dream.

Rona single, — again; two beautiful daughters from her first marriage making her life complete. Back to dinner, lunch, and tea with friends, each time showing up elegant — with her unique trademark, matching gloves, even in July.   On occasional dinners, we'd find out Rona still orders dessert first, before her dinner, to the laughter and shock of most waiters. Who does that?

***

Salons closed on Mondays, on one such morning during Lent I invited Rona for breakfast at my favorite resort, the fabulous Copperwynd overlooking Fountain Hills, where the view is spectacular. Attending Mass first, a distinct habit continually a part of our get-togethers. Rona's visit to a new and awe-inspiring church I had mentioned on the phone, left her completely surprised not to know about this majestic church in the desert, one of the most serene places to be at 8:30 in the morning.

As routinely, we dressed up, Rona with fine leather gloves evoking stares from everyone. Blue sky, a daily Arizona-thing, however, on this glorious morning the blue appeared more intense; bougainvillea's and the all in-yellow blooming Palo Verde trees were out in masses for two friends who had not seen each other for months. God was smiling at us.

Another such Monday, one of the finest yet, was my birthday, October the 18th. Church at **8** a.m. was written first on my endless list of typical day-off chores.

To attend Monday Mass instead of Sunday's Vigil, to fulfill traditional Catholicism had triggered a turning point into my isolated practice and belief when I became Lew's wife. Every week the faithful Catholics are obliged to attend Sunday Mass to fulfill an obligation, ingrained into me for as long as I can remember. This changed dramatically for one serious reason: the anguish of being sad and alone during worship. I tried. It became clear: one cannot have everything.

To ask non-Catholic Lew to join me, every week, I modestly wouldn't. Yet, in my heart, I hoped he'd offer. He did, a few times; one pulsating memory is the first time, Valentine's Day. That year on a Sunday.

In the late sixties, early seventies, as a result of the Vatican accommodation, a Saturday late afternoon/evening Vigil Mass was added to count as a Sunday Mass. Why not Monday, I asked, the morning after? How could that be wrong? I talked to the Lord regularly and many priests during confession over the years.

I call to mind attending Mass every Sunday as a child reading and repeating words of prayers dutifully. Now I prayed to hear God: *"Better on Monday than not at all?"*

As I prayed in the small chapel that birthday morning, the church I visited weekly for years, a dramatically dressed-up lady — Rona — sat next to me. Her gloves caught my eye, my gloves from the seventies I never wore I had offered her as a gift. She knew where to find me, knowing my Monday-Mass habit. She did not know it was my birthday. In my happy heart, I sensed a special angel got Rona out of bed on this specific morning — or coincidence? *Some things are simply meant to be.* It had been **8** months since we last saw each other.

After Mass, Rona tempted me to the new James Hotel for breakfast. A modern and exciting place I had heard about and wished to stop by for some time. Like dropping a bomb at the restaurant when Rona's entrance let everyone know of my birthday. At 9:30 a.m. a pastry with a candle arrived, compliments of the chef. One of the unmatched birthday delights — early in the morning — tasting that good. My friend Rona somehow always adept to get anything, anytime, anywhere.

It is the unexpected in life that has us wonder and smile. The surprise to see my friend let my birthday turn into big-bang awesome. Rona — a blessing to treasure.

By Christmas 200**8**, Rona worked part-time only at a salon where they idolized and valued her. No more facing agony of owning a salon any longer mixed with joys at times.

She had learned to be content is a special gift.

For a few years, retired-me did hair three mornings a month, thanks to Markus the young owner who had treated me like his mom. Still does. Not an early riser he let me use and share his station any morning I desired. Some of my since-196**8** customers added to my old-life I loved so long as an artist of hair.

Hair — still an eternal part of my new, exciting writing life.

One Wednesday before Christmas, Rona and I met at our favorite church on the outskirts of Scottsdale. Rona's place now to pray weekly, the church she found because I had taken her one spring morning.

The service had already started on that rare, freezing morning in the desert, I sat wondering, *where is Rona?*

Finally, ten minutes late she squeezed herself into the pew next to me, her effortless way of looking elegant absent. Rona hugged me longer than usual. Her cold face and hands shocked me. I whispered, "Why are you so cold?"

She had traveled on her turquoise-colored motor scooter. Her car wouldn't start. The half-hour distance from her house, riding in the cold, did not stop her. Calling me for a ride? Not Rona's way, she relentlessly has a backup plan. Plan B.

To know her is to love her.

On the way out after Mass, we chatted about the homily by a priest who believed in being a candle that can be lit by anybody who crosses our path in daily life. In other words, *Be kind to one another.* Rona had stopped in front of a display of beautiful candles where people put in money to light one, followed by a prayer of their choice. As she rummaged in her handbag, she pulled out a one-dollar bill. I gaped frowning at her outstretched hand — in absolute disbelief. My gaping belonged to a dollar with my writing . . . a dollar I had given Rona many years ago for doing one of my clients' shampoos — money she never wanted to take, except for this one time when I wrote on the dollar, *"God Bless whoever receives this bill."*

Rona put *that* very dollar in the moneybox. With her phenomenal smile, she lit a candle.

Life is a chain of moments, emotions, and events we don't expect. Many times, they surprise us, and when they happen, we can't believe it — the times they happen, when we least expect them. This was such a moment.

During our one-of-a-kind Christmas breakfast, at *our* place where we had gone before, up high overlooking the Arizona valley where the scenery and views are like a prayer, we exchanged gifts — fun gifts. Christmas had come early.

I watched my friend get on her flashy scooter parked right at the front door of the resort, the exclusive turquoise color shining bright in the sun. She wore a matching helmet in turquoise visible for miles — her mink jacket and fine leather gloves — a sight to behold. On the back of her distinctive motorbike, she had attached a big red, glittery bow with silver bells. In the front, a Christmas wreath — what a sight.

Waving goodbye on that exceptional morning, I gazed at Rona gliding down the road. She smiled and blew a kiss. I waited until she disappeared at the bend of the road. I stood mesmerized, knowing two friends had started a new Christmas tradition.

"The language of friendship is not words but meanings." —
Henry David Thoreau

Ronaleah Griego de Garcia — her real name — is from Spain: Valencia, Spain.

What is in a name, a name that sounds like a song? It spells Rona, a friend for life — my friend.

Rona's true name emerged one morning after Mass, years into our friendship. I asked her to sign an important paper as I collected signatures from various countries all over the world for and about soccer — the world calls football — my life passion. I had written a letter, about the World Cup 2006, an appeal for changes to the game, to President Mr. Sepp Blatter of FIFA, Federation International Football Association, headquartered in Zürich, Switzerland,

I had believed Rona's home country to be Mexico. Wrong.

A 'Spain' signature made my day and completed my letter.

Indeed, we don't know what we've got until we lose it . . . yet, it is also true we don't know what we've been missing until it arrives.

One more thing . . .

A bright purple orchid with a silver twig in her outstretched

hand Rona, a grandma now twice, rushed to sit next to me at Blessed Sacrament Catholic Church at 7 a.m. on Friday, December 14, 2018. A Mass I had ordered and paid for had started on this cold thirty-eight-degree morning in Scottsdale. My only remaining aunt back home, Maria Meyer, wife of Uncle Otto my godfather, had passed away on her husband's birthday in Wohlen, Switzerland.

Rona surprised her friend in need at a time of sorrow.

By the way . . .

Arlene, a jewel of assistants, Rona, and customers claimed she had agile fingers that gave a dreamy scalp massage, a most-even tempered worker with mind and soul in daily chores, she had a smile that lit up client's faces at the salon, anytime. Arlene and my attitude alike, we'd grin at a most favorite phrase: w*hat's done is done.* *W*hat I can do today, I don't have to do tomorrow.

One Saturday, chaotic and overbooked as usual, around noon I had misplaced my scissors. More turmoil. Arlene, known for finding lost items in a snap at crucial times, but not this Saturday. Her usual praying to Saint Anthony, the Patron Saint of lost things, had come to a halt at 1:00 PM.

"I believe Saint Anthony is out to lunch." Arlene's dry sense of humor echoed all around with laughter from everyone.

A stroke at her home ended this fine lady's career. A friend for life . . . we place flowers on her grave every season, still — knowing she would adore the red, white, and blue with a small flag before Memorial Day. A widow from Iowa, with hidden matter-of-fact humor, had one older sister, no children.

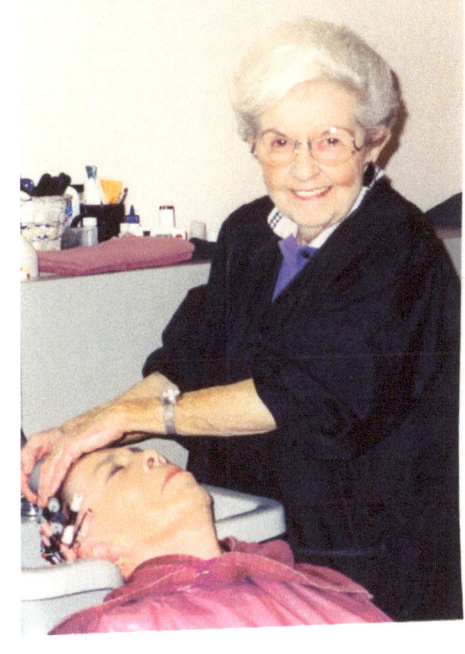

Arlene's constant good mood guided by the Spirit of God, interested in what clients had to say; she sincerely spoiled everyone with kindness. Yes, she got customers wet at the shampoo bowl, her flaw was my flaw reminding me of my early days when Mom barked, "Don't get the ladies wet." No matter what I tried did not help. Now I sounded like Mom, giving Arlene looks of *try harder*. Some clients got mad, complained, Arlene however, pampered everybody her way.

One wealthy business owner on his every two weeks early at six- haircut appointment handed Arlene 20 dollars — simply for bringing him a cup of fresh-brewed morning coffee.

The day Arlene arrived for her first interview, glancing through the mirror I spotted gray bouffant hair that aged the short, chubby lady standing in the back of the salon. I whispered to the client in my chair, "Is she too old?" The still employed decorator at 74 leaned over demonstratively, to see better,

"Hell, no!" Overly loud words that had me cringe would be proven right for 16 blissful years. (Rona loved Arlene.)

"I don't mind coming in early. I love the mornings."

Hesitant I asked, "At six?"

"Or earlier is fine with me, if you need me to." Arlene beamed. Not used to such a rare statement from any assistants during the years of showing up late and half-asleep most days, I spilled words in haste, "When can you start?"

Arlene's 65th birthday surprise lunch at the Sunburst Resort, sixty-one of us, my clients, Riccardo owner & our boss, a few stylists. A SURPRISE in every detail at its finest and the talk of Scottsdale, in December 1991.

Sports — Football/Soccer — Tennis

Beckham to "Rock" the American Soccer World

They say the American soccer world is a "small world," but, judging from the media frenzy, that "small world" is on the way to getting bigger, *the absence of glamour and money* when it comes to soccer in America is going to change dramatically with the arrival of a super football star from England, David Beckham. He not only knows how to hit a football with finesse and class that borders on spectacular, but he also started multiple male hair trends and fashion looks enjoyed by men and boys worldwide.

Beckham coming to America!

What a shot in the arm for a sport that has gotten little attention during the past years. The USA team at any World Cup is surely the *loneliest* soccer team in the wide world of football frenzy, qualifying without their nation's support.

Soccer — the world calls Football — was shown on Spanish TV channels **only** when I first arrived in the US ages ago. Will Beckham change the thinking of the not-yet-soccer-lovers in the United States of America?

America is a country with many sports, where soccer is just another game. When Americans are watching a match, will they understand to sit for forty-five minutes? *No commercial interruptions!* (There are two forty-five-minute periods during any game.) *No trips* to the refrigerator for another beer or more chips; moments of brilliance sure to be missed if you take your eyes off the ball at any game.

We who make up that "small soccer world" love all this *Beckham-mania.* We will be there when this millionaire, many times over will show off his skills and individual brilliance, over which the universe has marveled. However, we will watch and *not* forget the players besides him who have soooo much less, because salaries in Major League Soccer are unmatched in other countries . . . *in America? Imagine that!*

Scoring, a goal that changes everything. is what all players have in common. *Our guys* will run their hearts out — and step up to the challenge.

The world will be watching David Beckham, what magic he might and can achieve in this grand country of the United States.

May the power of the media shine . . . and be there.

May America find out — indeed, we don't know what we've been missing until it arrives.

SOCCER RULES . . . Will America finally care?

David Beckham would and did 'rock' the American Soccer World. He arrived in 2007. America woke up.

[*USA Today* published a shorter version of this article in the Sports Section, January 16, 2007. As well as in the *Scottsdale Tribune*, Friday, January 19, also in the Sports Section.]

One more thing . . .
How to win more fans in America?

Show the beginning of a soccer match, consistently, every game. In the tunnel, most moving when the players walk into the stadium onto the field holding onto children's hands, boys and girls — the future of soccer.

All TV games coverage, please do not leave out when the Anthem plays, the part that touches the world, when players are known to close their eyes and pray to their God.

America wake up — embrace and cheer your team!

It will be the kids of the United States someday who will run down those fields where miracles on grass happen, in any country where the World Cup might be. Fire in their eyes and a reason to win for their Nation during an epic showdown on grass, Soccer/Football will be in their blood. All soccer moms and dads will root for the right reasons, with all of America, that someday will belong on the biggest stage of that global sport.

"Passion at the World Cup is not measured by the steps you run down a field (and towards a possible better career), it is measured by the heart that beats for your country." — Anonymous

FIFA Letters: 1994 — 2010 — 2014

FIFA
Hitzigweg 11
Postfach
8030 Zürich

01/384 9595

Mr Sepp Blatter
FIFA President

Trudy B. Wells
7843 Via Marina
Scottsdale, Arizona
USA

August 08, 1994

Dear Sir:

Penalty shooting will cause a suicide some day.

The solution to your problem is in this letter.

WORLD CUP 1994, through the eyes of a Suisse girl in America.
It was the best - ever - 52 fantastic games. I watched them all.

Penalty shooting is the worst possible end to a championship. Here is the answer. When overtime starts, allow two additional substitutions. In the second 15 minutes of overtime allow two more substitutions. If the match is still tied after overtime, then the match goes to sudden death and two more substitutions are allowed.

If you saw all of the matches you know there were quite a few goals made by players brought in near the end of the second half. Give some of the guys a rest and others a chance for fame and glory.

I loved all of the other changes that you made to the game. I can hardly wait for the next World Cup!

Sincerely,

Trudy Wells

P.S.   I did cry for Bulgaria - that French referee - that was not fair!

P.S.S   I arrived in the States on June 18, 1965 - 29 years later
         Switzerland ties the USA 1:1 - I didn't have to be sad for either but
         in my heart I wanted Switzerland to win.

Copy of original letter sent in 1994.

Trudy Wells-Meyer

Mr. Sepp Blatter
FIFA President

August **8**, 1994

Dear Sir:

Penalty shootout at a final will cause a suicide someday.

The solution to your problem is in this letter.

World Cup 1994, through the eyes of a Swiss girl in America. It was the best — ever — fifty-two fantastic games. I watched them all.
Penalty shooting is the worst possible end to a championship. Here is an answer. When overtime starts, allow two additional substitutions. In the second fifteen minutes of overtime, allow two more substitutions. If the match is still tied after overtime, then the match goes to sudden death and two more substitutions are allowed.
If you saw all the matches, you know there were a few goals by players brought in near the end of the second half. Give some of the guys a rest and others a chance for fame and glory.
I loved all the other changes that you made for the game. I can hardly wait for the next World Cup.

Sincerely,
Trudy Wells
P.S I did cry for Bulgaria — that French referee — that was not fair.

How big is football/soccer? Do the math: it is the ultimate global sport, with worldwide dominance. Football's intense, mysterious powers give a trance-like quality to any World Cup every four years. Tiny countries — giant dreams. The contrast of emotions, where men cry openly in the agony of defeat; unbridled joy and delight beyond description when they win; dancing with strangers in a global language. That is the World Cup, an event that almost stops the world from spinning. Agony versa ecstasy.

Soccer/football has arrived in America and woke up to forty-five minutes of uninterrupted playing with **no commercial** stops. Will America, however, someday call soccer by its real name, Football — where feet do all the magic, and headers can put a country into a frenzy? One goal . . . that changes everything!

240

Thanks to my love of writing, in my first letter to FIFA in 1994, I believed Sepp Blatter (Swiss-born) to be the new president of the global addiction, (in 1994 he was *General Sekretär of FIFA*, I found out many years later.) I dared to ask for changes. I wrote with enthusiasm about concerns for the rules of the game.

(Did my ESP — clairvoyance — have Mr. Blatter in 1994 already at the helm of this Global frenzy, four years earlier?)

Years later. . .

Reuters UK, easyJet.com, published an article on September 27, 2006, that had me shriek, do a double take with hands covering my mouth. Skipping and clapping followed words confirming my letter, my concern about penalty shootouts.

FIFA President Sepp Blatter believed future World Cup Finals should not be decided by penalties. "A tragedy" he called it and informed the world, "Changes could be in place for the showpiece tournament in South Africa in four years."

REUTERS :D UK

You are here: Home > News > Sports > World Football > **Article**

HOME
INVESTING
NEWS

Top News
World
Business
Editor's Choice
Science/Technology
Health
World Crises
Sports
  UK Football
  World Football
  Cricket
  Rugby Union
  Golf
  Tennis
  Motor Sports
Entertainment
Oddly Enough
Motoring
Video
Pictures
MORE NEWS TODAY

Blatter wants to scrap penalties for World Cup finals
Wed Sep 27, 2006 3 20 PM BST

Email This Article | Print This Article | RSS **XML**

[-] Text [+]

By Sam Cage

ZURICH, Sept 27 (Reuters) - FIFA president Sepp Blatter believes future World Cup finals should not be decided by penalties and said changes could be in place for the showpiece tournament in South Africa in four years.

Italy's win over France on penalties made up for their 1994 final defeat by Brazil in a shootout, but Blatter said the manner of deciding it was "a tragedy".

He said a replay or gradually deducting players in extra time would be a better solution.

"We have four years or so, so I think we have time," Blatter told Reuters at a Swiss Chamber of Commerce event in Zurich.

"Maybe to replay the match if it's the final, you can't do that through the tournament because of lack of time. Maybe to take players away and play golden goal," Blatter said, adding that high-level discussions would start soon.

"When it comes to the World Cup final it is passion, and when it goes to extra time it is a drama," the head of world football's governing body said in an earlier speech. "But when it comes to penalty kicks it is a tragedy."

Friends and strangers signed my letter that summer. I

I collected signatures from eleven countries as I approached and listened to people with accents everywhere. Each time ready with a pen. To name a few: Norbert, our shoe repairman, the *Fussball*/football fanatic from Luxembourg. My monthly hair client Dr. Koppen, Holland. Zizzo, the alteration specialist from Italy enthusiastically agreed. The exchange student from Argentina understood Football with remarkable knowledge. Grinning she happily signed.

FIFA sent flags, pins in a response letter, and a thank you to fans who cared. During the next World Cup in France, 1998, a third substitute change was introduced to the glorious game of World Football. News that sent me to Football/Soccer/Heaven.

(Later still, FIFA used the Golden Goal, for a little while only.)

Dad, who loved *Fussball,* passed away of Lou Gehrig's disease at age 74 in 1989. He never witnessed his daughter's passionate writings — letters to the Swiss president of FIFA — not even the first letter when I suggested to change the two substitutions rule and allow three. FIFA complied in 1998.

Yet, I can see *Schgruna,* my *Tädi,* proudly smile in heaven.

Lugano, boat ride to Gandria, 1980

FEDERATION INTERNATIONALE DE FOOTBALL ASSOCIATION

Sweden

June 25, 2002

FIFA
Hitzigweg 11
Postfach
8030 Zürich

Mr. Sepp Blatter
FIFA President

Dear Sir:

Referee changes are essential!

A referee can **not** call a game where one of the teams has beaten his own country during the World Cup!

The match USA - Mexico - the referee is from Portugal – USA beat Portugal 3 : 2. That yellow card to the USA goalkeeper – what ever for – that was personal. South Korea – Italy - the referee from Ecuador – Italy beat Ecuador 2 : 0. I do not need to remind you of all the bad calls that happened during that game. 400,000 emails from Italy took care of that.

You have all these referee's from all over the world – use them! Do not give the fans heart failures – and be fair to the referees!

Mr. Blatter - from one Suisse to another – you were reelected because you **are** from Switzerland – the world is counting on fairness – that is what Switzerland stands for...

One more thing - The linesman - Assistant referees as you call them now – give them **better** training – some seem to not know what offside **is**...and have their eyes checked...

Sincerely,

T. Wells

Trudy B. Wells
A Soccer Fan for life
"Just a girl", from Switzerland, in America
over 30 years, who watched **all** 64 games

P.S.
This is for my Dad in heaven... He must have been shaking his head during this World Cup...

7843 VIA MARINA • SCOTTSDALE, ARIZONA • 85258-2826
TELEPHONE: 602-920-1561

MARCOS E. SOUTO — BRAZIL

(FRANCE)

Robert Vellooo (Oberhavlavels)

(GERMANY)

Yelhy Belev (RUSSIA)

Shirin Anvar (IRAN)

Les CeSulak (POLAND)

England

Rita Gallagher (IRELAND)

Urania Sylista (Czech Republic)

BULGARIA

Elvira Valenzuela (Mexico)

Marlert J. Kriel (LUXEMBOURG)

USA

CANADA

Minan Dobranm HUNGARY

(Italy) Kati —

Copy of original letter sent in 2002.

I wrote again and again. My letters involved more changes to the beautiful game that almost stops the world from turning. I hunted, listened, and found a selection of soccer-lovers (in unusual places) with accents, at restaurants, grocery stores, at the Mall. One ecstatic lady while selling bras and ladies' underwear proudly snuck in her signature from Peru as I searched for my valet to pay the bill. (Peru, a first)

Yodeling and skipping when I found a Brazilian, a handsome waiter, who wanted to skip along with me after he signed. I adored football/soccer-crazy Kenny from Bulgaria, the elite European cars auto mechanic, who frequently serviced my silver Mercedes 500 SL. France, Italia, England, and the Netherland signatures, the dominating power countries of world football, left me in seventh soccer heaven.

Mr. Blatter, president of the world's global tournament, answered my letters. What a dancing-like feeling to open a FIFA envelope. In one of his letters he wrote, "We listen to our fans. . ."

On July 1**8,** 2010, I mailed a letter to FIFA with 24 signatures, after the World Cup in South Africa which left us dreaming of what could have been. The sounds of the vuvuzelas had stopped; tidal waves of emotions, tears of defeat, and victorious countries were now a memory only.

Signatures included Germany, Spain, Portugal, Belgium, Sweden, Iran, Poland, Hungry, Romania, Ireland, Australia, Greece, and more. How about Trinidad and Vietnam.

No event defines the agony of defeat or a glorious victory as visibly as the World Cup. The world as we know it, for one-month stops. Costa Rica declared a National Holiday when their dream team, Costa Rica's best, played the opening game in Germany in 2006, against the host nation, the German giants. The first shot on goal — a beauty — by a defender stopped all hearts in Costa Rica, the hearts of a country and the world . . . 1-0 Germany. Then silence in the massive stadium in *München* . . . Costa Rica scored — disbelief for all Germans — the world. Costa Rica, a country gone wild, on their feet — screaming, dancing in the streets. The red, white, and blue Jerseys had caught my eyes and mind, a country I knew nothing of. I jumped and cheered for Costa Rica (sorry Mom — her dad, my grandfather, was German.)

The sounds of victory belonged to *Deutschland* — the final score 4-2 — but the best stories are not always about the winners. Anybody not convinced of the magnitude of the beautiful game of this universe does not know about nail-biting sensations ripping through our bodies as sure as we breathe.

Why is the World Cup so big? One month of emotions beyond words, the world united with countries all over the globe. They run for their country — for the pride of their nation and one goal can change everything!

32 DREAM TEAMS — each country's BEST — to qualify takes 2 years. The world's largest football scene — renamed only in America. Soccer. A country still learning the reasons why Soccer/Football rules the globe. One goal in 1998 stopped traffic in Paris, a goal by an American against Portugal, while America was sleeping. The US went on to win that game. My brother in Switzerland almost dropped his coffee cup when the winning goal echoed all over Europe. In France, the US for sure was the loneliest Football/soccer country in the world. No support (small only) from America. If only America cared . . . someday. . . .

Elections have been put on hold — Wars halted — problems forgotten. Ask anybody from Brazil, they postpone Mass until after the game, and in Dublin Ireland offices and stores have handwritten signs in the window "Closed for the match". Pubs are filled to the max. For one month every 4 years, when the unexpected will and does excel as the world watches. Senegal declared a national holiday after their win over France (champions.) In some countries (England, Nigeria), TV sets are rolled into school rooms, so the kids won't miss coming to school. In Italy, Spain, and Paraguay, thousands of candles are lit by the player's moms. For the China-Brazil game, an estimated 750 million people watched in China.

One may wonder if the economy will suffer during World Cup fever.

Football (Soccer) unites the world.

What is the prize?

A place for the name of the winning country on the very top of an elite list: the world's most impressive Football, soccer teams. A splendid trophy in gold to hold up for the most magnificent team after 4 demanding and grueling weeks for the whole world to admire and respect. Life-time careers and glory for each player and coach. A prodigious book records the all-time best over a significant period of time. Forever.

America, be there.

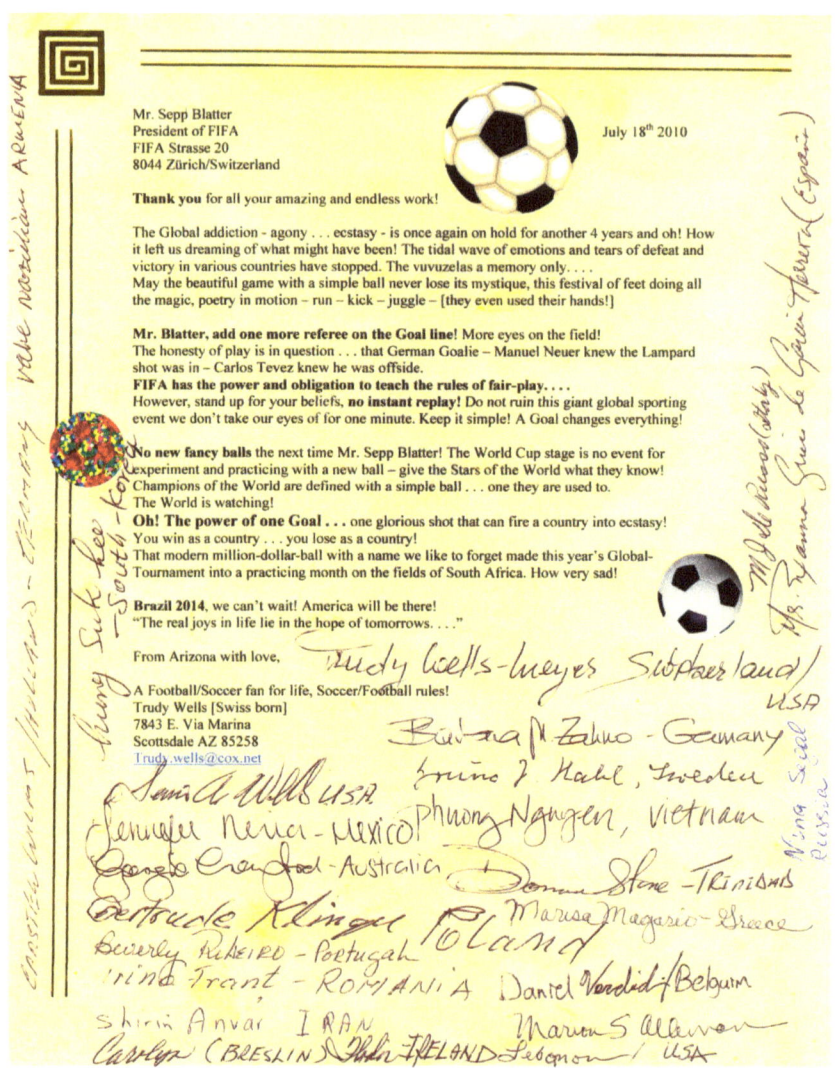

Mr. Sepp Blatter
President of FIFA
FIFA Strasse 20
8044 Zürich/Switzerland

July 18th 2010

Thank you for all your amazing and endless work!

The Global addiction - agony . . . ecstasy - is once again on hold for another 4 years and oh! How it left us dreaming of what might have been! The tidal wave of emotions and tears of defeat and victory in various countries have stopped. The vuvuzelas a memory only. . . .
May the beautiful game with a simple ball never lose its mystique, this festival of feet doing all the magic, poetry in motion – run – kick – juggle – [they even used their hands!]

Mr. Blatter, add one more referee on the Goal line! More eyes on the field!
The honesty of play is in question . . . that German Goalie – Manuel Neuer knew the Lampard shot was in – Carlos Tevez knew he was offside.
FIFA has the power and obligation to teach the rules of fair-play. . . .
However, stand up for your beliefs, **no instant replay!** Do not ruin this giant global sporting event we don't take our eyes of for one minute. Keep it simple! A Goal changes everything!

No new fancy balls the next time Mr. Sepp Blatter! The World Cup stage is no event for experiment and practicing with a new ball – give the Stars of the World what they know! Champions of the World are defined with a simple ball . . . one they are used to.
The World is watching!
Oh! The power of one Goal . . . one glorious shot that can fire a country into ecstasy!
You win as a country . . . you lose as a country!
That modern million-dollar-ball with a name we like to forget made this year's Global-Tournament into a practicing month on the fields of South Africa. How very sad!

Brazil 2014, we can't wait! America will be there!
"The real joys in life lie in the hope of tomorrows. . . ."

From Arizona with love,

A Football/Soccer fan for life, Soccer/Football rules!
Trudy Wells [Swiss born]
7843 E. Via Marina
Scottsdale AZ 85258
Trudy.wells@cox.net

Copy of original letter sent in 2010.

Mr. Sepp Blatter,
8044 Zürich, Switzerland   *July 18, 2010*

Thank you *for all your amazing and endless work!*

The global addiction — agony . . . ecstasy — is once again on hold for another four years, and oh! How it left us dreaming of what might have been! The tidal wave of emotions and tears of defeat and victory in various countries have stopped. The vuvuzelas a memory only. . . .
May the beautiful game with a simple ball never lose its mystique, this festival of feet doing all the magic, poetry in motion — run — kick — juggle — they even used their hands!

Mr. Blatter, add one more referee on the goal line! *More eyes on the field! The honesty of play is in question . . . that German goalie Manuel Neuer knew the Lampard shot was in — Carlos Tevez knew he was offside!*
FIFA has the power and obligation to teach the rules of fair play. . . .
However, stand up for your beliefs. **No instant replay!** *Do not ruin this global sporting event that we don't take our eyes off for one minute. Keep it simple! A goal changes everything!*
No new fancy balls *the next time, Mr. Sepp Blatter! The World Cup stage is no event for experiment and practicing with a new ball — give the stars of the world what they know! Champions of the world are defined with a simple ball . . . one they are used to. The World is watching!*
Oh! The power of one goal . . . *one glorious shot that can send a country into ecstasy!*
You win as a country . . . you lose as a country!
That modern, million-dollar ball with a name we like to forget made this year's global tournament into a practicing month on the fields of South Africa. How very sad!

Brazil 2014, *we can't wait. America will be there!*
"The real joys of life lie in the hope of tomorrows. . ."

From Arizona with love,
Trudy Wells-Meyer, a Football/Soccer fan for life.
Soccer/Football rules!

UEFA (Union of European Football Association, the confederation of world football's governing body FIFA,) did add one more referee on each goal line to the games. Five referees became a norm for a while, during UEFA Champion League playoff games, and, in some English FA Cup games, mostly final games.

In 201**8**, at the first-ever, new UEFA Nations League Tournament, 5 referees were used likewise. Not at the World Cup. However, VAR, (Video Assistant Referee) came to pass for the first time in Russia, in 201**8**.)

In 2014, after the World Cup in Brazil, where they shut down the Stock Market during games of World Cup magnitude, Germany declared the Champions, I sent a letter to FIFA, to Mr. Sepp Blatter, with 25 countries' signatures. Again, I had approached people with accents, everywhere: our dry cleaner from South Korea, my young model-gorgeous European assistant Ludmila, Czech Republic, the young, handsome, black fellow working at the carwash in Steamboat Springs, Colorado, who gave me a jumbo smile when I asked, "Do you like soccer?" His agreement and signature (in the men's room so as not to look like he was not working) represented Jamaica, his home country. My favorite signature that year, the WEST condo handyman, a Godsend who fixed the plumbing problem in our condo one hectic morning — his country, Argentina, enhanced my FIFA letter.

That same summer I needed an emergency dental root canal, known to be painful and not on my list of things I wanted to do. My long-time dentist sent me to a root canal specialist. With my mouth stretched open to the limits, I speculated about this doctor's unusual name, Dr. R. Sluyk — Holland? He must be Dutch. On the way out, with Novocain hardly allowing me to speak, I mumbled, "Doctor, do you like soccer — I mean *Fussball*?" His enthusiastic *yes* let me explain, on my follow-up visit I would bring a letter to FIFA. While for days I suffered the discomfort in my mouth, Holland, the Netherlands, was now at least secured as one of the signatures.

A USA signature, my American soccer buddy Brendan asked proudly for his name to appear on top, for everyone to see. Yes, there are soccer lovers in America who know it is real Football. *Fussball* in German.

Soccer . . . only in America.

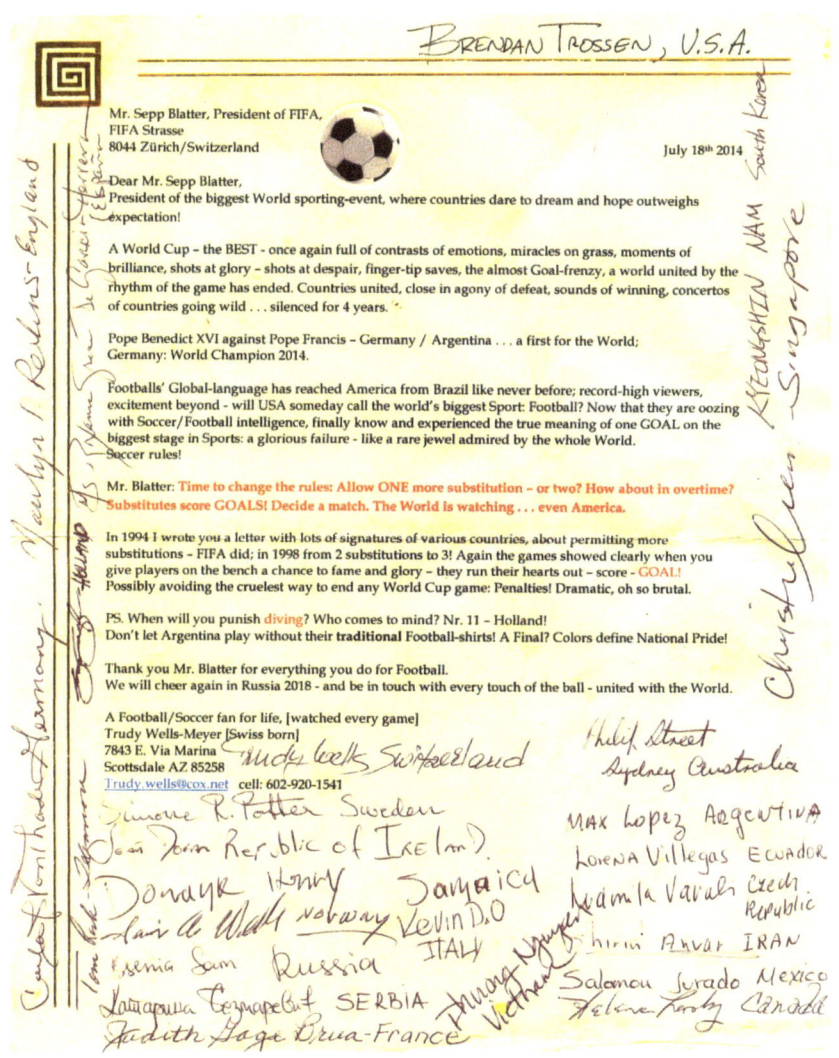

BRENDAN TROSSEN, U.S.A.

Mr. Sepp Blatter, President of FIFA,
FIFA Strasse
8044 Zürich/Switzerland

July 18th 2014

Dear Mr. Sepp Blatter,
President of the biggest World sporting-event, where countries dare to dream and hope outweighs expectation!

A World Cup - the BEST - once again full of contrasts of emotions, miracles on grass, moments of brilliance, shots at glory – shots at despair, finger-tip saves, the almost Goal-frenzy, a world united by the rhythm of the game has ended. Countries united, close in agony of defeat, sounds of winning, concertos of countries going wild . . . silenced for 4 years.

Pope Benedict XVI against Pope Francis – Germany / Argentina . . . a first for the World;
Germany: World Champion 2014.

Footballs' Global-language has reached America from Brazil like never before; record-high viewers, excitement beyond - will USA someday call the world's biggest Sport: Football? Now that they are oozing with Soccer/Football intelligence, finally know and experienced the true meaning of one GOAL on the biggest stage in Sports: a glorious failure - like a rare jewel admired by the whole World.
Soccer rules!

Mr. Blatter: Time to change the rules: Allow ONE more substitution - or two? How about in overtime? Substitutes score GOALS! Decide a match. The World is watching . . . even America.

In 1994 I wrote you a letter with lots of signatures of various countries, about permitting more substitutions - FIFA did; in 1998 from 2 substitutions to 3! Again the games showed clearly when you give players on the bench a chance to fame and glory - they run their hearts out – score – GOAL! Possibly avoiding the cruelest way to end any World Cup game: Penalties! Dramatic, oh so brutal.

PS. When will you punish diving? Who comes to mind? Nr. 11 – Holland!
Don't let Argentina play without their traditional Football-shirts! A Final? Colors define National Pride!

Thank you Mr. Blatter for everything you do for Football.
We will cheer again in Russia 2018 - and be in touch with every touch of the ball - united with the World.

A Football/Soccer fan for life, [watched every game]
Trudy Wells-Meyer [Swiss born]
7843 E. Via Marina
Scottsdale AZ 85258
Trudy.wells@cox.net cell: 602-920-1541

Trudy Wells Switzerland

Simone R. Potter Sweden

Sean John Republic of Ireland

Donayk Henry Jamaica

Clair A Wells Norway Kevin D.O ITALY

Ksenia Sam Russia

Latrapuwa Comapelsut SERBIA

Judith Hoge Drua-France

Philip Street Sydney Australia

MAX Lopez ARGENTINA

Lorena Villegas ECUADOR

Adam la Varals Czech Republic

Shirin Anvar IRAN

Salomou Jurado Mexico

Helene Koroty Canada

Hwang Nguyen Vietnam

Copy of original letter sent in 2014.

249

Mr. Sepp Blatter, President of FIFA,
FIFA Strasse
8044 Zürich/Switzerland   July 1**8**, 2014

Dear Mr. Sepp Blatter,
President of the biggest world sporting event, where countries
dare to dream, and hope outweighs expectation!

A World Cup — the BEST — once again full of contrasts of
emotions, miracles on grass, moments of brilliance, shots at glory
— shots of despair, fingertip saves, the almost-goal frenzy, a
world united by the rhythm of the game has ended. Countries
united, close in agony of defeat, sounds of winning, concertos of
countries going wild . . . silenced for four years.

Pope Benedict XVI against Pope Francis — Germany-Argentina . .
. a first for the World.
Germany: World Champion 2014.

Football's global language has reached America from Brazil like
never before; record-high viewers, beyond excitement — will the
USA someday call the world's biggest sport "Football"? Now that
they are oozing with soccer/football intelligence, they finally
know and experience the true meaning of one GOAL on the
biggest stage in sports: a glorious failure — like a rare jewel
admired by the whole world.
Soccer rules!

Mr. Blatter: **Time to change the rules: Allow ONE more
substitution — or two? How about in overtime? Substitutes
score GOALS! Decide a match. The world is watching . . .
even America.**

In 1994, I wrote you a letter, with signatures from various
countries, about permitting more substitutions – FIFA did; in
199**8** from two substitutions to three! Again, the games showed
clearly when you give players on the bench a chance for fame
and glory — they run their hearts out — score — GOAL!
Possibly avoiding the cruelest way to end any World Cup game:
Penalties! Dramatic, oh so brutal.

P.S. When will you punish diving? Who comes to mind? Number
11 — Holland!
Don't let Argentina play without their **traditional** football shirts!
A Final? Colors define national pride!

Thank you, Mr. Blatter, for everything you do for football.
We will cheer again in Russia 2018 — and be in touch with
every touch of the ball — united with the world.
A Football/ Soccer fan for life (watched every game).
Trudy Wells-Meyer (Swiss-born)

LE PRÉSIDENT

Mrs Trudy Wells
7483 E. Via., Marina
Scottsdale
AZ 85258-2826
USA

Zurich, 26 September 2014

Dear Trudy, *dear friend in football,*

Many thanks for your letter – nice to hear from you again!

I was delighted to receive a first-hand account of how popular is becoming in the USA thanks to the success of the FIFA World Cup in Brazil. I am also very pleased to hear how much your enjoyed the tournament – your positive response fills me with encouragement!

I have also taken note of your comments regarding possible changes to the Laws of the Game and diving, which I will bear in mind.

Wishing you continued enjoyment of the game of football in the years to come, I thank you again for writing in.

Yours sincerely,

Joseph S. Blatter

Fédération Internationale de Football Association
FIFA-Strasse 20 P.O. Box 8044 Zurich Switzerland T +41 (0)43 222 7777 F +41 (0)43 222 7878 FIFA.com

In ecstasy, I read Sepp Blatter's answer. At the World Cup 2018 in Russia for the first time, at the knock-out stage — loser goes home, FIFA used a fourth substitute in overtime at a crucial game. Russia played Spain. Russia beat Spain in overtime.

Russia, the first to enforce the new rule at a World Cup put in a fourth player during overtime, 30 minutes even more electrifying. (Stop at 15 minutes each way and switch Goals.) Fresh legs. Let the guys on the bench into the game with a chance for a miracle on grass and score. Fame forever.

Did my one Russian signature, the pretty hostess at a restaurant downtown at the Dells in Wisconsin, remember the FIFA letter she signed one summer in 2014? As the Europe-chic lady walked our group of four, (two school friends of Lew) to a table by the window we requested, I detected her accent. She never let me finish my question, "Do you like soccer/football?"

"YES, love it," she yelled, putting her hand over her mouth as if in shock for being too obvious. During her busy lunch mob crowd waiting to be seated, the 23-year-old found a minute to read and sign. Bsenia Sam agreed. Russia's signature on my letter sealed for FIFA, yeah!

I recalled Sepp Blatter's words on different occasions: *FIFA listens to its fans.*

By the way . . .

In 2018, at the final games of the UEFA European Championship, a fourth player in overtime also was to be used in the exciting yearly semifinal and the final.   Yet, at that particular final game, Real Madrid/Liverpool — 3:1 — the new change was not needed. Only when the match remains tied.

The first time a fourth substitution was used in overtime, in a FA Cup semifinal in England, materialized back in April 2017. As I watched with incredulous eyes, glued to the TV set, commentators enthusiastically debated and discussed this new rule. I freaked out. I danced around the coffee table in our den/TV room. Cheering at the top of my voice I applauded.

I wrote immediately to Mr. Sepp Blatter, not the acting president any longer. I sent him my heartfelt thank-you in the name of all the signed countries.

I enlightened *Herr* Blatter of our upcoming visit, for one week at the end of May, staying at the Hotel Storchen in Zürich on the banks of the river Limmat.

The day after our arrival in my homeland Switzerland, Sepp Blatter called the world-famous Storchen Hotel to speak to Trudy. We merely had left to meet my younger sister and my brother. Upon our return to the hotel late afternoon the concierge stopped us at the desk to inform me of Mr. Blatter's phone call. He handed me a message written on the imposing hotel stationery: An invite to FIFA's headquarters in Zürich. Utterly ecstatic, but dejected and worn-out, due to a mammoth family dispute/crisis over *Herr* Blatter. "Shut up!" (in German sounds worse) to my sensitive sister Beate, as I continued to defend FIFA's hero. (Swiss Press, not kind to Sepp Blatter, just like Donald Trump.) I came to regret unfortunate words exchanged. Our fighting, my sister not talking, lasted for days, months. Entirely changed and ruined plans. No visit to FIFA. I remained distraught, melodramatic for long after our return to Arizona for the missed chance and opportunity to meet Mr. Blatter, the soccer/football king. Pass up an invitation to the world legendary FIFA headquarters in Zürich?

How I wished and dream *Tädi* could have been a part of my FIFA association filled with Football/*Fussball* frenzy.

Erwin, *Ini*, his nickname still today, short for *Ineine,* our baby sister Beate gave him when she first started to talk, *Ini* speaks little English. Not enough to understand the FIFA letters. I translate a lot and feel the distress of his spellbound hanging on my every word. If only *Ini* could read these significant letters himself. Loneliness comes from family, relatives, friends from school never able to read my story — my book — poetry, or any essays — due to not speaking/understanding English.

Writing in my second language has many challenges and its cross to bear. Loneliness is one.

Erwin, who celebrated **8**0 years of Salon Meyer in 201**8** with his loyal clients, way back when his school buddies frequently needed an extra player, a goalie on their all-boys team. Next to the Catholic church, close to home, kids gathered to play (no organized boys and girls sports in those days). Enough boys did not always show up at the shabby grass soccer field. *Trudeli,* who tagged along wherever Erwin went (Mother's orders) a girl, asked to guard the goal? Erwin's apprehension, stamped in my brain forever, did not trust his younger sister. Whereas at any given time I was better than nobody and got the 'call' — a goalie at 9 years old. Erwin, time and again he'd come storming to help stop his buddies' shots and save the ball with his feet or head from bouncing into the goal. Undoubtedly, I learned young to be a nervous wreck, a worrywart right there on a *Fussball*/soccer field — to not let the boys down.

Our quiet father, with a hidden temper, never had time, his daily workload not permitting to observe his little girl (through teenage years) in action, in the goal that seemed to swallow her. I knew he secretly cheered me on. A daughter knows.

Most Sunday afternoons, in the next village to Tann, in Rüti, at the local *Fussball* field, home of Dad and Erwin's sport, is where I learned to cherish the moments when *Tädi*'s smile emerged. I adored him for throwing his arms in excitement. I learned cuss words as a young girl and the meaning of one goal. Fingertip saves — a goal denied by the framework, when woodworks, a crossbar, became a goalie's best friend — oh, and the heroism of one goal. Forever will I glorify a sport that unites us a lifetime.

Schgruna never knew of the close *Fussball* connection *Udi,* his daughter shared with him (still does) throughout any important football game. A lasting bond, all the more in his death. An attempt to retain a link of emotion: *Schgruna, sitting next to Trudeli, his Udi,* a never wavering bond. Raising arms, shouting words, and cussing like Dad. Cowbells ringing when the Swiss team played — like father, like daughter — a tradition lives on.

He loved *Fussball* — she loves *Fussball.* The real football of the world: America's Soccer — the world's Football.

Thank you, Dad, *Tädi*, my *Schgruna*, who remains the only one who called me *Udi.*

In 1994 during the exciting World Cup in America, Erwin and friend Heiri traveled on a tour from Europe and visited various selected US cities. My brother *Ini* loves to chatter happily about utterly gripping, impressive live soccer, *Fussball* matches he was lucky to attend.

Erwin's visit, 1984
Siegfried and Roy show
Mirage Hotel, Las Vegas

Amazingly in that 4-week tournament in 1994, the USA played Switzerland — two countries in the same group to cheer for this Swiss immigrant with dual citizenship. I cried. I prayed. They tied.

Wildly elated with the game's result, not to favor one country, although — who am I kidding? Deep in my heart — *Hopp Schwyz* — Switzerland — all the way. The red and white colors of a nation — the Swiss flags in the crowds brought rapturous tears.

Once a Swiss, — always a Swiss.

In 2006 at the World Cup in Germany, after the USA lost to Ghana, Switzerland was still to play its third game. As 'my team' stepped on the field in Deutschland, cheered on by all the fans who had made the trip across the border, I stared in amazement at a  sea of red/white Swiss flags in the stadium — a sight I will not forget. Switzerland has this many flags. When the National Anthem played before the game, familiar sounds of home, time stood still. A stream of tears rolled down my cheeks. Our home in Arizona, where we have the best TV coverage, had turned into 'little Switzerland'. Flags and cowbell waving.

Tädi, Schgruna right there beside me in spirit.

I waved 2 flags ferociously wishing I had more hands, a cowbell on my arm. The Swiss scored first against South Korea. Did I honestly jump that high? Cowbell-ringing would not stop, the pride of being Swiss not leaving me for a second . . . what a feeling!

Switzerland went on to win and led to the second round in a tournament where feet are doing all the magic and *Fussball* is played at the highest levels with each country's best. A small nation famous for the snow-covered Alps celebrating — in ecstasy. They dared to dream for more.

The power of goals — or no goals — that changed everything.

Still tied, including overtime, no goals at the end of the game against Ukraine. A hero Swiss goalie all tournament long and team Switzerland, with a Wilhelm Tell mentality, the only country not giving up any goals in 4 matches during the 2006 tournament was ready to face the final ordeal — Penalties. The knockout stage, when the score is tied, demands the agony of penalty-shoot-out to decide the winner. The torture started. Legs are gone, hearts beat faster, nerves takeover to be one of the selected players to face the goalie. History shows the best of the best have missed. The football world remembers the names of those who failed. Goalkeepers become heroes, stars for life. Championships have been decided because of one shot on goal — or missed. Oh, the power of one goal.

3 Swiss shots on goal did not go in . . . damn the belief in 3's.

'Lady Luck' already asleep, Switzerland did it as a team. Ukraine won.

That is the World Cup!

***

FIFA
FIFA-Strasse 20
please forward to President, Mr. Sepp Blatter
8044 Zürich, Switzerland   *May 28th, 2019*

"Retirement is about achieving your dreams and having time to say YES to everything."

Dear Mr. Blatter,

How are you? Remember me? I hope you get this letter.

Your call at the Hotel Storchen on May 30th in 2017 I so appreciated. Due to a family crisis while there, I never got to visit FIFA Headquarters — very upsetting.
Your legendary work in Football and the biggest world sports events during your reign, Mr. Blatter, will live on— I hope you are enjoying your well-deserved retirement.
"Life is not a rehearsal."

I am writing a book, the title: Some Things Are Simply Meant to Be (Coming to America — from Switzerland) A memoir as a collection of poetry and short stories. I would love to include copies of the three FIFA letters 1994, 2010, and 2014 I wrote to you about changes in Football and your answers.
Do I have your permission to do this?

256

THANK YOU in advance!

We will again be at the Hotel Storchen in Zürich, from July 15th until July 23rd.
I hope not to miss visiting FIFA Headquarters, the world's biggest football governing body.

By the way. . .
About VAR — I was wrong. Nothing short of sensational. I love the whole new level of drama (UEFA Championship games — the best this year) and I am glad referees now have help for fair and correct calls.
Mr. Blatter, your compassionate love for Football, known all over the world, lives in your heart and soul. We will ALWAYS remember.

"It is not true that people stop pursuing dreams because they grow old, they grow old because they stop pursuing dreams." —
Gabriel Garcia Marquez

*Soccer/**Football** rules!*

Herzlich,

Trudy Wells-Meyer a Football fan for life — thanks to my father.

In this particular letter to Mr. Blatter, in May 2019, I wrote for my personal need. Writing my memoir, my legacy, "*Some Things Are Simply Meant to Be,*" I found out, for my book, I needed to receive and ask for permission to include the 3 vital letters (starting in 1994) I wrote to the headquarters of FIFA, mailed to the President, Mr. Sepp Blatter. All letters about football/soccer changes, ideas, requests dominated with signatures from around the world, somehow, frankly had to appear visibly more dramatic and noticed. The first change implemented transpired at the World Cup in 199**8** in France — Sepp Blatter's first year as the FIFA's president, elected on June **8** (our wedding anniversary).

The envelope to FIFA headquarters in 2019, I addressed with a thank you in the left corner. I added, "Please forward this letter to Sepp Blatter".

Herr Blatter's response, where I mentioned his well-deserved retirement and wrote about our stay at the Hotel Storchen, arrived immediately, by e-mail. His phone number and contact information in Zürich in my inbox. YEAH! What an outstanding moment. He let me know *yes*, he would be in the Zürich area during the same week of our visit.

Continuing contact through e-mail and phone calls allowed a meeting with Sepp Blatter, the President of FIFA for 17 years. A retired and happy man visited Lew and me at the Hotel Storchen in Zürich, on July 16, 2019, where he was treated and received like the star he is, by staff and manager. Witnessing a scene like a celebration in the hotel lobby, and bar, warmed my heart.

Sepp Blatter had called the afternoon of our arrival at the sophisticated Hotel Storchen. I experienced tummy flip-flops from excitement. Texts and calls followed, and his sensational visit occurred the following morning.

The first time I had dialed Sepp Blatter's phone number, my hand trembled silly, while we stayed at the Capra Hotel in Saas Fee, a small, picturesque resort for hiking. (On our bucket list for years). Our dream had come true and astounded *Herr* Blatter immensely. He revealed knowing Saas Fe very well since his childhood home was close, in Visp, Wallis. (Valais, the same *Kanton* where the new FIFA President Gianni Infantino resided and grew up.)

What a stellar moment, one week later, when Sepp Blatter walked through the revolving hotel entrance and my outstretched arms ended in his enthralling hug. I strained to think of one single thing to say he had not likely heard a thousand times, no luck. Speechless, yet with a mammoth smile, I knew in an instant, in my heart — this man is in front of me because he has a heart of gold.

At the hotel Storchen's famous Barchetta with a view of the river *Limmat* Lew waited, waving his usual royal wave, slow and deliberate. He had reserved the corner seat Mr. Blatter aimed for and gave the impression to be familiar with. A perfect corner for stretching his wounded knee, still riddled with pain after an operation only a short while past. I witnessed a heartfelt handshake between the two men. I introduced Lew, a non-soccer-lover. Sepp Blatter's smiling face reminded me of a glass of warm spiced wine . . . yes, we had a glass of wine at eleven in the morning. Mr. Blatter ordered and treated his guests. Lew and me.

The best Swiss — from the Valais — wine.

Herr Blatter brought his newly published book, his name as big as life. A gift for me.

I showed off my book, a proof copy only, (nearly finished.) I promised to send him a copy as soon as possible, depending on publishing factors. A gift to him, hopefully soon.

My question for the permission *"Can I use the 3 FIFA letters in my book"* reason now for sitting next to this prominent man, left Sepp utterly humble. His hand clutched his heart.

"I am honored" included his priceless smile.

A stirring response beyond words. Like the icing on a cake that meant everything to participate in a fun time, together, with such a positive man who brought the World Cup truly to the whole world. Conversations flowed easily, like a most natural occurrence to sit across from this legend who was forced out of FIFA. Literally.

On May 27, 2015, on a Viking River Cruise from Amsterdam to Zürich, going home, I turned on the TV in our suite late afternoon: CNN reporting from the US of the raid, FIFA officials in Zürich being charged with bribes. I stopped in mid-air arranging my hair for dinner. My mouth open, jaw-dropping, I stared at the US *Attorney* General talking about accusations. Something was fishy . . . the timing for one. Two days before the possible reelection of Sepp Blatter? Why is America involved?

As I would tell Sepp Blatter, 2 years later, in Zürich,

"America, why America . . . they don't even like Soccer."

A phrase would remain with *Herr* Blatter, (and his lawyers.) Words that opened Sepp's ears big time . . . wondering.

I expressed "I wish I did not know so many facts . . ." He suggested I talk to a reporter he knows well. I declined.

Monday before our Arizona departure, Sepp Blatter joined us again, one more time, same hotel bar corner. I had mentioned on the phone when I called to thank him for the wine, fun, and classy visit, "You forgot to autograph your book."

"Oh, so sorry. *Ich chume no mal.* I come back. How about for *an Abschieds* drink? A goodbye drink."

Herr Blatter brought gifts. Eyes huge I held Nici, a brown Zürich Lighthouse Bear, snuggling him in my arms.

A FIFA gold key chain for Lew, the future soccer lover?

At the hectic full of tourists Sprüngli store on the Bahnhofstrasse, earlier Lew and I had found a gold heart (to match Sepp's heart of gold) a gift filled with a variety of in vogue chocolates. He opened the fancy package, held the gold heart to his heart, "Oh, *DANKE VIELMAL!* My favorite chocolates."

Uf Wiederluege Sepp Blatter! We will see each other again. . ..

Hotel Storchen @ the Limmat, leaving for the airport, Nici Bear ready

One more thing . . .

For the duration of the 2018/2019 UEFA Europa League season, not forced out yet by VAR, Video Assistant Referee technology with instant replay, fans still watched and cheered five referees, with two on each goal line. Four extra eyes. This one new rule was still in use; however, at the Europa League Final — Arsenal/Chelsea in Baku, Azerbaijan — for the first time VAR, the use of Video technology, with its added drama, and sensational and provocative moments was available. VAR would become a part of world football, nothing less than controversial, but oh so fair most of the time.

Fairness, a word huge in my Dad's vocabulary, he would have welcomed fair play but to change old-fashioned *Fussball?*

Probably not so much.

Trudy Wells-Meyer

Gold . . . Gold at Last

Olympic Gold 2008 through the eyes of a Swiss lady with dual citizenship.

The Olympics — an event that stops the world from spinning — emotions and sensations rip through our bodies, feelings for athletes we never knew or heard of before, feelings we don't even know exist. Moments of distinctive brilliance, mistakes that shape the future — sounds of victory — agony of defeat.

The world as we know it, for two weeks, stops . . .

The day when Roger Federer lost to James Blake, USA, in the quarterfinals in Beijing, China, showed the ultimate of despair in Roger's eyes; his dream denied again, Olympic Gold. However, the magnitude of his loss spelled much more. One of the most decorated tennis stars to have lost his magic. As he walked off the court, head down, hiding tears, he left the world wondering.

Even the red and white Swiss colors on the *Prince of the World in Tennis* looked faded. Heartbreaking. My heavy heart stopped dreaming for Roger Federer.

The sounds of victory belonged to James Blake — his first win ever (in eight games) against the Swiss phenomenon. In ecstasy James's march for a medal continued. What a monster moment for the American. A certain hush and mystique filled the world about an underdog finding a way to win at the Olympics. Impossible is nothing.

Saturday came — intuition — my getting up early turned into a morning to remember. I clicked the remote, which is not my habit in the morning. I stared in total disbelief. On the screen Roger Federer serving, the red and white never looked better. Oh! And there was Stanislas Wawrinka — on the second Tennis- Swiss-wonder's racket, a backhand winner crossed the net.

Awestruck, I witnessed the gold-medal doubles match, Switzerland versus Sweden. I had no idea about the match at this early hour. By an amazing chance of luck, I gazed at the "Fedrinka Team" playing for gold. For one hour I forgot to make my daily necessary cup of coffee.

They won. As a team. Roger won his first and only gold medal with Stanislas Wawrinka, his good friend. On their rackets giving Switzerland, the country of the impressive Alps, ecstatic happiness — a glorious victory. The Fedwrinka team brought home gold. *Gold in doubles* left the proud Swiss celebrating a long-awaited elusive gold medal in tennis.

A country, that never stopped dreaming for Roger, the icon of the world and role model of the century.

A certain rush of irony about a world-class player who faced his *chosen tennis life* alone for years, but oh, so victorious. As a team, on that day in China. Roger found out in Beijing: "Happiness is truly real when shared."

"Passion at the Olympics is not measured by the steps they run on the court . . . it is measured by the heart that beats for their country." — Anonymous

A tennis fan for life, I know in my heart Switzerland, the country of my birth, will be the country I am rooting for, first and foremost.

"Hopp Schwyz!"

["Gold . . . Gold at Last" was published in the Swiss Arizona Society newsletter *VALLEY ECHO,* September 200**8**]

Scottsdale Arizona, our home at Golden Heritage Village, since 1977 on McCormick Ranch

April 201**8**, at Horseshoe Bend, Page, Arizona

The Beginning — 1968-2020

Power of Possibilities

"If you live a life of love, you will love the life you live." —
Anonymous

Now that I have shared my world — our world — through words, and writing has become a lifestyle, a state of mind necessary like breathing, I am beyond thankful for the ability to form my life into words. Filmmakers create an emotional impact with image and sound — writers do it with words.

Writing . . . at the heart of this ambition is desire and determination to show people the world through my eyes — I guess a somewhat arrogant belief to have found a way to describe something worth committing to paper. At the age of 78, I held a proof copy of my manuscript, a book, my book enhanced with pictures. A legacy as a *Schriftstellerin,* (Author) to leave behind.

Writing, a revelation of one's reality feels like creating a world by the light of the mind, the heat of the heart, and finding music in words. What a comfort a pen is. . ..

Trough out my eventful American life, I tried to push away the echo of my past. Once upon my childhood and humble upbringing at the end of the war, at times when we were small not having enough food on the table and continuous hand-me-down; I hated ill-fitting clothes. Mom, the seamstress, could and would sew them to look much better when time permitted.

Now life had changed to horrors of the world and devastating news flashing on TV, to worries of low batteries on a Cell Phone, a common necessity to society, to an all-knowing google-time. Clicking, an agonizing frustration as well as the helplessness of my computer getting stuck. One more reason to have and own a book — my book — to hold in my hands. Oh, the power of turning a page, my words to read. No more dependence on a machine called a computer and hit delete by mistake.

Such is life.

After uncountable questions of, *"How could you leave a beautiful country like Switzerland?"* I now see the meaning of that repeated inquiry with grown-up eyes each trip home. I feel nostalgia — hidden, rare, but constant. While trees grow tall and change, the sky is the only childhood thing not smaller than you remember it.

"Where we love is home, home that our feet may leave, but not our hearts." — Oliver Wendell Holmes, Sr.

I learned there is something good in everything, and being a part of the flow of gratitude, I embrace those early days and unpretentious beginnings with appreciation. They led to dreaming of *Coming to America,* to step foot on American soil, alone. I went confidently in the direction of my dreams. I created a life in a foreign country. Choices of my elusive life guided me to find what I never dreamed possible.

What will be will be . . . *Some things are simply meant to be.*

Motivation to learn taught me you can never completely remove yourself from the place that raised you through mere distance. Homesickness is laced with nostalgia, longing for what we don't have, including neither speaking (oh but trying) nor understanding a language — truly helpless at times.

Now that English reigns in this inner multi-dynamic of writing in my second language, I don't miss *'the tortured affair with language'* — Chang-Rae Lee's words. To feel *at ease* with speaking English one dreams about and does not identify nor comprehend until years later.

My limited English vocabulary for so long didn't allow anyone to recognize my sense of humor handed down from my father. To search for the right word anytime but in a punch line? My accent still evident, (they say) *"Where are you from?"* is a constant. A friend claims European women put on an accent and work at it on purpose, a statement I never understood and relentlessly irritates me. One of my precise answers is, "Try to speak in a different language . . . and write."

With fondness, I think of Mrs. Le Cornue, with white beauty-parlor hair, who taught me English. A summer hairdressing job in 1963, at "Touch of Class" salon, from the first of June to the end of October on the Isle of Jersey, included a place to live, walking distance from the salon. A loft room with no door, squeaky stairs, and a low slanted ceiling was my temporary home at Mrs. Le Cornue's adorable, small English cottage in St. Brelades Jersey, an island between

France and England known as the Honeymoon Island of England.

My first time across the border, away from Switzerland.

With inadequate knowledge, my few English words disappeared as my wrinkle-faced teacher, with a jolly grin expected everything of me. A floppy, worn-out cushion on an old wooden chair, my assigned daily seat, faced an amazingly green garden with countless roses and flowers. A widow for years, my new-found English grandma, my educator had me sit for hours. On my day off, in the evenings I wrote every word on a piece of paper before speaking it. If once I knew how to write a word, I would remember.

When learning a new language as an adult, one tends at first and for a long time after, to translate every word, every sentence in one's head — a word salad at its best.

One catchphrase I knew well: "How would you like to have your hair done?" Customers proceeded to tell me and mumble on, to my distinct horror of feeling lost. I purchased a photo album and cut out at least one hundred hairstyles I had found in a range of magazines: short hair, long, curly hair, red, blonde, bangs, straight hair, updos, etc. That hair album, a tremendous help, I packed in my suitcase when I left on my across-the-ocean journey, *Coming to America.*

Mrs. Le Cornue had to endure sounds from upstairs — constant music from a tiny, blue phonograph that played only 45-single records, my proud, precious possession purchased with tips from clients. I adored American hits — Elvis Presley, my favorite, and other English records I didn't understand and tried desperately to translate the words with my small dictionary. I played the same songs over and over until they wore out. As my mom used to say, "Trudy plays records until she is unconscious."

For years I stayed in contact and wrote to this kind English lady with stiff hair that didn't dare move in the strong island wind. She had a small family only, no grandkids to tell her, "Grandma, you put too much rouge on your cheeks."

Each time I wrote postcards from all over the States and letters to my unforgettable teacher, I hoped she would not find one mistake. I used extreme measures to perfect my new language — American English, — British accents were now absent, I would only hear them occasionally. The impact of that lady being proud meant the world to a pupil a continent away who never forgot her English educator. Never will.

***

Lew and I are tied together by shared memories: all the reasons Lew hooked me — grateful to be caught, and by the future of maybes and what-ifs . . . May love live on.

"Those who don't believe in magic will never find it." — Roald Dahl

As I started to write this book with my aged hand in 201**8,** a memoir, a collection in poetry, essays and prose about life, it is fifty years ago in the spring of 196**8** when my car turned onto Orange Blossom Lane in Phoenix, Arizona, **8**501**8**.

At an early age, I had learned how everyday life can turn on a small decision. Events in life become doorways into intense realities that stem from mysteries. Certain moments remain dynamic as I think about that fateful spring morning after I arrived in Scottsdale, Arizona. In search of a place to live, I turned left on Camelback Road in the grand American car I had spotted in a car dealer's showroom in downtown Washington, DC. I did not pay for it like my old-fashioned dad instructed his children: "If you can't pay for something you can't have it." Dad's belief due to a strict childhood upbringing, as one of fourteen children — the second youngest — number thirteen. His motto never changed, a belief the difference between luxury and necessity is directly proportional to your ability to pay for it.

Did Dad know about my monthly payments to a bank back East I did not know? Silence can be (was) golden.

Why did I turn left on Camelback Road to drive south on 56th Street? A foreign area, not knowing I was in Phoenix, why did I cross a busy intersection, a street called Indian School Road? Why another left turn, on a small street, before Thomas Road the next traffic light as my enormous car headed into an alley lined with tall palm trees. A street sign had caught my eye: Orange Blossom Lane — that sounded like a song.

Everything in life happens for a reason. . ..

I drove toward a long, three-story building, facing Camelback Mountain. I detected a huge name high up *Allegro;* and I spotted a white sign with black writing: *2 and 3 bedrooms for rent.* With an apathetic look that translated to *not what I need,* I slowed down anyway, wondering with dreamy eyes what the view must be like from the top floor. An older gray-haired gentleman rushed out of a street-level apartment next to the big for-rent sign. A surprisingly calm voice asked, "Can I help you?"

I rolled down the window, "No thank you." I pointed to the sign, "I am looking for a studio, possibly a one-bedroom." With a resigned look, I tried to turn my car around, wondering if he could understand me.

Mr. Libas walked to my car and introduced himself. "I am Max, the manager of the building. You simply must-see number #31**8**, the vacant two-bedroom jewel on the third floor." He insisted. "Come, let me show you a view you won't believe." The number **8** echoed in my ear.

"No way. Too big, too expensive."

Mr. Libas had become aware of my accent. "Where are you from?" My Swiss German startled him.

"I lived in Germany" he commented.

Whatever compelled me to get out of the car? *View*, a magic word — 31**8**, a pulsating number.

Some things are simply meant to be.

I followed Max Libas up the stairs.

In the background of my memory looms forever the moment when Mr. Libas opened the door of apartment 31**8** as my lucky number **8** hit me in the eyes. Memories are not always as they were, yet this one remains clear as yesterday.

Max gently pushed me through the door. "Go!"

I walked in. "OMG! Paradise."

My hand covered my mouth. Camelback Mountain in the distance yet close as to touch it. Ignoring the kitchen on the left, I dashed to the massive, enclosed patio window; chills crawled down my spine. I pinched myself, staring at a golf course, its deep green baffled me. Palm trees everywhere. Gardens with magnificent flowers surrounded a huge swimming pool below. The desert has flowers like that? Are those tiki torches? Am I on a tropical island? Hawaii or heaven?

Could I possibly live here?

My heart played tricks and almost jumped out of my chest. The sight simply compelled my heart to leap.

I must live here is all I could think. How? Two bedrooms and two baths? The place was humongous for a Swiss Miss from tiny Tann.

Max Libas, with a grin, slipped me his phone number as I hurried to the car.

I drove with alarming speed to Carsten and his wife Sally's home, where I was staying. I had worked with Carsten in Atlanta. He had offered me a job in his new 5th Avenue Scottsdale salon. Maneuvering my great big car up to their house, I spotted him cutting bushes in the yard. His day off, salon closed on Mondays.

Spilling words, I hollered, "Will I have enough customers to afford this magical place I found? "

"Of course. Where?" Carsten yelled back.

"At the Allegro, overlooking the Phoenix Country Club."

I moved in.

***

Once upon a time . . . Destiny knocked, in the enthralling year of 1968. On Sunday, August 28th, at 10:30 in the morning, I stood at the enclosed balcony window on the third floor. I gazed out, as usual, mesmerized by living in paradise when I saw him. Standing by the pool: a slender, sun-tanned male body, tall, with dark, short hair and the longest sideburns I had ever seen. He wore blue swim trunks — with large pink polka dots. My love for pink confirmed — once again. A cigarette appeared to rest between fingers in the middle of his hand, a position I had never seen. Who does that?

A sun-tanned face. No wedding band.

My heart pounded, doing flip-flops. "Who is that?"

Nobody to hear me. My heart did.

Love at first sight?

I ran to put on a pink, newly purchased bathing suit I was lucky to have found early summer. A tennis dress look-alike, with a pleated skirt; I could wear my reliable bra underneath — a reason I positively felt more comfortable than in any other swimsuit, ever. My fat complex on hold, this miracle suit let me believe I appeared slimmer and less self-conscious of my fifty-pound-extra body. An urge triggered — to my total surprise — to head to the pool, head held high.

I could hardly wait to go.

Pool and garden in view, I stopped at the bottom of the stairs. Mr. Libas, in lively conversation with the tall, striking stranger, like they were friends, called my name.

"Come, meet Lewis Wells," he yelled. Max had grabbed Lew's arm and unmistakably pushed him, toward me. With his terrific smile, I heard Mr. Libas say to Lew, "Have I got the girl for you." He paused, grinning at me,

"Lew, this is Trudy, the Swiss girl upstairs I told you about." Max moved closer and looked straight into Lew's eyes, "Don't forget, if I was twenty years younger, you wouldn't have a chance."

Lew's belly laugh rang out, a sound I would come to know so well. My life was about to be changed forever. I had only to see him once, see his smile, — Lew reached for my outstretched hand — it is the Swiss way to shake hands when greeting anyone. His beaming eyes and an undeniably gentle but firm touch alarmed my heart.

Boom, boom. . . I felt my face get hot.

"How is Marco? We miss him at the pool." Bethany, my new friend's unwelcome, piercing voice interrupted from the other side of the garden near the pool. Single, from Michigan, with a dark chocolate-like suntanned body, paraded her love for constant Arizona sun and screeched, "How was his trip back to London?"

"Okay," I shouted back. My short, do-not-bother-me-now answer shocked Bethany. I surprised myself. I naïvely did not want Lew to hear about another man in my life.

London, 1963-64

Intriguing like in old movies, a cigarette hanging on the left of his lips when he talked, Marco, a headwaiter at the famous Dorchester Hotel next door to the Coffee Inn on Park Lane, was a regular. His mannerism had everyone look up when he entered, and his captivating, good looks one guessed him to be from Italy or Spain. He dressed like an English-working man on strike, time off from the hotel demands of a waiter's starched uniform. His choice of casual attire, a sweater over his shoulder tied like a scarf would be noticed anywhere. He had a knack for tying scarves in unique ways long before Paris launched the scarf fashion for men. My eyes pursued Marco anytime I worked behind the coffee bar. Sadly, I never sensed him noticing me other than serving his most days Cappuccino enduring a polite thank you.

In November of 1963, I first encountered London fog, mysterious dim lights in semi-deserted dark streets. I learned the meaning of pouring rain. My hours at the elegant Coffee Bar on Park Lane were long and hectic, filled with fear and anxious moments. Toby Knight, the owner, had hired me without a work permit. The result: low pay and fright of being found out.

A summer job on the Isle of Jersey, at the contemporary "Touch of Class" salon in St. Brelades, a short bus ride from the capital, had come to an end in late October.

Theresa, a client I met at the beauty shop for her weekly shampoo and set, knew Mr. Knight, the English gentleman who hired girls at his Coffee Inn, which naturally served tea, an English custom, primarily in the afternoon.

"You mean I don't need a work permit?" I asked my friend in utter surprise.

"No, you won't," Theresa indicated convincingly.

The hair salon owner in St. Brelades, not a stylist, had obtained my permit to work on the island and sent it to Switzerland. I had only papers to sign and hand to the customs officials the day I arrived on the Isle of Jersey. The permit was for five months only and now had expired.

That season I not only learned English but what it meant to have no parents say no — freedom — in exchange for unknown responsibilities until you face them. Daily and constantly.

Theresa, my divorced English friend from Germany, a waitress in a smashing resort hotel near the ocean in St. Brelades for the duration of the island's vacation season, had lived in London for years and had offered to help me find a job in the big city. Theresa knew of my infatuation with one of London's professional football (American soccer) players, Ray Alford. I had met him in a bar during Arsenal's one-week summer training on the small island. He had asked for my phone number.

A chance to go to London and possibly see more of Ray? Possibly see him play at the Arsenal Stadium? Trudy's dream, her destination-wish and, need to find work were like an open book.

Guilt, however. over not wanting to return to Switzerland just yet bordered on agony at times.

Time to rebel, to stray from hairdressing and non-stop hair on my mind. Be a waitress. As a little girl, I had turned the family kitchen into a make-believe restaurant. I used the old wooden chairs as tables and played with my mother's dishes in the cabinets. Spoons, forks, and knives I found in the drawers. Silver coins, play-money I had received as a Christmas gift. I hand-sewed a small half-apron with dad's old, not-to-be used-any-longer white shaving towels from the barbershop. I added a tiny pocket for my tips.

Juhui — yeah, my waitress dream came true in London.

The chubby Swiss girl who had a troublesome time with English money and the language (although managed when hair was involved) got a job at a long, curved bar, with a few charming tables in the corner and daily fresh flowers. One of the most well-liked tables, with a cozy bench, faced Hyde Park and the hectic London Street. Customers were mostly employees in hotels on Park Lane and tourists asking for English tea. The Coffee Bar was sandwiched in between the Dorchester and Hilton hotels. German and Swiss guys stopped frequently for coffee and a small bite to eat before and after work. Hearing and speaking German — even Swiss — how enormously helpful and morale-elevating, creating a feeling of home away from home. We named The Coffee Inn *who-has-the-heaviest-accent* club.

Days were filled with chores I had to learn, carrying dishes with no wobbling, exchanging English money, pounds and shillings often confusing and worrisome; yet I found my new job unexpectedly fun at this international gathering place, — until the day my infatuation with a professional English football player ended with a jolt. He did not call as promised.

Theresa, my caring friend, investigated and located Ray's address. I stood at an old heavy iron gate, off to the side;

apprehensively I watched two small children with a narcotically beautiful, stunningly dressed blonde leave the front door. They climbed in a waiting car on the curved paved driveway.

Ray Alford — married with two children. While on the isle of Jersey, did he keep his wedding band in his wallet, the European way?

Surprising — no — yet disturbing. My efforts to come to London were based on a falsehood. He should not have kissed me.

Ray never called.

I remained an Arsenal fan, however, throughout my life.

Still today.

***

To this day I remember one densely foggy November day, the first time my weekly pay, in cash, disappeared — stolen from downstairs at work, where a tiny corner was assigned for employees, enough room for a purse and a coat.

Happening again and again I speculated. I knew who did it: the manager, a short guy who looked like a thief, with sleazy eyes that undress you while they rob you, eyes so narrow I wondered, *How can he see?* Oh, he saw everything and more. Customers knew of the manager's despicable manners.

What was I to do? Go to the police? Regularly the identifiable United Kingdom Police Force, in pairs, walked by the Coffee Bar, too frequently. I was sure they noticed guilty me through the no-curtain window behind the bar. An illegal at work.

Feeling extremely poor, with money relentlessly on my desperate mind, a norm to be depressed and gather pity along the way. How would I pay rent for the tiny room I had found in an old, gray, typical brick English apartment house, five stations away by Metro? London's Underground railway, the world's first, the only way I knew to get to that shabby, smelly room. Deflated my distress showed on my face and evoked questions by concerned customers, constantly asking,

"What is wrong?"

Nonetheless, my tips had a way of growing enormously and let my smile resurface.

One heavenly day dashing Marco, with long, sexy hair ready for a shampoo commercial adding to his aura of mystery, finally smiled an extra smile. I served him his predictable cappuccino; afraid my nerves would let me down and spill the brew. That extra wink with his chestnut eyes and an extra shilling was how a romance began — slowly — in my dreams mostly, for weeks consisting only of incomparable smiles and extra pleasantries across the bar.

I lived for Marco the Brit's cappuccino stops at the Coffee Inn, close to the elegant Dorchester, where he worked extended hours. The short times we saw each other, my communication skills non-existent, I nervously scrambled to find the right words, worrying about the loss of words not necessarily due to my limited English vocabulary.

Christmas in London, the intriguing city, arrived. Marco's family holiday tradition was unclear to me with an English dad, his mom from Italy. He still had not asked me out. I blamed his heavy work schedule, but how could I know for sure? I imagined another woman.

No plans for Christmas, my first away from home for this Swiss Miss. On Christmas Eve I decided to attend Midnight Mass at the famous London Westminster Cathedral. I worked until closing time; the Coffee Bar's usual 10 p.m. With enough tips on that day, I hailed one of London's recognizable taxi cabs.

I won't forget crying during Mass, feeling alone, all the more when I stepped out after the long-drawn-out Christmas service at 1:45 a.m., searching for one of those famous taxi lights on black cars that could be noticed anywhere, even in the fog.

No luck. A taxi nowhere to be seen. Now what? The lump forming in my throat felt like a stone. I started walking. The crowds had left. Semi-deserted streets downright disturbed me, and with no idea which direction to walk. I guessed. To make matters worse rain started, a drizzle in the fog to match my tears.

Do not panic, I prayed, shivering.

Horrified and frightened, I kept walking. What else could I do? On one of the massive streets, I saw a few cars speed by in the cold night. No taxis in sight. No payphones. The glowing streetlights reminded me of Christmas. Would they guide me home? Where was home?

A sound of a whistle pierced the stillness. A small car had stopped. A black man rolled down the window. His white teeth jolted me into reality, it was 2:30 a.m. on Christmas morning. Soft-spoken words by this mystery man confirmed, "No taxis on Christmas." He added, "One day off, once a year."

His voice kept talking. "Would you like a ride?" Like opening an overdue love letter, I was struck with an impulse to stretch out my arms. A Christmas angel from heaven, sent to me?

How could I be certain in the dark, foggy light above? Somehow, I failed to fear the man behind the wheel.

Shuddering from the cold, I got in the old, dented car. I ignored what my father taught his kids with stern words: "Do not go with any strangers! Ever." I hoped the extra candle I had lit after Mass would shine on. Sorry, Dad.

On the night Christ was born, the angels watched over me and sent a man who drove me home to my faraway Kensington address. Safe.

While I was searching for the house number, heavy fog set in — classic London. It had stopped raining. The car clock showed 3 a.m. My angel/driver got out, walked over to my side, and opened the car door. He walked me up the stairs of the weathered exterior building lit by dim streetlights. I hugged him, hoping it showed my gratefulness. His return bear hug lingered for years to come, his simple way of saying good night. Merry Christmas!

An intense Christmas memory hanging on and resurface so far as today. In a world filled with excessive evil and racial division, goodness triumphed, and history was made with the kindness of taking advantage of nothing.

A lost kind of paradise.

That African Englishman, my Christmas savior, stopped at the Coffee Inn to my surprise. Each time I served Jamal one of the Inn's specialties, a slice of delicious apple pie, my favorite. I would eat one every day for lunch. My slice belonged to Jamal at no charge when he startled me with a visit. As for the manager with his familiar sneer I knew too well, he made certain the price of the pie got subtracted from my paycheck, every time.

A fortnight after Christmas my cash was stolen the third time. Learning about money the hard way, the lack of it had turned to new heights. On the edge of desolation, I called home: "Dad, help." His strict voice offered to pay for a Swissair ticket to fly to Zürich. In return, I had to work at my parents' salon to pay the money back. My time in London ended abruptly, the same week, Marco on his day off had the guts to invite me to a movie theater.

The last evening at work, he waited until the bar closed. His prolonged goodbye hug, passionate kiss, and tight hold left me deeply flushed.

"When will I see you again?" His whispered words sounded like music letting me rejoice while feeling sad. A pledge turned into a long-distance, letter-writing relationship — drawn-out, waiting for answers. My letters got longer as my English improved, yet not more often. Absence makes the heart grow fonder — maybe. For a little while?

In June 1965, when I boarded the *Bremen,* for New York, a German ocean liner in Southampton, England, Marco stood at the dock and waved. He had traveled from London to see me board the floating city; he had asked for the day off from work.

His words dallied like an echo: "I will come and visit you in America." He did.

I saw his handsome face again, on American soil, in Arizona, early August 1968 — two weeks before I met Lew on August 28, 1968.

September 1968 — Phoenix, Arizona

Love is born with the
    pleasure of looking at each other.
It is fed with the necessity
    of seeing each other.
It is concluded with the
    impossibility of separation. — José Martí

What is LOVE?

A pinnacle of pain was more typical in my young dating life. New nonetheless, unrecognizable sensations, unfamiliar trembling when I saw him. Staring down to the pool too frequently. Anxiously, too often, I found myself searching for a certain red sports car parked at the Allegro, a convertible Austin-Healey. *Is Lew home?*

Love for Lew sizzled in my body, a few weekends after I met the tall, new resident on the third-floor end-unit, on that life-changing Sunday, August 28 downstairs by the pool.

I drove to Sedona in my dreamy car, top-down, by myself to

attend Sunday Mass at 11 a.m. at the world-famous Chapel of the Holy Cross, where millions of people from all over the world, including many Europeans, stop and pray on their sightseeing tours.

Not knowing any of these facts, I drove around a particular curve on the narrow road I would come to know so well, the majestic red rocks in full view at the outskirts of Sedona left me hypnotized. Each time a pinch-me-moment and thoughts wander to Karl May, the German author's influential descriptive novels about the Wild West and Arizona.

On this Sunday in September, sitting on a stone bench, mesmerized by the view through a massive glass window behind the altar, red rocks in the distance yet so close, I prayed in search of answers. One vital answer, a crucial one: Should I return to Europe? Marco, my London long-distance boyfriend wished I would come back. Possibly marry an English man and live in London? My fluttering heart implied — maybe? My mind, however, struggled with leaving Arizona and an amazing job where clients asked for Trudy — no other stylist would do.

I prayed for a sign.

"Listen to your heart. The heart has reasons that reason does not understand." — Jaques Bossuet

That afternoon, during a scary drive home on a hectic highway, I had nearly fallen asleep at the wheel. Shaken up and elated to be back safe at the Allegro, I rushed to the window: Who was at the pool? I peeked from my enclosed balcony. Yeah!

Lew in pink polka dots.

I watched him sit alone, his bare legs dangling in the water. In haste, I hunted for my new pink swimsuit. Nervousness slowed me down in rushing to get to the pool as soon as possible. I blessed the day I found that pink suit, fashioned like a pleated, short dress. My insecurity to be seen hidden at least for the moment, eagerly I headed downstairs. Swirling thoughts filled my brain; Lew in pink polka dots and me in pink — we matched. Years later, with a jolt, I would come to comprehend we were color-coordinated the first day we saw each other — before we met. Pink — Lew would come to call — Rose.

"Where were you?" Lew hollered in a voice I had not heard that loud before. Did he have a frown on his forehead? How did he know I was gone? He missed me?

I sat down on a towel near him, my legs in the smelly chlorinated water on this hot September afternoon.

To cover an unfamiliar uneasiness and give me something to do, I grabbed the suntan oil in my canvas bag. Eyes startled by his closeness, Lew stood behind me, pink polka dots looking bigger. He reached into his bathing suit pocket and produced a cigarette, matches right there. To find the right words — all at once — essential to use nothing but the perfect words. "You smoke?" is all that came out.

"You didn't tell me where you were," again Lew asked.

"Sedona," I mumbled. I distinctly remember not telling him I went to Mass. I left that part out. I worried what he might think.

"Alone? You drove alone to Sedona?" he continued with a concerned voice.

"Yes, why not?" My lack of a clever answer was evident.

Lew inhaled his Lucky Strike in the process of sitting next to me. His strangely speckled brown eyes and his startling smile assembled themselves into skin-tightening charm. My impulse to splash him did not happen.

Legs lower in the water to cool off my whole body, sun blazing in the cloudless sky, I started nervously to mess with a band-aid on my index finger. I ripped it off — a cut from the salon started to bleed again. A problem I was used to — a frequent occurrence.

I informed Lew, "I joke with clients every time a slip-up happens with shears that guarantee a good haircut when mixed with a little blood."

"You need to be more careful." Lew's words sounded like a kind order. With a gentle touch, with hands that did not look like he worked hard at anything, he picked up my hand to cradle my bleeding finger in a gesture I had not seen outside the movies — similar to as my hand could break. Tenderness beyond measure, as if he held a treasure. A touch that would follow me to the end of time. His eyes watched me intensely, my heartbeat sky-rocking, as electricity surged through mind and soul, down my spine like I was hit by lightning. Does love feel like that?

Lew jumped up in a search of a band-aid.

First Date

Weeks passed. New to Arizona 4 months, my older, over-tanned neighbor Bethany, who spent more time by the pool than in her second-floor studio, she and I had become close friends. On weekends we drove all around in the Arizona desert, admiring the sights and scenery we both adored and explored for hiking trails, not minding the heat. We shared a bond of firsts, our first time in glorious Arizona.

One evening during dinner at Coco's, our beloved food hang-out, I listened to babbling Bethany about a possible get-together when her boyfriend from Michigan would visit for one week. A dinner at Reata Pass, a steakhouse with dancing in the desert. She proceeded to tell me she already had asked three couples.

"What if we met for a drink at your place with the superb view, hint, hint, at about six?" Her words showed hesitation in what I might say.

"Grand idea, but I don't have a date."

"Ask Lew, the guy at the pool!" Bethany proclaimed.

"I won't ask Lew. He'll think I am after him."

"I will," she replied. "He likes you." She referred to all the times we'd see him and chatted at the Allegro Garden pool.

"I will be at Trudy's apartment 31**8** at six." I clutched my heart that missed a beat and turned skittish when Bethany called and told me Lew's response.

I started cleaning. It was only Tuesday.

At five on Saturday afternoon, the last day of Bethany's handsome, much older boyfriend Dale's visit, the shrill ringing of the telephone left me tense. A voice in distress, "I don't feel well. I already called everybody to cancel. You can go out with Lew anyway. Call him."

"Bethany, I am not calling Lew," I shouted. "Sorry you feel sick, but I will never call Lew. You call." Not believing the turn of events, getting upset I reasoned, why was I the last one to be called? My super-clean apartment for nothing? Extra pretty napkins I searched and found at a fancy gift shop, crackers, and cheese wasted — who will drink the wine?

Ten minutes later the phone rang, again. Did the color drain from my face at Lew's strong voice? Bethany had given him my phone number.

"Would you like to go out anyway and hear Dolan Ellis at the Peppermill?"

281

Knees buckling, I stammered, "YES." I slowly replaced the phone in its cradle, hoping my *yes* did not sound too deliriously happy.

Dolan Ellis, Arizona's official balladeer, a title offered to him in 1966, Lew undoubtedly must have overheard conversations by the pool, where Bethany and I raved about that popular weekend act in Scottsdale, near us, on Indian School Road.

On a cool October Saturday evening, ready to be seen with perfect hair, in a smashing short red dress-coat and new black boots, feeling safe and confident to appear less fat, I heard knocking. I opened the door. I experienced a reaction of horror, hopeful it did not show on my face as my eyes zoomed in on bright, multi-blue plaid pants and a blue shirt that matched one of the blue shades in the hideous trousers. Over his arm, he carried a blue multi-colored sports coat. Lew wears pants like that for a first date? Who does that? Where is his good-looking swimming suit with pink polka dots? Lew's sideburns appeared longer than ever. My sense of style worked overtime. I could not dump my guilt of hoping nobody would see me with him. My dislike for blue had begun.

While I loved the pinch-me moments to sit in Lew's red Austin-Healey, both of us nervous and not used to being alone, the drive to the bar where Dolan Ellis performed dragged on in uncomfortable silence. Astounded at the early crowd, we were seated at the last available table in the back. I looked around; my eyes stopped and stared in shock. Who sat across the crowded room in the corner, snuggling and lovey-dovey? Bethany and her boyfriend Dale. I freaked out, my mouth open, but no words came out. I tried to act nonchalant and ignore the couple.

Had Lew seen the two — Bethany, the supposedly sick one? Yes, he had. Lew's quick-to-laugh way was silent. The whole thing, confusing yet baffling, left us solely bewildered. Our obvious edginess continued all through a show of Western ballads. Lew knew most of them to my surprise. Momentary, awkward minutes climbed to unbearable heights in the parking lot. The waiter ran after us, catching up as Lew opened the car door for me. Lew had forgotten to pay.

Driving home, words were sparse. Anxiety took over. What must Lew be thinking? A date gone bad.

Days later Bethany paid me for the unopened wine, and with a mysterious smile she informed me, "Dale and I wanted to be alone on our last night together." The romance had heated up.

"Tell Lew!" was all I could muster.

At the salon ten days later, a favorite customer, with a gloomy demeanor handed me two *Cabaret* tickets, at the Celebrity Theater in downtown Phoenix. She sadly was not able to attend. In her loud voice she announced, "Here, this is your chance to ask Lew." She smiled knowingly. In astonishment, I clutched the amazing tickets for fifth-row seats. My first live musical.

Lew's phone number unknown to me, I had to wait for the right time by the pool. Feeling safe with familiar voices around, I asked bravely, "Do you like musicals?" Lew's shrug meant no. Waving two tickets, I continued, "Would you like to go with me on Saturday?"

Lew wore another disappointing suit when he picked me up. Olive green — Lew wears a suit like that? He selected that color and paid money? My horror in full display, he proclaimed, "I hate to shop. They don't make my size." Embarrassed, not knowing what to say, I recall what I was thinking, *"I could change that."*

Another uncomfortable yet exciting evening out had started.

After the sold-out musical, Lew walked me up the stairs. At the door, he simply said, with smiling eyes that held mine, "Thank you, the show was terrific. Good night. See you around."

A gentleman. No inviting him in.

"Do you like the zoo?" Lew asked one Sunday morning near the pool, splashing in full swing; a crowd had gathered early.

"Love it," I answered, surprised at the question.

We marched all over the Phoenix Zoo, my first time. All afternoon, aware of being close to Lew, we searched for animals hiding under any shade on a still-warm, late October day. One memory is as clear as ever: I longed and hoped for Lew to hold my hand . . . but no, he did not.

As we reached his sports car hours later, Lew asked, "How about a bite to eat at Coco's?" The restaurant my crazed and baked-in-Arizona-sun friend Bethany and I went to frequently and raved about to everyone during pool gatherings.

Lew ordered shrimp. Shrimp, I wondered. Exotic seafood?

"I hate seafood," I uttered.

"Honestly?" He sounded surprised. "Why?"

"An unfortunate memory growing up," I added. "My angry old maid teacher with ugly hair pinned like a snake on her head ordered me to eat fish that still had eyes staring at me. I vowed when I grow up -- never again."

Lew's untimely belly-laugh seemed out of place for my hated childhood memory that included having to eat fish every Friday.

With a jolt, my hand on my mouth I informed Lew, "Oh, I didn't go to Mass today." My voice was almost a whisper.

Lew sighed, "You are Catholic? My mom was." My gaze hung on his lips, eager to hear more.

"My family is Lutheran. Well, essentially, I am nothing."

"Nothing?" I concluded almost whispering.

We continued to dine in silence.

Walking up three flights of stairs to my place, at the door I thanked Lew for a lovely day and dinner.

"See you around," I said, my eyes never leaving his. I closed the door.

I fretted all evening about not going to Mass that Sunday. The devil was not going to win. I attended early Mass the next day, Monday, my day-off, and my own *Monday Rule* started. The first time I asked God, "Is it okay to attend Mass on Monday?"

Better on Monday than not at all? Words I hoped to hear.

Two weeks passed. Lew's call at the salon created a buzz, three hours to closing time. The receptionist's loud yell had everyone look up, "Trudy, a call for you. It's Lew."

"Would you like to see Elvis?" My heart danced, triggered by his excited voice as I tried clumsily not to smear any hair dye on my hands holding the phone receiver. Wow, attend an Elvis Presley concert? Music by Elvis repeatedly played in my dreams of coming to America. Lew had won two tickets on the radio early that afternoon. Elated beyond description not to have other plans, I accepted enthusiastically.

Sitting next to Lew at the massive Colosseum buzzing with an immense crowd restless for Elvis, the icon of the world, to appear, a pinch-me moment for sure. To my left in tan-colored polyester pants and the same navy shirt as on our first date, sat Lew, a man with hair with Sonny Bono bangs to his eyebrows, who had me guessing and wondering day and night. Up on the stage a star, Elvis Presley, walked out to greet his adoring fans singing: *It's Now or Never*. Screams and shouts cascaded down the stands. He wore an opulent, eye-catching flashy suit the universe would come to expect.

I found myself rising from my chair, but my screaming, sounding like a shriek, stopped. No sound came out to join the overpowering noise of the gigantic crowd. Puzzled I glared at Lew, the only one sitting. Slowly I sat back down — his eyes pulling me — like a kid caught at doing something wrong. I held my smitten, teenage love and, adoration for Elvis in check for the rest of the evening. I could not bestow a sense of my fluttering heart.

After the loud, ecstatic, and crowd-erupting concert and sounds of his final song *Can't Help Falling in Love*, we drove home in uncomfortable silence. I felt awkward talking about a giant man to the one that left me trembling and anxious.

Lew walked me to my apartment. He took the keys out of my hand with a touch that left me wondering. *A man is that gentle*? He opened the door wide to 318 and grimaced startled at two massive hair contest trophies on the floor in the hallway.

"What are they ever for?"

"Cooking," I replied with a tinkling giggle that turned to a forceful laugh. A laughter-getting response each time anybody asked about the Potomac Styling Champion 1966 trophies. Today this lame line was not comical. I tried to ignore the ego-boosting side effects of hairdressing-awards; this time my answer sounded simply awkward.

An instant later, Lew's kiss on my forehead, his electric hold on my shoulders for a few seconds, left me paralyzed.

"Good night." With a prolonged look into my eyes, he turned and left. I clutched my heart conscious of the closed door for an eternity. His expression of affection played over and over in my dizzy mind. I forgot to thank Lew for asking me to the Elvis show.

Puzzling agony — yet smiling mysteriously — a norm throughout days that followed and nights; nonetheless, I experienced occasional gratification when I'd see his red Austin Healey parked in his spot . . . Lew must be home.

Trudy Wells-Meyer

Thanksgiving Day, 1968

"Wisdom is, knowing what path to take next . . . Integrity is taking it." — Robyn Elpruhzlein

Thanksgiving, an American family holiday, for a Swiss-born is solely a day off in the middle of the week.

"You can't be alone on such a day. You belong with us," Doretta, one of my darling customers proclaimed, as she turned to other clients at the salon like she needed approval. I did not accept another of her invitations, like on Labor Day, celebrating with her family. Spend Turkey-day at her home with friends and family? Putting the final touch on her red hair, I informed her with a heartfelt thank-you for an additional kind invite, "Oh, I have plans already."

No mention I'd sit in the garden by the pool, maybe write some overdue letters, and . . . possibly see Lew?

My hidden hope, bottled up in my mind, was that Lew would ask me to do "something" — anything.

Ready for what — in brand-new, white bell-bottom pants with navy polka dots and a matching navy top, (no white shoes in November), I headed downstairs to the Allegro pool area. The weather too cold for a bathing suit. God in heaven cooperated with a glorious Arizona November day. Not believing the rare silence with nobody around, I obtained the ideal lounge chair. I covered the lounger with a towel to protect my clothes. In perfect view of the amazing flowers and garden, I set out to write postcards and a letter to my parents.

Interrupted by sounds of someone approaching, I looked up and saw Lew appear around the corner, a pile of laundry in his arms.

"What are you doing all by yourself?" He jumped back as if shocked to see me. Lew's dazed, embarrassed gesture left me speechless. I smiled and kept writing. A short while later I peeked as he left the laundry room located at the end of the lengthy building. He walked over. I had never seen him unshaven, with dark stubbles on his handsome face. Towering over me, he asked again, "What are you doing all by yourself? Aren't you with friends to celebrate Thanksgiving?"

A simple "No" left my lips.

His face transformed into a vast smile. Trying hard not to show my happiness to see him, eyes lowered, I managed not to stare. He wore his tight, doing-the-laundry jeans I had seen him wear — the tightest jeans I had ever noticed on any American man. (Gay guys in Europe yes)

I remembered Lew's words: *"They don't make my size."*

I revealed to Lew about my client Doretta's invitation for Thanksgiving dinner with all her family I had declined, feeling guilty for saying no.

"Would you like to go for a drive?" Lew asked, still standing. My ears perked up; my answer blurted out too fast. "YES."

"How about the Apache Trail to Canyon Lake?" Lew continued.

My all-time favorite drive? He knows that scenic trail in the desert, at the foot of the Superstition Mountain?

Too excited I stammered, "I can bring sandwiches."

Ready to be asked and beyond clever I had shopped on Wednesday, after work, I had bought cream cheese, French bread, and chocolate chip cookies.

Specifically, in my mind about that life-changing day remains my worry about hair flying in the wind, messed up, apparently not ready for Lew to see me that way. My headscarf would not stay on in his dreamy, top-down red Austin-Healey. Oh no!

My long-ago teenage dream, to have a boyfriend with a red sports car was as vivid now driving in one on the much-loved picturesque winding road in the desert, Arizona State Route **88**. The same road where my mom would see Winnetou the Indian chief on a horse, thirty years later.

Ecstatic feelings were mixed with too many worries. What will we talk about while driving for two hours? Did I bring food he liked, enough to drink? What if I must go to the bathroom; I did not know about primitive public facilities at the lake.

In Apache Junction, on a scenic road seemingly to nowhere, deep in the desert, we arrived at Canyon Lake and found a spot where my fancy blanket looked too pretty to lie on grass and desert dirt. Lew expressed surprise.

"Don't worry, it can be washed," I told him as he sat down carefully, facing the blue desert Canyon Lake, surrounded by red rocks.

Lew's admiration of nature's beauty was evident to a girl whose headscarf fluttered in the desert breeze. He loves the desert as much as I do; he didn't stop talking about its beauty while I served cream cheese sandwiches. I learned later; much later Lew hates cream cheese. Luckily, he devoured all the cookies.

On the long drive home, we found a soda machine. I was so thirsty but drink more? How do you tell a guy you are smitten with, *"I have to go to the bathroom?"* You hold it — and hope your bladder does not burst.

Lew's red 1962 Austin Healey 3000 at the Allegro.
Camelback Mountain in the background.

Arriving at the Allegro, Lew parked his car in its normal spot. He jumped out and rushed to open my door and pointed to the leftover picnic stuff, "I'll help you carry everything."

I rushed up the stairs.

I came out of the bathroom when Lew entered the front door, I had left open, his hands full of paraphernalia he dropped on the kitchen counter. Eyes on the enclosed balcony decorated with silk plants, to my surprise he raced towards the window. Trying not to be obvious, I glanced out of the corner of my eye not to miss his reaction to what I loved so much; a sight that mesmerizes.

An eternity passed before Lew turned around with affectionate eyes and sat down at the bar by the kitchen. He pushed the barstool around, toward the window, so he could still look out, shaking his head, "Your view is amazing, even better than from my place on the other side. We live in paradise."

Words like an echo . . . a million-dollar view we had in common.

Our first partner look, summer 1970
Allegro, 5656 Orange Blossom Lane, Phoenix, AZ **8**501**8**

Trudy Wells-Meyer

First Kiss, Thanksgiving 1968, at 7 p.m.

As the hour descended on our desert outing, Lew still sat on the last barstool close to the wall. His blue shirt that matched my outfit was unbuttoned lower than the average man's. Head tilted, he leaned over the bar and in his cool manner reached for his *True* menthol cigarettes.

True — like Tru . . . dy? Could he — did he change brands? I had noticed the mystery package out by the lake. I remembered Lucky Strike when we first met in August.

On occasions I smoked True Menthol by the pool, at parties, basically to look cool.

"Would you like one?"

I declined.

The language of our eyes added to the charged tension in the air. Lew's rare way of holding a cigarette was more evident at this electric time. He refused left-over cream cheese sandwiches. I sat down on the tall stool next to him. The bar seemed to get shorter. Unconsciously I stroked my soda glass, wishing it were wine for courage. Lew checked his watch as the wall clock struck seven. *Is he ready to leave?*

What indeed happened, I can't be sure. (I write this fifty years later, 2018, in Coronado, where we celebrate every Thanksgiving.) One instant we were talking and the next I leaned forward parallel with his eyes — my hand on his arm — clearly giving him a hope transfusion. A crackle . . . by the sheer contact, a leap through space and time. Nothing ever would compare to Lew's gentle grip at this moment in time, his touch caused not just my body but my soul to shiver. A silent crescendo when the man of my dreams, who would become my life and love that promised to last forever, kissed me for the first time.

Love in a tightly sealed compartment of my heart exploded. A set-your-heart-on-fire moment. An earthquake on the third floor — a transition into hushed serenity and immeasurable quiet . . . a connection of hearts and souls. His arms around me — finally, in each other's arms. Safe. Nameless feelings, a spell we both were under, sealed by a kiss, built a fine luster of knowing I wanted to be wherever Lew was.

A lifetime, a future awaiting us, when souls became one.

Love is a sigh that draws a smile . . .

Tann, Switzerland — Christmas 1968

On the TWA Phoenix-Chicago flight, on a cramped seat sandwiched between two overweight guys, I opened a small, crumpled bag Lew had handed me at the departure gate. He had driven me to the Phoenix airport in his sports car to see me off and wave goodbye. A Christmas gift from Lew?

I found a small, black velvet box in a brown paper bag. With shaking fingers, I opened the tiny jewelry box; inside lay a silver heart necklace with one diamond inside the heart. I closed my eyes. Spellbound, I thought about the guy who hates shopping.

Love beyond the stars . . . found in the Arizona desert. Only I did not know yet.

Up in the air, close to clouds on an all-night flight to London, a trip planned when Marco visited Arizona and booked one week after he had left Phoenix to fly home to England, nonrefundable tickets we reserved together, long-distance, I sighed heavily. On the bumpy flight, I held on to Lew's surprise gift close to my heart, a heart like it could break but spelled love. In a trance I pictured Marco waiting at London Heathrow to join me on Swissair to fly to Zürich, to meet my family on Christmas, who awaited us at the arrival gate in Kloten. Marco was the first man I had ever brought home: my English boyfriend with his stylish dark-long hair like an Italian had visited Arizona in the summer, two weeks before I met Lew.

For weeks riddled with guilt and squirmy nerves, mixed with a horrendous gloominess I didn't fully understand, never had I experienced such restless nights. Lew's smile in my brain, his earthshaking kisses on my lips, and now a heart-shaped diamond necklace around my neck — emotions left me dismal. I wished the prearranged trip and intense worry about my family erased from reality. Everything encircled me as if I were a prisoner of my heart's confusion.

Marco's customary attention-getting, nonchalant manners, his sweater over his shoulder tied like a scarf, did not impress my parents. He showed no nerves. When his feet, with shoes on, ended up on Mother's newly polished coffee table, especially shiny for Christmas, Dad's fury had me trembling. He acted more upset than Mom, as he judged a Brit who spoke no German and consequently never had a chance to say the wrong thing.

How could a merry family Christmas plan go so wrong?

My promise to call Lew right after arriving safely at home in tiny Tann failed miserably. Never happened. (Convenient cell phones unheard of.) Amidst all the commotion of an Englishman with Mediterranean manners visiting our humble home, I merely forgot. An eight-hour time difference did not help. Nightmares continued for a long time over a promise I did not keep. Lew's worry and anguish, wondering if I was okay, kept haunting me for a long time.

Marco failed the test of family. Ending uncomfortable hours for almost everyone, he left a day early to fly back to London. Or did he essentially leave because of my news, finding the truth of meeting Lew while I wore a sparkly diamond heart necklace?

Marco guessed. A joyless embrace upon arrival at the London airport one can blame on jet lag only so long. Love letters between Arizona and England had become fewer during our long-distance relationship to an occasional phone call only.

Beate, my eleven-year-younger sister, smitten with Marco, expressing sadness and sorrowful eyes handed him her beloved Teddy bear when he hugged her goodbye. Beate's favorite bear peeked out of Marco's travel bag as he rushed out of the house to the waiting cab.

Marco packed his bag upstairs when my sister had yelled, "Mail from America." A Christmas card from Lew. What timing, as I was on the brink of attempting to hug Marco Adieu. In haste, shocking my little yet tall sister, I ripped the envelope. I found a poem on white notepaper. Lew wrote poetry? For me? My heart skipped multiple beats.

His words. . . (Lew's Original Poem, 1968)

I see you walking in the snow
The air is cold but not so bad
You can't be sad
You should be glad
If you stop, look up, it's beautiful, I know.
There's a guy, thinking of a girl he can't see.
The Allegro's not a happy place anymore
Because up on the third floor
There is a locked door
I stop, and remember, "What will be — will be."
The nights are sad, the days are very long;
I think I am beginning to believe in Three
No Christmas tree
No place to go, or you here with me
My whole world has stopped since you have been gone.

During the Christmas holiday in Switzerland, I phoned Els, the friend whose influence, immense encouragement, and help was vital in booking my voyage on the ship, the *Bremen,* to New York in 1965. We met for lunch in Zürich at the famous Sprüngli Café on the hectic Bahnhof Strasse, her most beloved restaurant. According to Els, I talked nonstop about Lew. She read the poem. Intensely she waved the flimsy white notepaper in the air and announced, "He is the one you are going to marry." Too loud for a public place, she continued to wave the paper at smiling ladies who gawked at us from several tables around the room.

"Him?" I shouted back.

Els would repeat those words over and over to anyone who would listen, words that came true on June **8**th, 1972.

TWA arrived two hours late from New York. Lew waited at the Phoenix airport.

"That coat is beautiful." Smiling he pointed to the glamorous, latest Paris fashion attention-getting, above all going-through-customs, maxi-coat I had purchased in Switzerland. Lew's eyes focused on the heart, the platinum silver heart, his Christmas gift visible dangling on my black sweater. We embraced his gentle earthshaking kiss on my lips once again.

With a typical Lew grin, he managed to put all my luggage in his red sports car. He opened the door, his eyes fixed on mine as I climbed in, casually asking, "How is Marco?"

Feeling a long international flight in my bones — it was five in the morning in Switzerland — with no enthusiasm I answered sleepily, "Marco? He flew back to London a day early; my parents did not like him." I hesitated as he started the Austin-Healy. "I met somebody new, Oliver, a Swiss guy. We met at a school friend's house, Suzanna's parent's New Year's Eve party." Never will I know what Lew suffered from the bombshell news that had left my mouth. (Guessing still)

Lew's baffled open mouth found no reply.

Awkward silence consumed us all the way home. Feeling cruel for having blurted out another guy's name I fingered a pearl ring on my little finger. I explained teary-eyed, "Dad handed me a tiny jewelry box when he held me close at the Kloten airport. A ring like the one he had shocked Mother with on Christmas. Dad, my *Schgruna* had observed his daughter *Udi* admire and love the jewel." I sobbed.

Lew said nothing but smiled reaching for my hand.

Nobody, not Lew, could conceivably know how heartbreaking and emotional it is to say goodbye to parents, family, and friends. The lingering pain of not knowing when the next time of seeing each other will or would happen. Will we meet again?

Airport drama is not for a sissy.

Torn between the two countries, a constant never gets easier.

Father's sad face had lit up instantly at the Kloten airport departure gate when he met Oliver, a young, charming, well-dressed Swiss man who had come to wave *Adieu.*

Pleasing your parents is unending, and to see a father's happy face meant the world for a daughter far away. At 28 and not married, parents must wonder: *How come nobody wants our daughter? Is she too picky?*

Are friends betting: *When will she land a guy? Or won't she?*

I had introduced Oliver to my startled family, he had asked for time off work and traveled to the airport to see me off. Would elegant Oliver, with his dashing looks, the bluest eyes, and impeccable manners, bring Trudy back to Switzerland? For good?

Everyone wondered and no one was surprised at yet another new guy in my life. Yes, I was popular, and oh so natural for me to meet anyone, anywhere.

Nonetheless, the question of sleeping with a man, often expected to, after a dinner out, a drink, a walk in the park — sex — ended any of my relationships on the spot, with my favorite line, frosty words at times: "You will remember me because I did not sleep with you, not because I did."

Throughout my young life, plenty of admirers never let me forget my parent's strict upbringing and values embedded in me as to just kissing a guy was not proper. I can still hear: "*It will lead to sex.*"

The romance of a relationship innocent beyond levels possibly not understood in today's world. Waiting for a look — a smile — a wink of an eye — a tender word — an unpretentious touch as readers of Jane Austin's novels, a famous English author's description of innocent love and romance, have come to adore.

Finding Love beyond the Stars

One week after my return from Christmas in Switzerland, on a cold January Sunday in 1969, I fell in love. Permanently!

The Monday evening before, Lew called. A date for Saturday "Would you like to go to dinner at a restaurant of your choice?"

"I better not," I answered in dismay. "I have to get up early on Sunday. I signed up with the Phoenix Ski Club months ago for a ski trip to Mount Lemon in Tucson." I rambled on, "Do the Santa Catalina Mountains have enough snow? I am not convinced, how can skiing in Arizona be any good? In the desert?"

To find snow, a two-hour drive away, on a first such trip, left me in total awe,

On Sunday I woke up early to attend nearby Mass at six, before meeting the ski group at 7:30 in a parking lot in Scottsdale. Still dark, as usual, my eyes wandered to a red Austin-Healey convertible in front of the long apartment building. I walked to my parked car — I stopped in total shock frowning at an empty slot. Lew's car not at his parking space? At 5:45 a.m.? What is a girl to think? *He is with another woman.*

Utterly waiting for my brain to make sense of what I was staring at and now awake, I marveled, he had gone out with someone else.

In a minibus with a bunch of cheery skiers driving to Tucson, with a perfect window seat, my face stuck to the glass all the way. My eyes searched for red — an Austin-Healey. Any red car. Not today, no red in sight. My dream of having a boyfriend with a red sports car vanished in thin freeway air. Skiing was dreadful, my turns close to falling constantly — a hopeless ski day to forget.

The weekend I fell in love — Love is forever. . .

Monday evening, after one disastrous ski experience — I blamed the Arizona snow and lack of — the wall phone jangled. Cheerful Lew asked, "Do you want to go skiing next Sunday?" The nerve. I knew he did not ski. His question caused me to lose patience as nothing else could with flashes of an empty parking slot when I heard his words stringing together: "I went skiing at the Snowbowl in Flagstaff over the weekend." Time stood still.

"You?" I shouted. Immediately I covered my mouth, regretting the tone. I bounced between overwhelming anticipation and disbelief.

Lew kept talking. "I flew to Flagstaff. I parked my car at Sky Harbor. I bought a book on how to ski and ski clothes at the Alpine Ski Keller."

"You did what???" I could hear the whine in my voice.

Lew continued, "I rented skis in Flagstaff."

By now I had arrived in a state of delirium.

Pointblank unreal to me as to who flies to Flagstaff got shoved to the back of my brain as the far more important question of the missing red Austin-Healey in the parking lot was answered with Lew's amazing words.

I was so happy. I was close to tears.

Miracle Sunday, skiing with Lew, arrived. The doorbell rang louder than anticipated drowning out the sound of my beating heart. I opened the door wide and felt like the luckiest girl in the world. With a swirl of jubilation, I stared at a vision — a dashing and well-dressed skier who did not know how to ski — yet. A sense of dreaming left me speechless. Lew's choice of a ski pullover in an exceptional mustard color and matching ski pants had me speculate: *Did someone at the Phoenix ski store help him select this stylish combo?* A brown, color-coordinated ski jacket over his arm added to the fashion statement. His sideburns, bushier than usual, did not bother me at all this early morning.

"Are you ready to be seen on the slopes with a want-to-be skier who only had two days to learn?" Lew's heavenly smile ignited the morning. Delight had no curfew.

I trusted Lew to drive my Pontiac Tempest. He had decided a big car would be more comfortable for a four-hour ride filled with two pairs of skis, sticking out between us on the front seat. Poles, ski jackets, gloves, and hats filled the back seat, along with rented boots for Lew, mine touching his. Driving away from the Allegro in my cherished automobile nobody else had ever driven, he educated me, "You know the Snowbowl in Flagstaff at 12,633 feet is as high as Switzerland's mountains."

I responded, "*Whaaat*? I don't believe that." Lew, of course, turned out to be right. Skiers, due to the high-altitude inhale hard, walking up to the chairlift, I found out gasping for breath.

Glancing at Lew in awe, this magical turn of events — skiing with him — I tried to move closer, skis in the way, yet close enough to peek at each other's eyes in the rearview mirror above us for the duration of the long drive.

We parked in the crowded parking lot. It started snowing. The wind from the north howled, cold and scary.

The extended lift line turned massive and restless. The chairlift not taking skiers up, why?

Weather did not permit the start of the lift.

At the small, overcrowded indoor restaurant sat one content guy smoking his *True* cigarette with a giant grin — the only smiling face in the restaurant. A not-yet-skier, embarrassed to be seen on skis just yet, spared for now to face the mountain with a Swiss woman he assumed to be a fabulous skier purely by being from a country with snow all year.

Delayed agony.

Whereas the girl he was in love with, did not think nor believe she lived up to admired Swiss skiing.

***

Two weeks later, Lew planned another ski trip. He had managed to find a report on the superb Snow Bowl ski conditions. On this glorious blue-sky Saturday, I was lucky to get time off from the hectic weekend salon, three hours earlier.

An overnight stay — in a motel in Flagstaff? Nerve-wracking thoughts and qualms swirled in my brain. A first night spent with Lew. Bashfully I searched for a perfect nightgown to pack.

We arrived late at the motel in Flagstaff after a bite to eat on the outskirts of the Western town; two rooms awaited us. In a trance, I noticed the open, adjoining door. Impressed beyond words and dazed at the same time, I put my bag on the bed. Lew's enormous respect and admiration have graced our lives. It started there, that incomparable night in Flagstaff.

Lew looked up from arranging a few ski belongings in his room. His composure and aura of mystery that surrounded him left me fascinated. He met my eyes and sent me a ghost of a wink. Closing his eyes, he nodded with a smile. Heat and cold roused down my spine, spelling emotionally charged happiness.

An adjoining room meant everything. I had correctly guessed Lew to be a gentleman of a woman's dreams. Slowly I walked toward him. Lew held me close under the doorframe. I gazed up into his eyes, "What if we — went slow — real slow? Could you, would you sleep next to me . . . but no sex?" I asked softly, like a whisper. A question I had dreamed of for when the time was right. The boundaries of our intimacy were about to crumble . . .

297

I felt like floating on a cloud of tenderness in the peace of a night spent together that first time, near in bodies and soul, as his hand gently moved across, under the sheet, to belong where it's meant to be — on my heart. Bliss of sleepy kisses, holding hands close to our hearts, the sweet contact of toes — that underrated touching of toes in the middle of the night.

A sense of dreaming continued all day, skiing on the icy snow on the Snowbowl was like dancing in the sky. Lew, however, falling over and over again. I tried not to notice and ignore his crashes. Although, I prayed nothing cruel would happen.

The sun had come out when I skied down near Lew. As he watched me, my own and only Swiss yodel I knew filled the air: "*Youdeehui. . .*"

My nickname was born — *Youdeehui* — a name for Lew only.

I call Lew *Loudeehui.* Still. We both do — always will.

Partner look 1970, Snowbowl, Flagstaff, AZ
(I found matching sweaters and my brown jacket,
a ski season later, after Lew had bought his.)

Breaking Up

A marathon of love . . . Love bloomed as if happiness was too much to bear.

Lew possessed no capital unless one means his winning a white Austin-Healey in an all-night poker game, (then painted the car red, one week later). Or, his emphatically handsome face, his strength, and polite pleasant manners and a certain way of captivating my heart which chanted one word — love — morning, noon, and night.

When asked, "What do you do for a living?" his same answer every time, "As little as possible" — an answer that shocked me the first time I heard it. Never a mention of aerospace. Silence was a part of his job, a must, his government top-secret clearance at stake, unknown and not explained to me for years to come. Lew's strangely brown eyes twinkled; he was a mysterious guy with long, bushy sideburns,

who had no tolerance for stupid people. His "whatever" shrug and belly laugh at the wrong time bordered on embarrassment for the people he targeted.

Nerds can be sexy.

299

In February that year, Motorola sent Lew to Chicago, where his brother and two sisters lived. Separated for four drawn-out months, a time when separation looked as if too crushing to bear, a letter-writing time filled my evenings. I wrote day after day during his absence; however, my trips to the mailbox after work filled with anxiousness were painful; his silence like willful indifference. No mail from Lew?

I did not comprehend the absence of love letters but learned Lew perhaps was no writer. Although my dash for mail rewarded a few times turned vastly jubilant one evening amid late April showers, after a hectic day at the salon. I held an envelope from Chicago, trembling. Avoiding the rain, I ripped open the precious mail. My hands shook non-stop — another poem on yellow notepaper — Heaven had arrived at the Allegro. A flashbulb-moment: (Lew's original, second poem, April 1969)

Yes, I'm in love with you!
But when I'm away I'm so blue,
*   I don't know what to do!*

But I think that I shouldn't be sad
And maybe I should be glad
*   Because I got something others don't have.*

I got a Love that is so strong
That I know nothing can go wrong
And I'll be back with you before long.

Uninhibited elation rose in my throat at the power of words. My heart soared to the edge of heaven.

The Allegro full, no vacancy when Lew returned to Arizona in early June, already beastly hot, a five-month aerospace job-shopper employment had ended in the windy city. I visited once — a magical weekend. The sights of Chicago still a blur but not Lew's love, like a flame the wind could not blow out.

Lew moved into a tiny studio in downtown Scottsdale.

News of Lew's mother on her deathbed in Wisconsin hit Lew with a cruel blow; he had visited Mom at home only once while working in the giant city. Cancer claimed Margaret Wells' life on July 10, 1969. Lew had been working at his old job in Scottsdale for barely three weeks. Heartbroken and crestfallen he flew to Milwaukee and boarded a bus to attend the burial in his hometown. Mrs. Wells, whom I never met, was only fifty-nine.

My world and his were about to dive into a spiraling freefall. The rush of heavy silence overwhelmed me — it confronted us and descended on our love.

Communication alarmingly nonexistent.

Lew shut me out of his life. No call after his return from the funeral. Privacy of grief? I wondered. Dumbfounded, his silent voice was disturbing. Lew didn't talk.

Nameless emotions struggled in my heart and mind. Something I did — did not do?

"The single biggest problem with communication is the illusion that it is taking place." — George Bernard Shaw

We both held back — not asking — so as not to hurt and upset each other, expectations of everyday life ruled and destroyed. I still remember how Lew stared at nothing whenever the past came up — the irretrievable past. Enduring his silence and dark stare one evening in June as I held him in my arms longer than usual, I listened to words that touched my core: "You are the light above my darkness."

Lew cried. There is a sacredness in tears; not the mark of weakness, tears speak more eloquently than tongues and let you wonder.

Denial has its distinct protection. I had no knowledge of grief and the loss of a mother, a certain ignorance, not knowing how people grieve in different ways.

I had not yet learned grief has many faces.

The first man walked on the moon five days after Lew returned from Mom's memorial service. America rejoiced — the world in awe of Apollo 11's first landing on July 20th, 1969. I failed to understand its importance — yet enduringly remember that day. Lew, part of the aerospace world, with a fever-like brightness in his eyes stayed glued in front of the small TV, and nonstop cigarette smoking. Our inability to communicate had come to a crescendo in his shabby Scottsdale studio apartment next to Lady of Perpetual Help Catholic Church where I attended weekly Mass.

The world waited for the first man to step on the moon. I had noticed how feverishly Lew behaved for months at these history-making, extraordinary happenings. Nevertheless, I did not know then his aerospace engineering was in the business of flying in the atmosphere of Earth and surrounding space. I found out many years later Lew actually worked on the going-to-the-moon project.

"Would you like to come over and watch?" Lew had called and asked in his composed voice. He wanted me to join him?

I did.

He avoided talking. More stupefied at his invitation than before, as Lew l stared at nothing. I sighed and tried to relax in a romance unclear for too long. No moments filled with electricity and handholding.

Thoughts of Lew's loss of his mother kept tormenting me and left mixed feelings with a sense of not belonging. I did not know of Lew's heavy load of guilt for not going home to visit. Now being overshadowed by an event that held the world in suspense.

I got up and walked out on my boyfriend with sealed lips and eyes stuck on the moon frenzy only. As I ran to my parked car a rush of affection swelled up inside me, fused with extreme dejection. I opened the trunk and reached for a Denver shopping bag; a surprise meant for Lew. With excitement and joy I had purchased a pair of gray pants, a pink shirt, and a matching gray scarf (men's fashion in the late sixties) from an elegant man-store in downtown Denver, while attending the National Hair Show two weekends earlier. Sandy, a hairdresser friend from the Cordes & Hendreks salon in Atlanta had joined me. We lived and loved the perfect two-day weekend.

I stormed back into Lew's apartment. I threw the fancy bag on the pullout bed that served as a sofa throughout the day. Lew sat in the same spot, leaning forward, staring at the TV, a cigarette at the opposite side of two fingers nobody else does. A sly grin appeared on his face, almost malicious — no twinkling eyes. I saw what was not there. All too grown-up grief for his mom, as I would learn much later, and immense guilt for not going home for years when she was well. Lew out of the corner of his eye watched me, his measured voice silent and unsettling, unarguably painful in his deliberate muteness.

My voice raised to a high pitch, my screams only a whisper: "You don't talk to me." I slammed the door.

Speeding home, I turned up the car radio. A song blasted: *Someday we'll be together*. I cringed. Helpless tears, imagining a non-future, I listened to the transparency of sound and sheer melody that would become our song.

Music found in silence becomes more precious when there is less light, in haunting words during our break-up. A song by the Supremes and Diana Ross — its drumming echoed through night and day. A number one hit for one week in 1969 played over and over on the radio, a tune I had heard the first time driving home in absolute despair, at an intersection waiting for the red light to turn, cars honking behind — *Someday we'll be together again* — I listened to words that granted hope.

Music is the world's language: no translation needed.

Words to fit a relationship on the rocks for months, in my ears, in my head, in my mind . . . I fluttered in circles of hope; my desperate longing strengthened because of a song. The 45 RPM single record, that would become an all-time favorite played again and again on my credit-bought phonograph/radio, a piece of furniture decorating my home.

Lew did not call. I would not call. No change endures unless it is accompanied by a change of heart. Silence of hearts hurts.

Oh, the mystery of communication. . ..

Words and sounds remained a glimmer of light. Secretly in my mind and bones, I strained to hear from Lew. Reluctantly, I banished my fantasies to a dark corner of my imagination. Did Lew know the hit song, its words? Did he speculate how I wrestled with yearnings while fighting doubts I attempted to ignore and forget his face?

I tried fiercely to recollect what other words I had used at a time when my eyes could see silence only, when I stormed in with a gift bag I hurled at Lew. Our happy life in pictures — gone — in the past. Where was the color? My heart turned a deaf ear to his unbearable quiet and deafening silence.

With courage, that comes from desolation, I drove by his one-room studio apartment, too often, at infrequent times; an Arizona indigo sky and the moon over Camelback Mountain were of no help. Would I see Lew's red Austin-Healey? I hid my Pontiac Tempest under a nearby tree, seeking occasional contentment when I saw Lew's car, knowing he was home.

Trudy Wells-Meyer

Getting Back Together

"Faith isn't magic, it's a choice to trust God even when we are confused and sad." — Unknown

A butterfly effect struck when the phone finally rang. Lew's voice created chaos on a Monday evening in December. The call came from the second floor, on the other side of the Allegro building. Lew's younger sister Judith in Chicago, the one he was closest to, had told her brother "Call Trudy."

He did. One week after he had moved back into a one-bedroom apartment on Orange Blossom Lane. He'd been stuck on a waiting list for six months before a unit had become available.

In the midst of planning a Christmas party at my place, his hopeful-some-day call left me shaking. Two single guys I knew from the Phoenix Ski Club had already sent their RSVPs. With a surge of courage, I heard myself utter into the phone line, "Would you like to come to my Christmas party on Saturday at 7 p.m.?" I smiled nervously as the voice I had yearned to hear answered "Yes."

As if from a lack of breath, I thought my heart would burst. A sigh and a cheer climbed to immeasurable heights. How on God's earth would I handle three single guys at my Christmas party? I'd worry about that later.

Ten minutes to seven I anxiously answered the first knock on the door. All the decorations were in place for a party on the third floor for eighteen guests. I clumsily held on to the open door . . . a vision like destiny pushing me toward the climax of my life — Lew, more debonair than ever, in gray pants fitting perfectly, a pink shirt and a matching gray/black scarf tied around his neck. Knee-buckling happiness — I stared at my Denver-bought outfit for Lew, which had landed in a fancy shopping bag on his bed/sofa on that earth-shattering afternoon when words *it's over* started and began to rule days and nights.

I gasped with my mouth open, my eyes found the smile I had missed so much, as well as Lew's cool meticulous voice that sustained an underlying boom, "Thank you for inviting me."

Trying hard to hold back tears, in a daze, I let him in. Lew's surprise and glance at a Christmas tree with real candles glowing fell flat as other guests were knocking at the door. All

304

evening I sensed Lew's eyes watching me intensely, his gaze like a candle that never stopped burning.

Friends, neighbors, and guests, everyone arrived on time, including the two other invited men -- Bill, blond like a German with manners to match, and Allen, an older guy with a comb-over who owned a fancy private airplane. If they were surprised to see Lew at the party, they did not show it.

Close to midnight, two guys were prowling — Lew and Bill.

Carsten, my boss, and his wife had waved good night soon after everyone had left with joyful memories in amazement of a Swiss tradition, a Christmas tree with real candles that had burned down. No more lights flickering on a fully decorated tree with Swiss chocolate ornaments. New candles would be placed the next day, not lit again however until Christmas Eve.

In my mind, awkward moments would stay put — cast in stone — two guys waiting for the other to leave. Bill helped do the dishes — Lew smoked at the bar. *Tru* cigarettes — still?

Dishes done. Bill left.

Kissing Lew that night, we became two candles in twilight — small and hot, a crackle by the sheer contact of our bodies. The presumably nothing became something when Lew's intense hold translated you and me — together — undyingly — at last. I wiggled myself free. Not wanting to let go of his tight embrace, I rushed over to the beloved record player. With trembling fingers, I dropped the Diana Ross and the Supremes' number-one hit on the floor. With one more scratch, the music filled the air — *Someday we'll be together.*

Music truly is what feelings sound like. Lew had tears as he admitted how many times, he thought of putting that penetrating record under my door at 31**8**. I could hear the tears in his voice.

Indeed, there is power in intention. He smiled dreamily.

Lew's love intensified with each breath as he revealed, "My Youdeehui, I did not want you to witness my grief-filled with guilt." My face close to his I gently stroked the back of his head. A measure of profound remorse in his voice evoked memories of the past six months. The grief of losing his mom showed in his face, his eyes. "If only I had stayed in contact after leaving on the eve of my high school graduation. I never went home to visit, nor called. I did not mean to punish my hardworking mother. How could I?" Lew sighed heavily. "I never intended for her to suffer solely because I was angry at my father. Yet, I did."

"A mother is always close in the heart," I murmured, as I held him close. We both were filled with despair for a time one cannot change, nor ever bring back.

Lew's withdrawn and silent way, however, now belonged in the inalterable past, like the moon with its glint of light.

The night we got back together forever started. Our future, an infusion of glorious change, a life laced with eternal love. An embrace that would last a lifetime, like a fortress of love.

The gift of God had lit up two souls.

The peace of passion spent, a purity in lovemaking as though floating in a cloud of tenderness, moments when the world stops, the bliss of sleepy kisses and sweet contact under sheets . . . bodies close and souls united, we knew a lifetime awaited us.

The morning after we stood at the enclosed balcony window with a view we had in common long before we met. His strong arms around my waist let me smile with tears, knowing we truly see beauty with the same eyes.

Our perfect harmony in sync . . . again — when love shines pure.

Lew's amazing spoken words would become gospel:
Sex is a bonus.

We found gold in the Arizona desert — each other.

"I carry your heart in my heart — I am never without — I carry your eyes — wherever I go . . . you go." — Anonymous

***

On New Year's Eve 1969, our plan to drive to Purgatory Colorado to ski, after a famously hectic last day of the year at any beauty salon, got interrupted.

"Such is life" Lew's famed and frequent words with a smile I heard for the first time. A lingering cold had forced me to stuff cotton in my runny nose — not a good thing while one does hair for fancy parties. A concerned client, a doctor's wife, offered some of her prescription medication to stop my dripping nose like a faucet. She rushed home in a hurry to get drugs that would and did not agree with my stomach. I threw up and got extremely ill. Ardis, another kind customer drove me home.

Wishing I had not used the Swiss face cleaner that left me smelling like a flower, I worried about my mahogany-colored hair messed up when Lew found me home in bed later that day. I was mortified for him to see me with smeared makeup, sick and weak.

"You need food," he acknowledged with a concerned face.

He learned I love tomato soup. Lew rushed to the kitchen and opened a can of Campbell's soup he found on the top shelf, the only one in the cabinet. I could hear the spoon and dishes banging; the non-cook served the best ever soup on a tray he had found in the back of a bottom shelf. Romance is tomato soup out of a can, laced with love, stirring for over fifteen minutes leaving me to wonder, why *is he taking so long?* I had hopped out of bed to peek around the corner to check.

Sickness gone — miraculous — cured by love. Lew and I left the next morning for our road trip to find snow in Colorado.

A phrase from Lew, sealed with a kiss when our love was young "*Nothing else matters as long as we have each other.*"

A belief my deadline for being happy forever . . . in October 1969 I had turned 2**8**.

"You don't know where you are going until you know where you belong." — Anonymous

Partner look had arrived, our first matching ski-outfits found at the Alpine Ski Keller, in Phoenix, 1970.

Couples that match, stay together.

Trudy Wells-Meyer

Santa Monica, California — 1971-1972

In the fall of 1970, Motorola sent Lew to Chicago, again. He did not accept the offer. Intense realities set in. Out of a job for three months Lew finally found employment at a small electronics company in downtown Phoenix. The green company truck, the color of the suit I had frowned over on our second date, had no air conditioner, like his sports car — miserable in the beastly Arizona summer heat that starts early in the year. Lew did not complain.

In the sweltering June of 1971, Lew's new workplace offered him a manager position at the Los Angeles office. I grimaced at Lew with a silent *oh no* on my lips. I stammered in a voice virtually angry as though I wished it weren't true, "You are going." The news was enough to put me in a state of quivering anxiety. An alarm of sad familiarity in a world without Lew rang inside me.

His face lacked the hint of a smile. "An offer I can't refuse," he reasoned as I nestled in his arms.

What will be . . . will be.

***

Unbridled joy filled my heart when I watched Lew's red Austin-Healey parked at the Allegro behind my Pontiac for the second weekend in a row. The long six-hour drive from Los Angeles in his sports car, without air conditioning, did not look as if to bother him.

Deeply flushed with happiness, we went shopping late Saturday afternoon at Andrew's Gold Jeweler for matching gold engagement rings. A ring, a sign of eternity.

The day was July 18, 1971.

One week later, on Saturday evening, I flew to Los Angeles. Lew resided in a motel room, his temporary residence, a place where Tina Turner and husband Ike, still together at the time, performed at the dark motel's lounge on weekends.

On Sunday we hunted and found a one-bedroom/den apartment in a high-rise, number 928 facing the impressive ocean, with views I couldn't get enough of. Lew right by my side. On the balcony, he held me close in semi-silence. We discovered the sea significantly calming, the water below as clear as our realities.

By the way . . .

We would and did find another ocean view in 1976, a one-bedroom condo on the 10th floor in El Encanto, building **8** in Coronado, California. Same builder — the same type of high-rise as in Santa Monica. We bought the Model they leased back from us for their use — no payment for one year.

Lew planning the future in full swing.

I felt enormously bold when I gave up #31**8**. Unspeakably hard leaving paradise behind — the hardest part of all. The image of the view from the balcony journeyed with me when we drove away two weekends later in a packed full Pontiac Tempest. I sat on the bench close to Lew, a vacuum of thoughts of days when what lay ahead was not yet known. Not speaking much, yet love in the air and deeply connected, each pursuing a private interest, a common thread of love. Absence of fear — must be love.

Destination — Santa Monica, California.

"As long as we are together." Lew's words gave me endless strength. The distance between Switzerland and family had grown a void, an abyss of emotions an immigrant learns to get used to — yet never ends. Oh, and the guilt of not calling enough . . .

"Life is not something we go through or that happens to us, it's something we create by our decisions." — Kathleen Dean Moore

The moving van arrived on Monday with my limited furniture.

An unknown future, a bridge that waited to be crossed,

I had to find a job. Going to school, a first for me to find an American beauty school to obtain a California hairdressing license concluding with a grueling test. I studied never-heard-of words to allow me to do hair. Tough to learn about body and skin diseases, totally foreign in a second language. A requirement not making sense to this student. Why? To cut and style hair?

Assigned experts never checked my haircut on that scary day of tests for a Swiss, yet they judged by how much hair was on the floor around my station. The hair I cut on my model had to be dropped into a paper bag taped to the side of the chair. Not on the floor — no hair on the floor. Memory has its own story to tell, planted in my mind, no one tended to believe me.

"Well, that solely projected California sanitation's rules in the early 70ties," I explained repeatedly.

"Proof of love for Lew," I howled as I waved that hard-to-get doing-hair license with a supreme accomplishment of relief. A most difficult way of obtaining a piece of paper let me count my blessings, I never had to do all that nonsense in any other state.

Driving the hectic California freeway, a day-after-day norm,

I worked in a fancy salon in Beverly Hills, as a receptionist for a while, waiting for the license. Ronald, the Swiss owner, hired me solely because I was from his country. An upscale salon on Beverly Drive turned out not to be an easy place to build a clientele.

Nobody had ever heard of Trudy. How I missed my loyal left-behind clientele in Scottsdale.

Living in Santa Monica, where one compares life to the movements of the tide, was like one overwhelming dream. We walked on the damp, packed sand, soft stuff that sucks at your feet close to the ocean of our choice; yet, stabbed with guilt I wrestled with worries I tried to ignore. My parents back home did not know Lew and I lived together.

Or did they?

Mom and family planned a huge for-tiny-Tann church wedding on June **8**th, 1972, in Switzerland.

With tortured anguish, capturing hope that was disappearing like the last sliver of light that follows on the heels of a brilliant sunset, I wondered how and when would I tell them? Could Mom hear my anguish?

On a regular working day, Friday, April 2**8**th, 1972 — the **8** in the date the only thing reflecting *a lucky day* — our civil wedding took place, at the home of a stranger in Beverly Hills. A lady judge, one of my new clients whose hair I had

310

fixed only three times, offered to marry us. Mrs. Lapid had just become a judge. Ours — the first civil wedding she would perform.

Teardrops I had held back at the salon all day long formed in the elevator when we left our Santa Monica home at 5:30 p.m. Tears fell on pink roses, Lew's thoughtful purchase while rushing home from the office for the six o'clock wedding at an unknown house near Rodeo Drive. Roland, my Swiss boss, and his French-born wife Natalie joined the ceremony as witnesses.

The last-minute civil wedding decision lacked enthusiasm. A passport became the reason for the rush. In Switzerland, the legal civil ceremony takes place on the wedding day or the afternoon before. A church ceremony is not legally recognized by the Canton.

My skull-spinning idea to have a civil wedding in America, to have a ceremony in English for Lew (since I knew he would not understand the German service in my home church in June), had vanished into a reality I had a dreadful time accepting.

A wedding needed, six weeks early, because of a signature, a passport. I cursed the idea that backfired when we found out that the name Meyer, my maiden name, had to be changed on the passport to Wells, my new married name — a process that could take up to six weeks. I spent hectic hours, nerve-shredding stuff, filled with anxiousness to get the renewal of the passport in time for our planned trip on TWA for a Swiss church family wedding.

A sour taste had lodged itself at the back of my throat with thoughts of *Mime* and *Schgruna*. I teared up like I had a bad cold — a sea of shimmering archangel-sized tears, — make-up ruined as I held on tight to Lew's bouquet of sweetheart roses, the only thing reflecting romance during this business-like ordeal. Poor Lew, not sure *I do* would come out of my mouth, I tried determinedly not to choke up, yet the sound of this important sentence drowned — a dreamy quality missing — only surrounded by four staring people.

There is no free will without pain. I held my parents in my heart; they knew nothing of our shared circumstances.

I shed tears for Mom and Dad. Could they hear my agony? How would we announce, "Hey, w*e are married*"?

Well — possibly better than living in sin?

"So much of what is best in us is bound up in our love for family that it remains the measure of our stability because it measures our sense of loyalty." — Haniel Long

311

I am possessed with boundless fondness for my disciplinarian yet considerate parents. For years they ignored to mention our time in Santa Monica or asked about living together. I volunteered bits and pieces about our civil wedding, although found no reaction. Mom and Dad managed the nearly impossible feat of showing they cared without butting in and interfering.

Silence can truly be golden. Ignorance can be bliss.

Parents don't always do what we want — when we want — they try to do their best — Parents come through when we least expect it.

On June **8**th, 1972, at a poignant church wedding in tiny Tann, a celebration lasting all afternoon and into the night, Lew's Dad and second wife, two sisters, his brother, and now

my sister-in-law from Chicago, attended. Judith, three years younger, had the same smiling eyes as Lew. Riddled with breast cancer, she traveled with older sister Loralee, a nurse by trade. Two more American guests had accepted our invitation: a customer and husband from Carefree, Arizona, and Suzie, a client, and a friend from the Beverly Hills salon. My adored grandma from Davos, a mixture of Swiss relatives from all over

Switzerland, classmates from elementary school, and numerous family friends and clients.

On Tuesday, two days before the Thursday wedding in Tann, the Wells sisters, tall blonde Loralee and Judith, dark-haired like Lew, were sightseeing on the *Bahnhofstrasse* in downtown Zürich. Judith tried to hurry onto a streetcar when she missed the handle to pull her up. She fell back onto the cobblestone street. With sirens rushing to the nearest hospital, the cancer specialist gave her six months to live. Judith at 28 years old, received news of her breast cancer had spread to the bones, devastating everyone.

After a morning of torrential rain, the sun was out for the walk of the whole wedding party from my parents' house to the nearby church. A bus covered with white flowers waited to drive 36 guests of the bride and groom to an amazing restaurant up high with spectacular views overlooking Lake Zürich, after the ceremonial Mass.

Ten minutes before the ceremony an ambulance arrived at the front entrance of the church, urging insistent onlookers and countless staring people from the village to the side. Judith, in a wheelchair, her smiling face bloated with morphine, wheeled down the aisle to the front by a male nurse. She wore a gorgeous long dress planned for her brother's fairy-tale wedding in a country called one of the most beautiful in the world.

After Mass and ceremony outside the church on June 8, 1972

Three months into our marriage Lew received a most important and anticipated call. Motorola in Scottsdale wanted him back. A job offer he could not, would not, did not refuse.

Our return to Scottsdale, where you know you are in the desert when "waterfront property" means you are close to a canal, created reactions of 'going home'.

I had sent out postcards to clients I had addresses for. *"Thanks to Lew I am back to do your hair for you."*

The moving van arrived on my birthday, October 18th, 1972, at the Maya apartments on Camelback Road. It rained all day.

The mountains in the distance over rooftops our only view.

Christmas that year, our first as a married couple, we spent in Chicago at Judith's funeral. Bone cancer had claimed Lew's sister's life. She died on my brother Erwin's birthday, December 19th — as the doctor at the *Kantonsspital* in Zürich predicted: six months.

I reminded Lew of my one visit when he had worked in Chicago for four months as he drove around to show me the famous city's sights. Along with a variety of busy streets and sections of Chicago, I noticed funeral homes — one after another — too many. As I would lower my head in disbelief, I moaned, "Not another one." Lew worried about my behavior and its meaning — we did not understand this odd happening, an omen, — how could we have known then a funeral home would become a part of our first Christmas family memory as husband and wife.

***

Old photographs in an album show cherished memories, days in Santa Monica that would stay put for years to come — a flamboyant event — our first Neil Dimond concert. *Hot August Night,* at the Greek Theater in 1972.

Musicality in the senses, ready to fly each time when Neil Diamond sang *"Cracklin' Rosie,"* his first American number-one hit on the U.S. pop singles chart that climbed to the top in October 1970 — his third to sell one million copies. Unmistakably now, Neil Diamond sang to us only on that hot August night, his all the rage song meant the world to the couple in love, married now twice. Lew and I feel abundantly lucky to have attended a variety of Neil's concerts in our life together. (Early 80ties in Tempe Arizona, ASU Activity Center, front row seats.)

Nectarose-time, on our minds forever when we hear "Cracklin' Rosie." The tune a reminder of Lew's small bottle of Nectarose rosé wine in his hand when I opened the door to apartment 31**8**, for an evening together. I remember the first time staring at the mini bottle, my heart beating faster as handsome Lew entered and handed me the pink wine from France.

Lew knew the Rosé Trudy liked.

A guy who in his refrigerator kept no food, who dined out every meal, yet he stored small bottles of Nectarose d'Anjou.

The Neil Diamond *Coming to America* movie in 19**88** spoke to me intensely, all so familiar. I have no words for my enthusiastic feelings each time I watch again and again — understood by Immigrants only.

Total partner look outfits at Sunrise Villa, our first home,1974, shirts I found at the Clotherie, 5ᵗʰ Avenue, Scottsdale

Hiking Bryce Canyon, all the way to the bottom, remains one of the most spiritual hikes in my lifetime. . . March 2013

Sunset in Coronado, CA in April 2019,
from outside our building **8**, El Encanto.

Retirement 2005

There is Life after Hair

"Time is the most important ingredient in the recipe of life." —
Charles Darwin

Dumont lake outside Steamboat, CO, on **8/18/2018**

Retirement means having time to say yes to everything.

Retirement is about achieving your dreams. As we walk the roads of autumn's past, one thing is clear: Don't postpone joy — live for joy. Be aware of taking life for granted. Take time for each other — don't ever wish someday you had . . .. Every day is a gift.

We have seen the beauty of life together — essential magic. A miracle to find that perfect partner to make choices together. We interlace fingers (still after **48** years) wherever we go . . . to never let go. Holding hands — where romance starts.

"All the beautiful moments retirement has given us; we believe
we can care at just about any age so long as we can hold hands
and be together." — Trudy Wells-Meyer

317

We have lived in our dream home on McCormick Ranch, in Heritage Village II, since November 1977. Lot 33, we found one Saturday afternoon after a busy day at the salon. Thank God for a weekend, tired and not in the mood to look for a new house; nevertheless, too curious about a brand-new development Lew eagerly had updated me on. A subdivision facing a lake and golf course. Sue, a real estate client, had spoken highly of the opening to clients while I coiffed her hair.

We drove to McCormick Ranch, found a trailer in a dirt lot on Via de Ventura. A young chatty salesman drove us in a muddy-looking four-wheel drive through the bumpy dirt (no streets thus far) to the only available lot left for sale along the lake facing south. In total ecstasy, our eyes fixed in disbelief on the view.

"If the kitchen window is here, we can see Camelback Mountain across the lake while at the sink." Words we still giggle at because we can. We knew precisely what model and layout we desired, all rooms facing the view. Two weeks had passed since we visited the talked-about *Open Models* across town, by the same builder, wishing the model we adored had one extra room. We found out this development allowed the addition of a den.

Sunday morning first thing the trailer opened, Lew called the inexperienced salesman, "We will be right over." I heard Lew say. All evening and early morning he had done the math that convinced Lew and me this to be the top deal in town.

We showed up at the sales office before anybody else and found our guy extremely nervous, scratching his head, harshly saying hello. Engrossed in checking out the model's layout of houses, pool area, tennis courts, large green areas, Jim's words interrupted, "Sorry to inform you, but lot 33 is not for sale." Head bent he kept talking, "The redheaded sold pin had fallen out by mistake, to let us believe lot 33 was available."

Our hearts stopped. Lew and my gloomy, ominous reaction got the guy off his chair disappearing behind an adjoining door. Slow and nervous minutes later Jim stormed back with a grin,

"Lot 33 is yours. The builder had saved this fine lot for himself but told me over the phone, *sell it, give it to them.*"

Some Things Are Simply Meant to Be . . .

We never forget, we do have one of the supreme, prime lots. Nor take for granted the mindboggling views.

Our home in pale shades of celadon green and an accent color black includes a decorative touch of rose — Lew's name for pink — in every room. Dusty rose. Yes, even Lew's bathroom.

Sunrise from our patio, January 200**8**

The living room, bedroom, breakfast nook with bay window, and kitchen face a lake with magnificent views of the golf course, where sunrises and sunsets are like prayers. Why is paradise not in a guidebook?

Paradise does not belong in a book; it has to be found.

"A luxury once enjoyed becomes a necessity." —
C. Northcote Parkinson

As our love can hear the echo of unprecedented miracles, Lew's and my eyes look in the same direction. Still.

We gave each other — forever.

Love is like a magnet. Love is shared moments. Genuine love is happiness when shared, like snow-burdened pines from a chairlift any glittery ice-on-every-twig morning in January with blue skies above. Those unparalleled moments (skiing no more) are now in the past, photos in a drawer we forget, yet buried in our hearts and souls eternally.

It is wisdom that sees the ordinary with amazement. A truly happy person is one who can enjoy the scenery along a detour.

Retirement, a word with its hidden meaning of times past, I didn't want to hear.

"For the old, the rich" I'd say too often.

Perspective is everything — I sought a new name for retirement. Found it — love it —*Vacation.*

A long vacation — if you are lucky. Life is not a rehearsal.

"Let's go" — Our motto in all things.

Retirement means freedom. Time to choose routine when you trade work for time. Enjoy priorities, they rule lives.

The question of time — its elusiveness . . . Age is admitting we stare at sunsets a little longer. Young eyes and minds travel too fast to the next adventure around each corner. In age, eyes linger — take in beauty at a slower pace, with an ability to compare.

Appreciated and most soul-filling, beauty is to be cherished.

Self-knowledge growing old offers, possibilities begin to narrow. Sepp Blatter, once the world's FIFA president, said in an interview after he retired, "*We find ourselves up in age and hesitate to blow out candles on a cake — Light is life.*"

Lew's transition from hectic work, sleepless nights and occasional nightmares occurred as smoothly on the first day as for years to come. A quality I came to envy. I witnessed his daily smiling face, bigger now than ever, previous stress of his important job whipped. Now all in the past.

Let the *vacation* begin . . .

I had loved my life — I did not want to change one thing. My world, to serve and see my customers regularly at the salon should end? Working day after day at a job I often didn't call work at all — now over — because of age?

"*Age is mostly a matter of mind. If you don't mind, it doesn't matter.*" — Mark Twain

Adventure is in our bones; may it live on, and a belief to embrace the best is yet to come. I value the power of possibilities that have guided my life. No more one-week Coronado, or Steamboat, one ski week a year only.

A time to sample new wines had started — no more rosé only. We experienced terrific delight when we learned at a senior seminar for a healthy mind: "*A glass of red wine is good for your brain.*"

You are never too old for all the possibilities. We faced a mad dash to make up for the time we felt was lost when we were consumed by work. An unpretentious walk, where eyes take in beauty that borders on wonderment and takes on a whole new meaning — a blue stellar jay in flight — the breeze rattling leaves — a squirrel crossing our path — a red-tailed hawk reminding us of the importance of life. Simple things become your universe.

Time to smell the orange blossoms in early spring.

A smile of another hiker can touch your heart. I watch with pride as the often-cynical Lew says hello to strangers, joggers, walkers, stern looking-people, and to a pregnant woman, "Good morning to the two of you." Her return smile, a precious sight.

Smiling is infectious: you catch it like the flu.
When someone smiled at me today, I started smiling too.
I passed around the corner and saw someone grin
When he smiled, I realized I'd passed it on to him.
I thought about that smile, then I realized its worth,
a single smile just like mine could travel round the earth.
So, if you feel a smile begin, don't leave it undetected.
Let's start an epidemic quick
and get the world infected. — Jez Alborough

It's impossible to frown and smile at the same time. Remember the muscles we use to keep us looking younger.

Keep smiling — it is the fountain of youth.

Let the smile win.

We all have the seed of joy — nurture it is up to each and every one.

What is important is not what you are but what you can be. Don't ask for the blessing . . . be the blessing.

Embrace what you have become.

"Be the rainbow in someone else's cloud." — Maya Angelou

On a humbling Arizona day when the sun sets in the west, one draws a deep breath and is grateful to be a resident on earth.

Camelback Mt. across the lake from our living room in 1987

Time marches on — too fast. Wise words ages ago to an impatient teenager from Grandma, who I loved so much, today appear like an echo. "Just wait until you are older — time goes even faster." My cherished grandma in Davos-Dorf I recall mostly dressed in black, one of my fondest memories remains — her knitting my first doll in black yarn. I had a black doll named Lizzie in my leap through childhood.

I will perpetually love the color black.

"Age starts when memories are stronger than hope." —
Anonymous

When routine becomes the norm and honey-do lists, lists in general grow longer, yet the clock in our brain slows and senior moments happen frequently. We learn brain moments are and can be most valuable. I believe up in age we appreciate time much more, oh, and all beauty around us. Differences become far less important, and harmony more easily found.

I listen to Lew's gold wedding band clicking against his nightly glass of beer. However, my matching wedding ring, with 18 spaces (coincidence?) we did not count when we bought the rings, is now filled with18 diamonds. Every Christmas for 18 years Lew had one diamond added — at the same jewelry store where we found the rings on that magical summer day we got engaged, July 1**8**, 1971.

Lew's long-time evening cantaloupe-cutting for his wife to take to the salon the next morning has now changed to cleaning my glasses, every evening after I go to bed. In the morning I find them in the same spot where Lew knows I drink my early Swiss-made instant Noblesse Oro Café.

Be a gracious receiver.

"When I was young, I admired clever people. Now that I am old, I admire kind people." — Abraham Joshua Heschel

I learned there is only one way to be talented at something — you have to be willing to do it in the way you most want to do it. Customers' worries rang in my ears: "Who will do my hair?" Devastated voices didn't let me sleep at night for a long time. I missed the glamour of doing hair, a parade of human vanity.

I spend hours reflecting on the decline in popularity of the gift to change bad-hair-days and rescue clients into the delirium of feeling beautiful once again. I miss seeing a client in the supermarket, in a restaurant, or at a party, and her hair looking better than when I did it, knowing I gave her a good haircut. These memories surface and creep into my mind frequently. Still.

A memory with a human face on display.

At Fabiola, the same salon since 2000, the **8** clients I still see regularly, every six weeks or so, (we try to return home to Scottsdale in time), help me live and enjoy my "old life" for one day. Although on the way home, driving down Hayden Road, I reason, "Oh good, I don't have to go in tomorrow."

Salon memories remain forever. Delightful Sabrina, the young mother of one, had been promised by the new receptionist "Yes", Trudy indeed had an opening for a trim-only on her long hair. Not really. This one overbooked Friday, Sabrina entered the salon with her classic smile, stopped at my station holding the ends of her gorgeous hair. Pointing she uttered, "Not more than an inch, please." With undeniable worry about hair too short in her voice, she marched to the back of the line of clients waiting.

Close to an hour later, after I apologized for the long wait, as Sabrina sat down in my chair she bellowed out, "Trudy, I changed my mind. Cut a bit more. My hair grew while I sat here."

Everyone at the salon who heard the high-pitched voice and hilarious words roared with laughter. I worried my false eyelashes would come off.

One memorable Mahogany weekday morning, (my routine starting time was 6 a.m., often before six.) at 7:30 five customers had gathered: two under the dryer, one with hair dye on her head for thirty minutes back at the color station, one lady being shampooed by my assistant, one client in my chair. As I put rollers in her hair, the sixth customer entered to join the morning gang. Arranging messy hair, she had not bothered to comb before her early hair appointment, she peeked around in disbelief and stuttered "Can I use your phone to call my husband?"

A telephone located on the manicurist's table nearby (no cell phones yet.) Mrs. Anderson picked up the receiver on the salon landline phone. Her shrill voice echoed: "Honey, I am at Trudy's. Looks like it will be a while."

"It's Mahogany's," an angry voice yelled out of the tiny office next to my working area. Handsome, yet stern owner Ricardo, (sourpuss boss at times), had arrived early and left the door wide open. Stifled laughter escalated all around our corner, giggling making the situation much worse. Poor Riccardo.

After a fascinating life, a part of my hair-world ended on Saturday, June 11th, 2005, with a posh wedding on my last fully employed day. I witnessed the power of hair one more time for Kendra's special day. A precious client who adored unique and dramatic hairstyles from as early as nine years of age. When she grew into a teenager a promise started.

"I will do your hair for your wedding — someday."

Those words echoed at Mahogany's one hectic Saturday as Kendra, with exuberance, had approved her new asymmetric haircut by parading all over the salon like a model.

No other hairstylist would do when her hair grew long like all her friend's hair at school. Mom tried to spend less, save money, send Kendra to Super Cuts for split ends to be trimmed regularly. Not her daughter. She just let it grow.

Kendra learned loyalty from Mother.

I have cut Kendra's mom's hair for over fifty years now. Maya's red-high-lighted, chemically treated hair has now changed to her specific amazing shade of gray. The color numerous mature women wished they had. Color hassles can turn into a nuisance.

Kendra's one and only hairstylist, with husband Lew, attended the ceremony and exceptional event. We arrived at the church in time for last-minute touch-ups. The stunning bride, hair up in interlaced curls — a style I had applauded at a hair show in Chicago — and her elegant bridesmaids floated down the aisle, glanced at and admired by 200 guests.

Spoken words, a promise from long ago, had come true.

"To the world, you may be one person, but to one person you may be the world." — Dr. Seuss

We learned life is truly a trade-off. Contentment is a luxury. Each day is a new experience. Life is a chain of moments.

Even in age, we dream. When we are old, we don't regret what we did — we regret what we didn't do.

Don't be an *I wish I had. . ..*

Retirement is, when we need the pretense of privacy, and we learn communicating is sensibly more important than ever.

It's a time I rip sheets off the bed and am not sure "Didn't I just wash them?" In the back of my mind a fun story surfaces often, one client had told at the beauty shop that left everyone in stitches. "I snatched the sheets off the bed early one morning to do laundry when my hubby came back from the bathroom to hop back in bed. Perplexed he stood there,

"What the hell?"

"Hello — it's morning," his wife mocked.

"Never lose a chance of saying a kind word." —
William Makepeace Thackery

Another noteworthy comment by a dear client every Friday at **8** a.m. for thirty-five years, Billie was not happy when her husband retired. Her week-day life had become unhinged. Weeks into Fred's retirement and most days home all day, Mrs. Billie sat in my chair one Friday morning shaking her head, her southern drawl strained, "I told him for better and for worse, but not for lunch."

True love means you care for another person's happiness more than your own. The very nature of love is to give. The mystery of truth and myth of love is found in day-in-and-out events — our love was fed by mutual admiration, devotion, and dedication, during all our years together.

To be loved so completely and fiercely protected, I feel cherished in Lew's breathtaking actions. When he opens the car door in the garage, with nobody but his wife to see, he uses the language of eyes that smile.

When he neatly squeezes the toothpaste in my bathroom, (or one bathroom only while traveling,) so that brushing my teeth is not interrupted by a tube of toothpaste not pressed to the top.

A forever romance. . .

Couples who idolize each other are happier — stay together longer and feel no decline in relationship satisfaction. That reach of his hand finding mine, anytime — anywhere — that is love.

Reach for each other's hand — it's magic.

We share a marriage people talk about in tones of wonder and envy. Over the years loads of people have asked us, "What is the secret of your happy marriage?" To one bride asking, when I had finished her hair for an early May wedding, I whispered, "Always give him a reason to love you. Communicate!" Her eyes sparkled as if to say, *I will remember those words.*

I added, "I never knew how much or if I wanted to marry Lew, all I knew, I never want to be without him. . .."

To be married to the most knowledgeable man, (he created — formatted this book) a smart man like Lew, with an IQ so high I don't frankly always understand. I simply know I live day in and day out with his infinite dignity and strength. I think of a compliment Lew gave me eons ago after I came home from a demanding day at the salon, rambling on about amusing customers' stories.

"It takes a smart person to have as many clients and — for them to come back." Lew's words have remained in my head and heart. His recognition gave me a warm glow, coming from my sophisticated, often too skeptical husband. It is the most valued of all compliments from his lips.

Lew's waving-hand motion he uses often with a voice that could scare a fish and evoke cringing moments. I learned Lew has no patience for stupidity.

Smart guys do finish first.

A personal handyman at our home, Lew without a doubt fixes everything that breaks.

"I don't know what's wrong" is a phrase from his mouth I can count on one hand in our 48 years of marriage. Months ago, a TV reception and Internet outage occurred. A young yard guy had cut the cable by mistake, after no reception for hours due to a storm problem in the area since the night before. In the dark, with a flashlight, Lew temporarily fixed the outside cable. Two days later the Cox employee informed Lew, "You don't need me."

Tomato soup still rules when I am sick. When I hear the words "tomato soup" — I smile. Choice number one at any restaurant. When expert-soup-cook Lew serves Trader Joe's low-sodium tomato soup, he puts a small spoon on the tray, the fancy kind used for guests, that lets me wonder, *Oops, he did not find a big spoon in the drawer?*

"So you can enjoy the soup longer," he reasoned.

Non-stop romance lets love blossom and grow.

Life is what you make it. Romance does not just happen . . . make it happen.

Lew and I gave each other reasons to love one another.

Love, solid as stone — tender — made our souls sing.

Retired for 18 months, married 34 years, on the Thursday before Christmas we unloaded groceries. Oh no — we had forgotten mandarins — the smell of Christmas. Mandarins, the fruit reminds me of home and growing up. That treat from Santa Claus on December 6, every year, on Saint Nikolas Day, when he visited our family home with a brown sack over his shoulder filled with walnuts, apples, and mandarins. A bell rang in his other hand to announce his arrival.

Still, in my color-coordinated outfit from earlier grocery shopping together, I was in a hurry not to be late for my monthly facial appointment. I kissed Lew goodbye. He stood in the street — waving as usual until I turned the corner. When I returned two hours later, I stared at three mandarins on our brand-new granite kitchen counter. Confused for a second, I paused, "Did we have three leftover?" Then I saw Loudeehui's gentle grin. He didn't . . . Yes — he did. Back to Safeway he went.

One may wonder what the clerk was thinking as Lew checked out **3** mandarins. Or, impatient shoppers in the line behind him, shopping carts bursting with holiday groceries watching a handsome man in a black shirt with gold threads, a red sweater ready for Christmas, pulling out a credit card for three mandarins.

The brightness in Lew's eyes is like a flame no wind could blow out — I will always love Lew, truly, madly, and above all, deeply.

"You are everything I love about life . . . you are everything I know about love." — Anonymous

Believe in 3's

A belief, things do come in **3**'s continues.
3 mandarins.

Davos — Parsenn, Weissfluh Joch, one of our hikes in Switzerland, 2006

We ended up with **3** of *everything* . . . Three condos: sizzling and glorious Scottsdale, Arizona; dreamy home-away-from-home Coronado, California, and 'home in the mountains' Steamboat, Colorado — our Switzerland.

3 job offers in America, 3 States: Silver Springs, Maryland; Atlanta Georgia; Scottsdale, Arizona. **3** is a charm, they say.

I learned to believe things happen in threes ages ago — good or bad.

I can fill a whole chapter with *three stories* that possibly leave a reader with questions of — coincidence? Nevertheless, straightforwardly emphasizes the importance of the number **3**.

To mention a few:

Three Scottsdale homes with a spectacular view — we could see Camelback Mountain. The first, where we met, the Allegro apartments facing north. Lew and I enjoyed the unusual, animal-shaped mountain before we got introduced —

Sunrise Villa, (our first patio home) looking west across the green lawn and open space with flowers in bloom — and Golden Heritage on the lake and golf course views to the south. Camelback Mountain, a day-after-day reminder of the Allegro long ago in 1968 — from the other side.

3 teachers, champions of smiles, taught me to smile — always. *Schgruna*, my dad, Soeur Thérèse Espérance at the boarding school and positive Lew. People who smile win every time. If you can smile, also in challenging times, everything will set straight and be all right.

A memory flashing of one Switzerland-home visit. At the end stage of our trip what an awe-moment at the departure gate in Kloten, when my mom, *Mime* put the 18-karat gold necklace around my neck, valuable gold she had worn with pride and joy — a treasure I seldom wore ended up in a jewelry box in a drawer. Racked with guilt I contacted a refined jeweler. Three shiny gold bracelets I never take off, now decorate my right arm, to comprehend precious gold from my *Mime*. How glorious, her aged chain had the exact length to create 3 bracelets and fill me with constant love.

3 priests gave Lew communion:

Father, Pastor, *Pfarrer*, Guisep Jacomet, *Pfarrer* Tarcisi Venzin, in Tann, ZH (my hometown church) and Father Ernest Bayer, Holy Name Church, Steamboat Springs, Colorado.

Father Jacomet at our wedding Mass, June 8, 1972, in Tann and again, in Domat Ems, GR, twenty-five years later, at our Silver wedding anniversary Mass on Sunday, June 8, 1997.

Pfarrer Venzin, a relative, a cousin of Father Jacomet, both born in the *Engadin,* Grison (where Mom grew up), at our father's funeral Mass in Tann in November 1989, Pastor Venzin handed Lew communion. During a time of sorrow, I thanked and praised the Lord, my God, for that uncommon gesture. A gift of intimate connection to my *Schgruna* in heaven.

Father Ernest, Steamboat, Springs, Colorado, Holy Name Church we watched built and emerge as a jewel of God in the Rocky Mountains. During my broken bones, ski accident recovery, Father Ernest visited our condo at *The WEST,* on

Valentine's Day February 14, 2014. To watch in awe, Lew granted communion — I did not ask for — as well as me, is etched in my heart. At our "Little Switzerland" Colorado home, what a blessing! I had however told Father Ernest of our wedding/church ceremony in 1972 when *Pfarrer* Jacomet handed Lew — the Protestant — communion.

Thank You, God, my Savior, who creates all things possible.

At weekly Mass, the congregation kneels when the priest lifts the bread, offering the body of Jesus Christ in prayer. **3** rings of bells fill the church with multiple small bells by an altar boy — now girls (no more boys only) — **3** rings again, during the offering of wine, the blood of Jesus. I count every time.

3 outstanding firsts at our age, we found **3** spectacular hikes in one month, the same year, spring of 2016.

West Mitten Wildcat Trail, at Monument Valley, Utah April 2016

Hidden Canyon Trail, at Starr Pass J.W. Marriott, Tucson in March

Treasure Loop Trail at Superstition Mountain in Apache Junction, late March 2016.

> *"Each moment of the year has its own beauty — a picture that was never seen before and will never be seen again."* —
> Ralph Waldo Emerson

Treasure Loop is now one of my favorites, a sea of yellow flowers in the spring, where Winnetou-feelings, the Apache warrior emerge for this Karl-May-books-loving Swiss, and nostalgia — to compensate for the neglect of my home country — a sense of melancholy repeats like a distant train whistle.

Still today, I attain pride, and a feeling of my own smallness next to this huge country — America — I have come to call my home.

FIFA changed rules **3** times after I wrote letters in 1994, 2010, and 2014. I collected numerous fan signatures from countries all over the world. Help from loyal supporters signing a petition to plead and hope for fair games in the future, in the world's most-watched sporting event of football (soccer in America) especially the World Cup and every year's UEFA championship.

My enthusiastic determination to watch Football games (soccer) allows me each time to be close to my father in heaven. In April of the 201**8**/2019 season, in one week, **3** of my most esteemed football/soccer teams lost. They played to advance to the final that spring. Atletico Madrid, Borussia Dortmund, and Arsenal — two on the same day, no winning triumph in their important title game race match. Arsenal played **3** days later, on Saturday, and missed a chance to move up in the Premier League. Arsenal lost — Everton won. Devastated I simply knew of Arsenal's end to glory; a day of cursing my belief that *things* do come in **3**'s — satisfaction once again put on the back burner. In a short week, **3** of my favorites, all-the-rage world teams, lost the possibility of reaching the top that year.

Sedona . . . We try to continue 'our tender as a love poem' tradition and once-a-year fix — Sedona — for **3** days, knowing in our hearts — true happiness truly is to want what you have.

Hiking in the red rocks, as long as we can . . .

In March 2019 we went even when it rained — **3** days.

The Holy Cross chapel we visit each time, where my anguish from ages ago surfaces "go home or stay" a decision I prayed for at the Holy Chapel in 196**8** (when sitting on a wooden bench praying, you admire a view of the mesmerizing red rocks through an oversized window behind the altar).

Today, a decision as clear as a mountain lake in the Swiss Alps:
Lew had entered my life . . .

Our awesome pink jeep tour — in 1991

Cathedral Rock Trail, Valentine's Day 2016

Devil's Bridge Trailhead, February 201**8**

An interesting question lingers, one we have been asked too often to count. Between our **3** chosen places, Scottsdale, Coronado, and Steamboat, "Which one of the three is your favorite?" Our answer, every time: "Wherever we are at the moment."

May our current adventures create a wealth of noteworthy stories, essays, and poetry to share. **3** things we hope not to live without any time soon: hiking — travel — the ocean.

Trudy and Lew 1977

Lew's white summer shirt with golden/yellow flowers I had found in the International Male Catalog while sitting on our patio, a pure find, smart and sharp.

Two months later I browsed at Sakowitz Department Store on my Monday-spending-money-day-off when my eyeballs stopped at a dress for me to see. . .

same fabric!

The sales lady hardly understood my exhilaration, my rambling on of *my husband has a shirt like this dress*.

Some things are simply meant to be.

Together Forever

My memoir of a life in poetry, essays and prose is filled with quotes — words I saw written, admired, loved, and lived by during our blessed lives. As far back as in my young adult life, I wrote passages, special lines, and viewpoints in a pretty *Poesie Album* I had decorated with pictures of flowers. Now displayed in our den/library in Scottsdale. I still reach for it now and then. Valued, meaningful words in German about Life — Love — Let Live.

Words, a powerful weapon, speak to us; the power of words lives on.

One of my favorite quotes is, (especially with politics in recent years):

"It is never about just one opinion, yours or mine, but it is always about the truth." — Anonymous

My 'Monday-am-mass-rule' exists no more — Saturday late-afternoon reigns — Lew and I attending Mass together.

"The reason you all are here today — you did not choose God, — God chose you." Words at the beginning of an impressive homily spoken by Father John one Sunday at 6 a.m. service at Lady of Perpetual Help in Scottsdale (early in my marriage). I cried uncontrollably that morning over Lew's absence, only too aware of not sharing this important conviction instilled in me for eternity. My religious upbringing haunted me.

Lew now by my side in church weekly, in cities all over the world. He searches for locations and Mass schedules before we depart on any long trips. Sometimes, throughout our extended traveling, if luck has it, our stay falls on weekends to attend Sunday Mass. In Barcelona, Spain, June 2017, a First Communion ceremony in Catalonia at the Basilica de Santa Maria del Mar. A ceremony everlasting in my mind, even Lew's.

During one class reunion weekend in Mauston, Wisconsin, Lew's hometown, we attended Sunday service at St. Patrick's Catholic Church, where his Catholic mom used to worship before Lew was born. His dad was Lutheran. Lew's parents married outside the Catholic church.

On a Viking River Cruise from Amsterdam to Basel, Switzerland, in May 2015, one of the highlights, a weekend Holy Mass in German, my native language. My watering eyes like a fountain, yet wordless joy as treasured memories flooded at the Köln Dom, Europe's world-known cathedral.

St. Charles Church — the famous Baroque *Karlskirche* — in Vienna, Austria, luckily within walking distance of our hotel, a useful bonus.

In Wyoming, in Mousse inside the Grand Teton National Park, we attended a late Saturday afternoon Mass at the Chapel of the Sacred Heart. The glow over the snow-covered Tetons from the setting sun in the distance reminded me of home — Switzerland. More tears.

In Scottsdale, we visit different churches, taking turns: Blessed Sacrament, St. Bernhard's, Maria Goretti, and St. Patrick's. In Coronado Saturday 5:30 p.m. Mass at Sacred Heart, in Steamboat Springs, 5 on Saturdays, in the new divine Holy Name Church. Our names and the year 1971, (the year we first visited Steamboat) grace a memorial/paver, an impressive granite stone, at the entrance to the magnificent church surrounded by a variety of parishioners who had donated to the parish.

Our Saturday Mass routine every week includes Lew's beloved Mexican restaurants in each place — Lew's choice for a late lunch before Mass. Miguel's in Coronado, his favorite.

In any church of the world, we admire the cross of Jesus, the Son of God, reminding us the deepest love can carry the deepest pain.

Life comes to us in seasons. A prayer that will carry me always, a reminder: It is not about having the best of everything but seeing the best in everything.

Happiness is a journey, not a destination . . . there is no road to happiness, happiness is the road.

Hopefully, with years yet to come and our awareness of the passage of time, we attained the knowledge being young at heart is better than being young. My internal humming is like an aged song as I listen to stories my husband tells a dozen times over, involving the family. Lew's genealogy hobby fills his days and time he says he has little of. Lew's unending interest and searching for family history warms my heart. Close to his roots and family in his meticulous way, transpired not too late.

"What do you do all day?" A question we hear abundantly.

Laughing his inept laugh and shaking his head, Lew's latest answer, "If I had 3 minutes, I would make a list for you."

The pinch above Lew's eyes, his occasional smugness, and defensiveness as he thrusts a toothpick back between his teeth, his tone sends an alarm of gloomy familiarity something is wrong. His voice can reach the level of roaring.

"Don't yell at me," I demand. In his cool, unhurried voice, even at times when the sky seems to be falling, he says, "That was not yelling — that was barking."

"Humor is mankind's greatest blessing." — Mark Twain

The importance of humor in a marriage is like a breeze that scatters; close to a number-one rule of any good relationship — Respect.

Let there be laughter in your heart; do not wait for tomorrow.

Husbands have ways of correcting wives, and words can drip with sarcasm. Spouses do it in return. A human weakness. Sometimes I shake my head and wink at Lew as if to say, *"You don't give me much credit."* Lew is the champion in correcting me. He blames my Swiss accent. Still.

If only foreigners could hear themselves speak. I did, on a tape recorder, and never could believe it, "I sound like that? No way — that's me?"

As people I meet continuously ask, "Where are you are from?" I wonder, will they ever stop asking, "When and why did you leave Sweden?" Yes, the world gets Switzerland and Sweden confused and mixed up — constantly. If I had a dollar for each time. . .

I had become an American. I am American, Swiss-born.

Suisse Ambassador Ball, at the Hyatt Regency, November 2004

Retired Lew learned and enjoyed online shopping. Whereas, he still shows dislike entering most stores, especially at a mall. One exception — the upscale Sakowitz Department Store he never forgot. Years ago, in the seventies, Mrs. Sakowitz, a glamorous, from Texas, client of mine, invited us to the grand opening of the new, elegant family-owned Scottsdale fashion store. Lew spent his time admiring every plant and flowerpot that decorated the entrance, downstairs, upstairs, and near the high-tech moving stairs. He had no eyes for merchandise all evening — everyone else did the staring at exclusive, sophisticated, never-before-seen tastefully displayed items.

Nonetheless, since retirement's gift of time to use as one pleases, I had taught Lew to enjoy shopping, for both of us, especially at Christmas time. I acquired a stillness in order not to get annoyed any longer when he grimaces with a look *Honestly — do I have to?*

Obsessive attention to detail and perfection ruled my life, still evident, always will. Lew never wears anything I don't like. I started to buy his clothes ages ago to add to his stylish elegance. They do make his size — he ultimately did not know (no helpful computers) where to go or, cared to find out. He is a perfect 39 Regular in a sports coat, size 32 trousers changed to 33, shirts mostly small — and shoes? Yes, I bring them home to try on — in peace. Lew loves the no-hassle attentive shopping by his wife.

In horror at times, trying on a red or purple shirt, *You want me to wear this — but not to work?* One of Lew's frequent questions *is now* a phrase of the past.

Angel's Landing Trail at Zion, a well-known, strenuous

most popular trail in the park (and feared on top), male hikers

340

voted Lew as the best-dressed male on the mountain. Everyone glared at Lew's white jeans. Men taking second looks. Compliments Lew had become used to from our Rocky Mountain hiking days in Steamboat. Each time, nevertheless, his gigantic grin lights up, at all the color-coordinated reactions and comments.

People's questions, asked too often to count, "Who decides the colors in the morning?"

"Oh, I lay out the clothes for her." Lew grins. I giggle a lot. He did not have to shop for any of it. I do — I did — for years.

The way a man feels about a woman in a relationship depends ultimately on the way she makes him feel about himself. And vice versa.

Kindness has its own rewards. Give praise a chance.

Remember — you praise and cuss by parting the same lips.

"Kind words can be short and easy to speak, but their echoes are truly endless." — Mother Theresa

When patience dwindles (it does — it will), practice tolerance — it grows with age. Although, I admit I still shake my head or kick Lew when he laughs during a tear-jerking movie (in a theater especially) or at a funeral. At some stage of serious arguments, I simply walk away.

One nagging flaw, his inappropriate, habitually quick laugh, will I ever understand? Love endures all things.

Patience — a magic word in any marriage — try to use it, tirelessly. Patience is an art.

"Love me when I least deserve it because that's when I really need it." — Swedish Proverb

Shared experiences are what love is all about. I often think of people along the way who could not bear to see the display of marital unity and spark between Lew and me, the spark absent in their marriage.

To be successful in various things: Hair — Love — Life — Writing — it all has its cost, sadly including friends that drift.

A cocktail of envy.

When reasons end and are no longer adequate, as we age, we find more ways to deal with tragedy, knowing so many lives deserve prayers. Will the world become a better place as we cringe at the giant TV screen with its flashing, disastrous crawl?

Now that I am too old to die young, I know what Love is . . . an eternal flame. I married a man I loved on the soil of the country of my dreams, a country I loved before I learned and recognized how to love anything else.

Lines in Lew's face are like a map I cannot always read, but I do know love does not require us to look at each other but compassionately look in the same direction.

Marriage is . . . the ultimate of *I love you.*

Loudeehui and Youdeehui — together forever.

This I will remember the rest of my life, the finest thing I've ever done is loving Lew.

I want your heart my own to be. . .

"*To have lived the dream of a love so true is to have seen a glimpse of heaven.*" — Anonymous

Lew's love is like the air I breathe. I hope I never find out how vital it is to live without.

Someday we'll be together, our song for life and in death. We share an embrace that lasts beyond the hold each time that melody appears wherever we are. The Supremes/Diana Ross will sing at our funeral, along with Neil Diamond's "Cracklin' Rosie."

Love is . . . endless gratitude. Love has no limit, no end.

By the way . . .

April 28th, 2019 — our 47th civil-wedding-in-Beverly Hills-

anniversary, we strolled to the exciting car show at Star Park in Coronado, CA, enjoyed every year by old-car lovers; they come from everywhere. Lew, one of those nostalgia-bound fans, all excited we left our condo early before a crowd would arrive. The winner circle caught our eye. The sight of a red Austin-Healey putting both of us into delirious exuberance. Just like Lew's!

A larger-than-life awe-moment on a bright, California blue-sky Sunday morning. The same car — I had seen first — before Lew. Before we met.

Some Things Are Simply Meant to Be.

We live by our motto:
"*Nothing else matters as long as we have each other.*"

Our fun motto: We drink to that . . . we have, we do. Still.

Brienz, Switzerland, (a trip home for 3 weeks) July 2019

"*All I have seen teaches me to trust the Creator for all I have not seen.*" — Ralph Waldo Emerson

Christmas dinner with friends at Orange Sky, top floor
at a Casino on the Indian Reservation, December 2019,
about **8** minutes from our home.

Home is where the heart is . . . Arizona's desert and
Camelback Mountain — a city's mountain in Phoenix, known
worldwide — our lives surrounded by the vision of a camel's
back . . . our mountain.

Each morning when I make the bed, I can see Camelback
Mountain in a mirror, framed and oversized attached to our
king-size bed as a headboard, across the patio with various
pink and a few yellow roses of all sizes and cerise bougainvillea
— the lake and golf course . . . what a view.

One last thing . . .

"My daughter can do anything!"
Mime's unexpected, atypical words in a world of strict
upbringing I overheard peeking around a corner, months before
I journeyed to America, are like an echo from the Swiss
mountain tops . . . in my head everlasting.

A growing collection of memories, 'little me' proved Mom,
our *Mami,* right.

The power of words. . ..

Gertrud (Trudy) Brunhilde Meyer-Günther, picture taken in 1979.

*"Faith goes up the stairs that love has made and looks out of the
windows which hope has opened."* — Charles Haddon Spurgeon

Trudy Wells-Meyer

Trudy Wells-Meyer
Summer of 1968

Author / *Schriftstellerin*

Picture from long before writing entered my mind and soul.

About the Author

Trudy Wells-Meyer lives in Scottsdale, Arizona with her husband.
She is a successful retired hair designer and writes in her second language.
Prose writing has become her American life since 9/11 when she wrote her first inspirational story, "The Power of Prayer", one of her readers' claims is of rare storytelling and makes you believe in fate . . . and God.
The dynamics of her writing world include essays and poetry published in six Goose River Anthologies, 2014 – 2020.
Poetry, the most precise form of expression language has given her when emotions find words, is published in *ABSOLOOSE* volumes 1 and 2. Trudy has won several awards in writers' contests. Her first poem, written in 2008, won $250.00, 1st prize.
Her work has been published in ten books . . . book number **8**, *Some Things Are Simply Meant to Be,* (2018) is her first full-length manuscript. '*The Ring*' is published in Baby Boomers 2019 (book 9). She has various soccer articles published, even in USA Today. Her immense love for soccer, the world calls Football, involves writing to FIFA, changing rules. (Now implemented rules).
Trudy, a legal immigrant who waited eleven months for a green card, a working visa, dreaming of *Coming to America,* the power of possibilities took over her life at a young age — an urge to go confidently in the direction of dreams, hopeful for a place that would change her life. She believed something extraordinary is possible . . . she dared to dream, wondering how life would turn out — her boldest guess could not have been near the truth. She learned how truly fascinating daily life can turn on a small decision . . . mystery and a leap of fate, as she still marvels at the job offer at a well-established German salon in Atlanta, Georgia. Life's unpredictable effect-events at their finest.
What will be . . . will be. Walking off that ship in New York, speaking and understanding a little English, Trudy inhaled a dose of determination, as her thoughts strayed to her stern and oh so strict mom, her amazing, bragging words: *My daughter can do anything!* This was the moment to live up to extraordinary words. Eventually was now. Years later she would come to understand from a tiny seed of such praise would emerge an exceptional will to cause her mom to be right. Thank you! Trudy's parents smile in heaven. . ..